MIKE MEYERS' CERTIFICATION
Passport ★

Security+™

TREVOR KAY

 OSBORNE

New York · Chicago · San Francisco
Lisbon · London · Madrid · Mexico City
Milan · New Delhi · San Juan
Seoul · Singapore · Sydney · Toronto

The McGraw·Hill Companies

McGraw-Hill/Osborne
2600 Tenth Street
Berkeley, California 94710
U.S.A.

To arrange bulk purchase discounts for sales promotions, premiums, or fund-raisers, please contact **McGraw-Hill/Osborne** at the above address. For information on translations or book distributors outside the U.S.A., please see the International Contact Information page immediately following the index of this book.

Mike Meyers' Security+™ Certification Passport

90 DOC DOC 0198

Book p/n 0-07-222907-1 and CD p/n 0-07-222906-3
parts of
ISBN 0-07-222741-9

Publisher
Brandon A. Nordin

Vice President & Associate Publisher
Scott Rogers

Editorial Director
Gareth Hancock

Acquisitions Editor
Nancy Maragioglio

Project Editor
Patty Mon

Acquisitions Coordinator
Jessica Wilson

Technical Editor
Glen E. Clarke

Copy Editor
Marcia Baker

Proofreader
Pat Mannion

Indexer
Karin Arrigoni

Computer Designers
Michelle Galicia
Kathleen Fay Edwards

Illustrators
Kelly Stanton-Scott
Melinda Moore Lytle
Lyssa Wald
Michael Mueller

Series Design
Peter F. Hancik

Cover Series Design
Ted Holladay

This book was composed with Corel VENTURA™ Publisher.

About the Author

Trevor Kay (aka Y2Kay) is an Information Technology (IT) consultant and computer book author. From London Ontario, Canada, he started his IT career working for a local museum as a desktop publisher. From that time, Trevor has held many positions—IT helpdesk, computer/network technical support, and network administrator. To learn more about Trevor and other certification-related titles he's written, please visit www.trevorkay.com.

About the Technical Editor

Glen E. Clarke is a Security+, Microsoft Certified Systems Engineer (MCSE), Microsoft Certified Solution Developer (MCSD), and Microsoft Certified Trainer (MCT). He holds a number of Prosoft certifications and is also an A+ certified technician. Glen currently works as a technical trainer for Polar Bear Corporate Education Solutions, one of Canada's largest technical training centers, where he delivers the MCSE and MCSD curriculum. Contact Glen at gleneclarke@hotmail.com.

Dedication

This book is dedicated to all my family and friends, who have always given me their tremendous support throughout my writing career.

—*Trevor Kay*

Acknowledgments

First, I want to thank Nigel Kay for all his input, his contributions, and the many hours he spent on this project to make this book the best it can be.

Thanks to everyone at McGraw-Hill/Osborne, especially Nancy Maragioglio, Glen Clarke, Jessica Wilson, Patty Mon, Marcia Baker, and Gareth Hancock. To all the people in the graphics and production departments, I thank you. Without your hard work and dedication, this book wouldn't have become a reality.

I also want to give special thanks to my family and friends: to my mother, Hazil Kay, Sharon Kay, Clare Steed, Hamish Humphray, Dell Errington, the Testolin family, Mary and Al Haskett, Alan and Yvonne Corfield, Steve and Tara Hutson, Lynda Pomfret, Judge Walter Bell, Maxine Lewis, Joe Piotrowski, Rob (The Sculpture Heath), Kevin Benjamin, Rico Leppard, Russ Francis, Scott Johnston, Barry Connolly, Mike Pressey and the boys at Williams Form Hardware and Rockbolt (Canada) LTD, Katie Feltman, Melody Layne, Amanda Munz Peterson, Brian MacDonald, Christopher Clark, Geoff Robins, Roger Bruce, Berle Conrad, Bill Lake, Tom Carter, Linda Young, Natasha and Trent Francis, Roger LeBlanc, Jim Esler, Lisa Mior, Beth Crowe, Ricki Fudge, Elena, N. Ranchina, Greg and Irina Stephens, Henry and Leanna Westbrook, Steve Marino, and Ken DeJong for their support during this project.

Contents

13 Policy Procedures and Privilege Management 299

14 Forensics, Risk Management, Education, and Documentation 319

Check-In

May I See Your Passport?

What do you mean you don't have a passport? Why, it's sitting right in your hands, even as you read! This book is your passport to a special place. You're about to begin a journey, my friend, a journey toward that magical place called certification! You don't need a ticket, you don't need a suitcase—just snuggle up and read this passport—it's all you need to get there. Are you ready? Let's go!

Your Travel Agent: Mike Meyers

Hello! I'm Mike Meyers, president of Total Seminars and author of a number of popular certification books. On any given day, you'll find me replacing a hard drive, setting up a web site, or writing code. I love every aspect of this book you hold in your hands. It's part of a powerful new book series called the *Mike Meyer's Certification Passports*. Every book in this series combines easy readability with a condensed format—in other words, the kind of book I always wanted when I went for my certifications. Putting a huge amount of information in an accessible format is an enormous challenge, but I think we achieved our goal and I'm confident you'll agree.

I designed this series to do one thing and only one thing—to get you the information you need to achieve your certification. You won't find any fluff in here. Trevor packed every page with nothing but the real nitty-gritty of the Security+ Certification exams. Every page has 100 percent pure concentrate of certification knowledge! But we didn't forget to make the book readable, so I hope you enjoy the casual, friendly style.

My personal e-mail address is mikem@totalsem.com and Trevor's e-mail is trevor@trevorkay.com. Please feel free to contact either of us directly if you have any questions, complaints, or compliments.

Your Destination: Security+ Certification

This book is your passport to CompTIA's Security+ Certification (exam SY0-101), the vendor-neutral industry standard certification developed for foundation-level security professionals. Based on a worldwide job task analysis, the structure of the exam focuses on core competencies in general security, communication security, infrastructure security, the basics of cryptography, and operational/organizational security.

Whether the Security+ certification is your first step toward a career focus in security or an additional skill credential, this book is your passport to success on the Security+ Certification exam.

Your Guide: Trevor Kay

There's only one thing to say about your author Trevor Kay—don't mess with him! Oh sure, he's a Canadian, so he'll fool you with that Great White North laid-back attitude, but that's just a ruse. First of all, Trevor is a proven author with a number of books already to his credit. He's a writing machine! To back that up, he has a stack of certifications as long as your arm and plenty of experience in the real world—don't mess with him on the technical stuff!

When Trevor isn't creating another one of his outstanding books, he's hammering away on one of his Fender Stratocasters, testing the integrity of his house by grinding out hundreds of decibels of pure overdrive.

Trevor loves to work out and figures if technology ever loses its appeal, he can always join Vince McMahon and the WWE!

Why the Travel Theme?

The steps to gaining a certification parallel closely the steps to planning and taking a trip. All the elements are the same: preparation, an itinerary, a route, even mishaps along the way. Let me show you how it all works.

This book is divided into 14 chapters. Each chapter begins with an *Itinerary* that provides objectives covered in each chapter and an *ETA* to give you an idea of the time involved in learning the skills in that chapter. Each chapter is broken down by objectives, either those officially stated by the certifying body or our expert take on the best way to approach the topics. Also, each chapter contains a number of helpful items to bring out points of interest:

Exam Tip
Points out critical topics you're likely to see on the actual exam.

Local Lingo
Describes special terms in detail, in a way you can easily understand.

Travel Advisory

Warns you of common pitfalls, misconceptions, and downright physical peril!

The end of the chapter gives you two handy tools. The *Checkpoint* reviews each objective covered in the chapter with a handy synopsis—a great way to review quickly. Plus, you'll find end-of-chapter questions to test your newly acquired skills.

CHECK POINT

But the fun doesn't stop there! After you've read the book, pull out the CD and take advantage of the free practice questions! Use the two full practice exams to hone your skills and keep the book handy to check answers.

If you want even more practice, log on to http://www.osborne.com/passport and, for a nominal fee, you'll get additional high-quality practice questions.

When you're acing the practice questions, you're ready to take the exam. Go get certified!

The End of the Trail

The IT industry changes and grows constantly, *and so should you*. Finishing one certification is only one step in an ongoing process of gaining more and more certifications to match your constantly changing and growing skills. Read the "Career Flight Path" at the end of the book to see where this certification fits into your personal certification goals. Remember, in the IT business, if you're not moving forward, you're way behind!

Good luck on your certification! Stay in touch!

Mike Meyers
Series Editor,
Mike Meyers' Certification Passport

General Security Concepts

Access Control
and Authentication

ETA	NEWBIE	SOME EXPERIENCE	EXPERT
	4 hours	2 hours	0.5 hour

The simplest and most often overlooked aspects of security are the concepts of access control and authentication. In many business environments, access usually involves a single login to a computer or a login to a network of computer systems that provides the user access to all resources on the network. This access includes rights to personal and shared folders on a network server, company intranets, printers, and other network resources and devices. These resources, however, can be quickly exploited by unauthorized users if the access control and associated authentication procedures aren't set up properly. Access control concerns permissions applied to resources that decide which users can access those resources. Authentication goes hand-in-hand with access control and identifies that users are exactly who they claim to be. After you've been authenticated, then you can access the resources for which you have permission.

Careful consideration must be employed when creating access and authentication policies for your network. Basic security practices such as logins and passwords must be augmented with advanced techniques, such as the use of long, nondictionary, alpha-numeric passwords, regular password rotation and expiration, and regular system account auditing. The security of the account and password databases themselves must be taken into consideration. The databases must be protected with stringent access properties, and the contents protected through the use of encryption. Finally, the protection of personal and shared data resources on network file servers must be maintained through the use of directory and file access permissions on a per user or group basis.

Access control and authentication might seem like a simple topic but, without careful consideration of the authentication methods and policies, the weaknesses in your network and system security can be quickly penetrated by unauthorized users both within and outside of your network. Access control and authentication work together to provide the first line of defense for your computer network.

 **Objective 1.01** **Access Control**

A ccess control is the first line of security for a computer network. Access control methods determine how users interact with other resources and computer systems. The resources must be protected from unauthorized modification or tampering. Access controls must be enforced on a network to ensure unauthorized users can access neither its resources nor the network and computer system infrastructure itself.

Users and Resources

To create an access control and security policy for your network, you must first define who the users are and to what resources they need access. A "user" in this sense doesn't always mean a specific person. A computer might act as a user when it tries to connect to the resource of another computer system. A *user* of a resource might also be a computer account used by a system to back up other computer system's resources and data to a tape drive. This *backup* user account needs to have its access control defined properly, so it can perform its job function.

Just as your users must be carefully defined, the resources offered by your computer network need to be categorized and access controls defined for the resources' security. A *resource* can be anything from a simple text file on a file server, to a network laser printer, to an Internet proxy server. Your resources must be categorized with the following attributes in mind:

Sensitivity   How confidential is the data from this resource? Should it only be seen by certain people or should access be open to anyone? An example of sensitive data would be payroll or human resources data. The capability to access this resource should only be available to users from those departments.

Integrity   Should users only be able to read from this directory or can they modify the files within? If the integrity of the data is vital, then this resource should have its access permissions set to read-only. For example, a datasheet of released company financials to shareholders should never be modified after distribution.

Availability   How available should the data be as a resource? Does this data need to be available at all times or only during certain time periods? Is this information so critical that it must be available whenever a user requests it? Typically, availability decreases with increased security, so the needs of protecting the data must be balanced with the needed level of availability.

Travel Advisory

In real-world situations, some friction exists between management and the Information Technology (IT) department over the need for availability against the need for security. IT departments must stress to management the need for security over ease of availability and balance the requirements accordingly.

Security Models

A *security model* is a way of visualizing the relationships among your users and groups and the resources they need to perform their jobs. For a network administrator to assign access permissions individually to resources on a per-user basis would be inefficient and extremely time-consuming. For small networks, this might be viable. But for mid-sized to large corporate networks, it would be an unwieldy strategy. Grouping your users, depending on similarities in their attributes, is much more efficient. Typically, you can identify groups of users in three main ways:

Job Function   Users who perform the same job will most likely need access to the same resources. For example, a number of data entry operators might need access to the same data directory on a specific file server. By grouping these users into one entity, you can assign the resulting group access to the data without the need to perform this configuration for every user. This model can also be defined hierarchically, as shown in Figure 1.1, where management might have more access to resources than nonmanagement personnel.

Department   Users who belong to the same department in an organization will probably need access to the same data and resources. A department doesn't always have to be physically in the same location. Because of the virtual nature of a large corporate network, a sales employee in the United States might need access to the same sales database as a sales employee in Japan. All users from the sales department can be assigned to the sale group: Sales. The network administrator only has to configure access to the sales database once for the Sales group, without having to assign it for each individual sales person. This model is shown in Figure 1.2.

Physical Location   A company could only be located in one building, several buildings, or have offices in different cities and countries. Many companies have

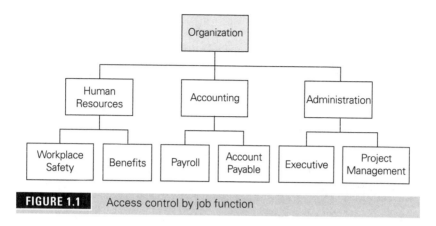

FIGURE 1.1   Access control by job function

their resources divided among physical locations, so an office in New York might not need access to resources to a file server in Los Angeles. In this way, the security model can be set up by physical location, where users are grouped depending on what office they belong to, as shown in Figure 1.3.

To ensure the most efficient security model, data resources should be organized on need-to-know criteria. Resources should only be available to the users who need access to that information. In most cases, the users in a sales department wouldn't need access to the data resources of accounting or human resources. Each resource must have its access controls specifically set to allow only the users authorized for that resource. This also flows down into more granular levels of security, where a user might have access to read a file, but not to modify

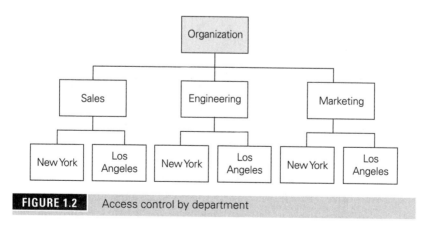

FIGURE 1.2   Access control by department

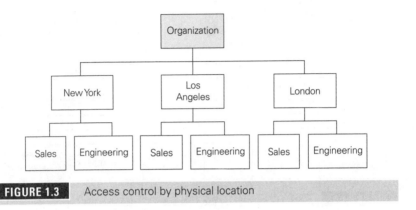

FIGURE 1.3   Access control by physical location

or execute it. For example, an employee assigned to print a directory of documents should need only read and print access to the file, not access to modify or delete. The best practice is to give only the lowest level of access permissions a user needs to perform their job.

Travel Advisory

When setting up a new network, it's extremely important to create a user hierarchy, based on one of the previous security models. Trying to change the model down the road can be difficult to do once a model is already in place.

Access Control

Before a user can access a resource, several levels of security must be passed. These three main levels are as follows:

- **Identify**   The user must initially identify themselves as a valid user for that network. This is usually provided through the form of a network login ID.
- **Authenticate**   The user is then authenticated to the network, using their logon ID and a password. If these two criteria are matched with the database of user logon IDs and passwords stored on the network, then the user is granted access to the network.
- **Authorize**   Finally, when a user tries to access a resource, the system must check to see if that user ID is authorized for that resource and

what permissions the user has when using it. Just because a user has been identified and authenticated to a network doesn't mean they should be able to access all resources.

Once a user has been authorized for that resource, they can use it according to the access rights they were granted.

Exam Tip
Be aware of the differences between identifying a user, authenticating, and authorizing. In a secure access-controlled environment, these terms specifically correspond to different steps in the process.

Access Rights

Access rights define how a user can access a resource. Several different access rights can be assigned to files and directories on a computer system. This is typically defined as an access control list (ACL). The ACL contains a list of rights a particular user has for that resource. The following are the most common access rights that can be assigned:

- **Read**   The capability to view the contents of a file or directory.
- **View**   The capability to view the contents of a directory. Even though you can see a file exists, this doesn't give you permission to read the contents of the file.
- **Write**   The capability to save a new file or write to an existing file.
- **Print**   The capability to print a file.
- **Copy**   The capability to copy a file from one location to another. The write permission would also be required in the destination directory.
- **Delete**   The capability to delete a file or directory.
- **Execute**   The capability to execute a program file or script.
- **Modify**   The capability to modify the attributes of a file or directory.
- **Move**   The capability to move a file from one location to another. The write permission would be required in the destination directory. The delete permission would be required to remove the file after the move is completed.

Exam Tip
Be aware of the differences between the various access permissions, especially which ones pertain to files, directories, or file attributes.

Determining Access Rights

The most basic levels of security that can be set on the resource level are full access or no access at all. This is a bad practice and it must be avoided through the use of more granular security. The ACL for every resource should be created for every type of user or group. When you first create an ACL for a resource, use no access as a default. This enables you to begin with a clean slate, where no access is the default permission. Then add access permissions based on the needs of the particular user or group, giving them only enough access permissions to perform their job function. Never give write or modify permissions unless users need to make changes to a file.

As an example, consider the following situation. A sales database is used to keep track of clients and their pertinent information. Employees in the sales group need to read and modify this information frequently. They also need the capability to delete and add new users to the database. The administrative staff will sometimes initiate or take calls from clients and needs access to the database to look up information on a client, and then print the results. The administrative staff doesn't need access to modify the contents of the client records in the database. To perform system maintenance and administration on the database, the database administration group needs access to perform all functions, including changing the file attributes of the database file. The sales group, however, doesn't want the database administration group to have delete access. In this scenario, the following access rights should be defined for each group:

User	Access Rights Assigned
Sales	Read, Write, Delete, Copy, Move
Admin	Read, Print
Database Admin	Read, Write, Copy, Move, Modify

Travel Advisory
Never give access rights to users if they ask for access to something they don't currently have without first verifying their need for the access with their manager.

Network Access Control

Although ACLs tend to be thought of as only for file systems, they can also be used on the network level. By enabling access lists on the components of the network, such as the routers and switches between other networks and subnets, network traffic can be separated and monitored to prevent access from unauthorized users. Allowing only specific protocols or network address ranges on to specific parts of the network can prevent someone from gaining access to the network using the wrong protocol or address.

Access Control Models

Access control models are policies that define how users access data. These policies form a framework based on the security and business goals of the organization. The rules of the framework are enforced through access control technologies. There are three main access control types:

- MAC   Mandatory Access Control
- DAC   Discretionary Access Control
- RBAC   Role-based Access Control

MAC

In a mandatory access control model (MAC), the operating system (OS) of the network is in control of access to data. Data owners are able to assign rights to their own files and share them however they see fit, but OS access controls will override any data owner settings.

Users, when defined on the system, are given certain access rights representing a certain level of trust. The data resources themselves also have certain security classifications. This classification defines the level of trust the user must have to access the data. If the user doesn't have the appropriate access rights to use the data, they're denied access.

This model is used with highly confidential data, such as government or military institutions.

DAC

Discretionary access control (DAC) allows the data owners to specify what users can access certain data. A data owner could only own one file or, if the data owner happens to be a manager, might own several directories of resources.

This is the model used by most computer networks. Access control is based on the discretion of the data owners. These policies can be implemented by themselves or through the network administrator. Users themselves can usually authorize access to their own data. For example, a user might share out their hard drive to another user without the need for a network administrator or manager to authorize or operate the procedure.

RBAC

Role-based access control (RBAC) is also referred to as nondiscretionary access control. This centrally controlled model allows access to be based on the role the user holds within an organization. Instead of giving access to individual users, access control is granted to groups of users who perform a common function. Certain roles, however, might only be held by one person. These groups can be hierarchical, with certain groups being part of an even larger entity. For example, a user might be a regional sales manager in a larger team. The user would have access to data particular to that region, but not others. Users above him in the hierarchy might have access to the data of all sales regions.

Exam Tip	
Know how the different types of access control models—MAC, DAC, and RBAC—control user access to data.	

Objective 1.02 Authentication

Once a user is identified, they must be authenticated to be able to use the resources of a computer system or network. Authentication is the act of verifying the user is who he says he is. The most common form of authentication is requiring a user login and password, but other schemes can also be used, depending on the type of access. Methods such as security cards, tokens, personal identification numbers (PINs), and more advanced techniques, such as voice or face recognition, offer additional forms of authentication. When a user logs in to a system, they supply a set of credentials or login identifiers that must be matched against the same credentials that are stored in a special authentication database. If any of the credentials don't match, such as user ID or password, the user is refused access to the system. Authentication methods are only as efficient as the amount of time and planning that's made to set up and configure the authentication system properly. The more complex the login process, the more difficult it will be for an unauthorized user to gain access to a system.

Types of Authentication

The methods used for authentication are greatly dependent on the resources that these security mechanisms are trying to protect. Most computer networks rely on a login and password type of authentication system, where the user must supply a list of credentials that must be matched to credentials stored on the network system. If the credentials don't match, the user is refused access to the system.

For physical location security, the use of pass cards or key-code locks is most often used. The use of dial-up or virtual private network (VPN) accounts might require the use of encrypted communications on top of the typical user login and password process. Each authentication system must be geared specifically to the circumstances that define a user and a resource, and how those resources need to be protected.

Physical Security

Physical security represents the effort to keep users out of the physical vicinity of a resource and only allow entrance to authorized users. The nature of this type of security and authentication typically relies on the use of keys or security cards to enter through a locked door. The resource can be anything from an entire corporate building to a certain floor or room of that building. Sensitive human resources and accounting information could be stored within these rooms, or within a computer server room, which houses the center of the corporate computer network.

Exam Tip	
A network server room should have only one entrance and that entrance should be secured.	

The most common form of physical security authentication is the use of a locked door, which must be opened with a key, or the entering of a password on a numeric or mechanical keypad. This is the most basic level of security, but the main problem associated with having every door or room secured with a lock is every user who needs access requires a key or the code. In large buildings, the administration of all the keys and passwords quickly becomes a daunting task.

If employees resign or are terminated, all the key locks and password codes need to be changed to prevent their unauthorized access in the future.

To alleviate this problem, modern physical security has turned to the use of an access card for physical security. The access card, magnetically coded with information about the user, must be swiped or waved in front of a card reader device, usually installed beside the entry door. The credentials saved on the card are then compared with a central database of user information and authenticated to ensure this user is able to enter into the secure area. In most corporate buildings, all employees carry a security access card to enter into the main building. A central database keeps track of which areas of the building employees can enter. For example, a janitor might have access to the building and its various utility rooms, but be denied access to a sensitive network server room.

For high security areas, such as government buildings or military institutions, the use of more advanced security techniques is employed. Access cards can be easily stolen by an unauthorized user who can then enter into any area for which the original user had access. New high-technology biometric security methods, such as voice recognition, retina/iris scans, and digital face recognition, create a strong wall of security that allows for the most accurate method of user identification and authentication.

Local Lingo

Biometrics   A technology used to authenticate users by a personal, biological attribute, such as an eye scan, a fingerprint scan, or voice recognition. The system is extremely accurate and secure, but is also expensive to implement.

Computer Network Authentication

The most common method of computer network authentication is through the use of a login and password. In early computer systems, when networking wasn't as available as it is today, each computer contained a set of resources the user would access. If users wanted to access the resources of a computer system, they had to use a specific login and password to gain access. Each specific computer and its resources needed a separate login and password. This was tedious for computer users and administrators alike because of the frequency with which login accounts and passwords had to be reset for each computer if users forgot them.

Nowadays, modern networks provide resources that are spread throughout a computer network that can be accessed by any user from any location. The user can be onsite on their own computer, logged in from home, or on the road by using dial-up methods or through the Internet. With the vast amount of resources that can be contained on a large computer network, the concept of multiple logins and passwords for each resource has been eliminated in favor of a single logon to the network. This way, the user only has to be authenticated once on the network to access the resources for that network. This type of centralized administration is a much more efficient way for a network administrator to control the network. User account policy templates can be created and used networkwide, to remove the need to configure each user's account settings individually, except a unique login and password. The policies can set account expiry times, and password aging and rotation for all accounts on the network. The use of access control methods, such as directory and file permissions, are used to provide more granular security on the resource level.

The following are some other popular methods of authenticating users on computer networks.

Kerberos   *Kerberos* is an authentication system designed to enable two parties to exchange private information across an insecure network. It works by assigning a unique key, called a *ticket*, to each user that logs on to the network. The ticket is then embedded in messages to identify the sender of the message.

PAP   Password Authentication Protocol (PAP) is the most basic type of authentication that consists of comparing a set of credentials, such as a user name and password, to a central table of authentication data. If the credentials match, then the user is granted access. Although the password tables used by PAP are encrypted, the actual communications aren't, allowing the user name and password to be sent over the network in clear text. This can easily be captured by an unauthorized user monitoring the network.

CHAP   The Challenge Handshake Authentication Protocol (CHAP) is much more secure than the PAP protocol. Once the communications link is completed, the authenticating server sends a random value to the client. The client sends back the value combined with the credentials and a predefined secret, calculated using a one-way hash function. The server compares the response against its own calculation of the expected hash value. If the values match, then the client is granted access.

Certificates   Certificates are a form of what is called *mutual authentication,* which uses a third party to establish the identity of a user for access control purposes. A certificate is like a digital piece of paper that contains your credentials. Digital certificates are used mostly in dealing with secure web communications and encryption. Each user needs that user's certificate to authenticate another user before exchanging secure confidential information.

A user obtains a certificate by registering with a third-party service. To receive the certificate, the user must supply credentials such as a driver's license, Social Security number, address, and phone number. The certificate authority then issues a certificate to that user, along with any encryption keys they're using. This certificate proves the user is who they say they are. See Chapter 9 for details on certificates and public key cryptography.

Communications Security

If a user can't be at a location physically to log in to their work computer, there are other methods to gain access to the system from home or while traveling. The use of dial-up modems enables a home user to call out from their home computer using a modem and a telephone line to connect directly to a system at their workplace. The first line of security for this type of communication is a remote access server (RAS), which typically contains the dial-in modem, or a bank of modems for large-scale implementations, and authenticates the users through a login and password database separate from their regular network authentication. Once users have gained access through the remote access server, then they can supply their credentials to authenticate to their network resources.

To augment these security measures and also to streamline the authentication process, some remote access servers authenticate the user to the network database of logins and passwords, rather than keeping their own separate lists.

To add more security to this model, the use of a security card or key token is used to ensure the user is authorized to log in to the network. These security tokens or cards cycle through a special algorithmic set of numbers that change every minute. The security token is compared to the current number on the server and, if they match, then the user can begin entering their login and password. For example, if an unauthorized user happens to find out the login and password of a user, and is able to dial in to the network with a modem, that user will still need the security token before being able to use the stolen login and password. This is called *multifactor authentication,* where it takes more than knowledge of a password to gain access.

The most modern form of remote access communication is the use of a VPN, which is a special encrypted communications tunnel that allows a user to access a corporate network from the Internet. In this model, the user isn't dialing in to an actual machine on the corporate network but, instead, is dialing in or connecting to a local Internet connection. Once the user has a connection to the Internet, they can then activate the VPN, which creates an encrypted tunnel through the Internet to the corporate network. Once the user is connected, they can log in with their user ID and password in the usual manner.

Account and Password Management

Although the most common form of system authentication is a login and a password procedure, this is also considered one of the weakest security mechanisms available. Passwords generally tend to be weak because users use common dictionary words or personal information that can be easily guessed by an unauthorized user. Many users use the name of their spouse, pet, or birth date as a password. They often tell these passwords to others or write them down in conspicuous locations, such as a note taped to their computer monitor. Unauthorized users often resort to social engineering, the act of using everyday conversation to provide clues to someone's personal information, which can be used as an attempt at guessing their password. By enforcing the use of strong passwords, which aren't based on dictionary words or personal information, but include the use of alphanumeric, and uppercase and lowercase letters, the ability for an unauthorized user to guess a password is greatly diminished. To ensure the usefulness and efficiency of logins and password, account and password policies must be created and strictly adhered to.

Account Policies

To strengthen the security of the logon process, several policies can be created for login account use. By setting restrictions on user accounts, you can effectively narrow the risk of having your network compromised by an unauthorized user. Some of the most effective restrictions include the following:

- Detailed naming conventions
- Limiting logon attempts

- Establishing expiry dates
- Disabling accounts
- Setting time restrictions
- Restricting machine access

Naming Conventions   When you first configure and set up a network, a best practice is to enact some form of naming convention for your accounts. The most common convention is using a user's first initial and last name, or variations of it, for an account ID. Never have account names that represent job functions. A user account called "admin" is much more likely to attract the attention of an unauthorized user if they're trying to hack an account. They know the user ID could be the main administrative account for the network and, if they're able to compromise that account, they will have full control over the network. Other names such as "human_resources" or "accounting" will also be more likely targets for an unauthorized user.

Limit Logon Attempts   This parameter sets the maximum amount of bad login attempts before disabling an account. This is an important feature because many hackers simply repeat attempts at getting into an account, using different passwords each time. If no login attempt restrictions exist, hackers can continue this brute force attack until the account is compromised. A best practice is to limit logon attempts to approximately three to five times. Once this limit is reached, a user must contact the administrator to enable the account again.

Expiry Dates   Setting an expiry date on a user account will disable it when the target date is reached. This is most useful for contract workers, who might only be working for the company a short period of time. When the contract is finished, the user's login is immediately disabled. Over a period of time, it's easy to forget when a contractor started and finished work. By setting an expiry on the account when a contractor is first hired, it won't be forgotten and the account will be automatically disabled when the contract is over. If the contract is renewed, the account can simply be enabled again and the expiration date changed to the new expiration date.

Disabling Accounts   When an employee has left the company, it's important to disable their account immediately. This is especially important for employees who are suddenly terminated for any reason. By immediately disabling the account, you deny access to any further attempts by that user to get back into their account. Reasons for disabling an account could be the employee doesn't work for the company any longer and shouldn't have any access to the corporate network whatsoever.

Another best practice is to disable accounts you don't recognize as valid. Unauthorized users could have broken into the system and created their own "dummy" accounts to perform their activities unnoticed. If the account is valid, the user will contact you because they can't log in. You can then verify whether the user should have access to the system.

Time Restrictions   If your company only operates during certain hours a day, it could be useful to set time restrictions on access to the network. After hours, only a select few users might need access. For everyone else, you can set their accounts to be able to log in only during operating hours. This will reduce the risk of unauthorized users trying to use an employee's account off-hours to break into the system.

Machine Restrictions   Like time restrictions, you can similarly only allow logins from certain machines on the network. If you set the machine restrictions to any computer on your current internal network, this can prevent anyone trying to access the system using an outside computer or laptop. Machine restrictions are usually set using a computer's network card MAC address or the network address.

Local Lingo	
MAC (Media Access Control) address A unique hardware identifier coded into every network card or device.	

Exam Tip	
Be aware of the different types of account restrictions that can be set to increase the security of user accounts.	

Password Management

The implementation of account policies is only one half the battle against unauthorized intrusion of your network. The most important aspect of login security is password management. A user account is only as secure as its password. An unauthorized user can easily find the names of accounts they can use to get access. Guessing a password for a user account is much harder but, with simple password discovery methods and weak passwords chosen by the users, this might not be as difficult as you think.

The typical user most often uses something easy to remember for their password. This includes names of family members, pets, phone numbers, and birth dates, all of which can easily be discovered by someone who knows them. These passwords can even be discovered by a complete stranger who, through simple social engineering, only has to ask the user a few questions about their personal life. Sometimes users, in an effort not to forget their passwords, write them down and leave them in a conspicuous place for anyone to find.

Other types of passwords that aren't secure are those based on any word found in the dictionary. Many password-cracking programs are out there that can discover any password in a short period of time if it's based on a common dictionary word. Passwords should always be at least six to eight characters long, and consist of a variety of letters, numbers, symbols (if allowed) and contain both uppercase and lowercase characters. Even common dictionary words can be reworked using numbers and symbols to create the same word visually, so it's still easy to remember. For example, the password "largerthanlife" can be changed to "L@rG3rTh@Nl!F3" by simply substituting symbols and numbers for certain letters, and by mixing uppercase and lowercase letters together.

Some important password policies can be set by the administrator to enforce strong passwords:

- Minimum length
- Password rotation
- Password aging

Minimum Length   The minimum length for a password can be enforced by the network administrator. This prevents users from using small, easy-to-guess passwords of only a few characters in length. The recommended minimum password length is approximately six to eight characters.

Travel Advisory

Don't set your password minimum length too high. If you do, users will begin to forget them more quickly and this will create more work for the administrator, who will then have to reset forgotten passwords and enable locked accounts.

Password Rotation   Most login and password authentication systems can remember the last five to ten passwords a user has used and prevent them from using the same password over and over again. If this option is available, it should be enabled, so a user's password will always be different.

Password Aging   The longer a password is in existence, the easier it is to discover, simply by narrowing down the options over time. By forcing users to change their passwords regularly, this will prevent the discovery of a password through brute force attacks. The recommended age for a password is usually one to three months. The smaller time of validity, the more secure the system. This, however, has a drawback because users will be more apt to forget their passwords because of these frequent changes, causing more administrative overhead. You might have to choose between security and convenience.

Exam Tip

Be aware of the various password policies that can be set to increase password security.

Administrative Security

System security has more to it than merely setting policies and standards for login names and passwords. Although these are important, maintaining the security of your network requires constant vigilance through the use of auditing, intrusion detection, and the security of the administrative account and password databases. Your network must be constantly monitored for behavior that might indicate unauthorized activity.

Securing Authentication Databases

Much of the network administrator's job is protecting the user accounts and passwords from abuse, but who's protecting the administrator's account and the central database of passwords? If an unauthorized user were to gain access to the administrative account or the password database, they would have full control over the network.

Securing the Administrator   The first task in securing the administrative account is to ensure the name of the account doesn't reflect the job function. For example, the first account an unauthorized user would try to crack is any account named "administrator" or "supervisor." One way to prevent this is to rename the administrator account to something that doesn't reflect the job function. Another best practice for using administrative access is to create an administrative group of users, who all have the same access as the administrator account. This way, each user can log in with their own ID and password, which resembles any other user on the network. This also helps in auditing administrative access because now you can see the name of the person who logged in to perform a supervisory task. If the user was simply "administrator," it could have been an unauthorized user who broke into that account. Of course, any administrative account should also follow the password rules that apply to everyone else.

Protecting the Password Database   The password database itself must be protected against unauthorized access. If a user were to gain access to the password file, they could use a special password-cracking program to search through it and discover all the passwords quickly. The permissions for access to the password database must be set so only the administrative users can access it. Care must be taken to ensure certain system accounts don't have access to the database. For example, an account called "backup" might be set up, which is used by a tape backup program. If this program is set up to have administrative rights, it will be able to see the password database. If an unauthorized user broke into the backup account, they would be able to retrieve the database. Ensure that only a few accounts have administrative access and don't enable this indiscriminately.

Another method that can be used to secure password databases, which is enabled by default by many OSs, is to encrypt the contents of the password database. If someone were to get access to the password file, they would still need to crack the encryption somehow. This can be extremely difficult, depending on the level of complexity of the encryption.

Local Lingo

Encryption The act of translating normal text into a secret code using some form of cipher of encryption key. To decrypt the file, you need the corresponding code.

Account Auditing

Your network computer system records every login to the network. Many OSs can even go further: they're able to record the actions of each user and what resources they're using at any given time. It's important for the network administrator to scans these logs regularly for unusual behavior. For example, the administrator might notice someone is logging on at 3 A.M. every day with the account "administrator." This should send a red flag to the administrator that someone has hacked into the account and is using it during off-hours.

Your login and password database should be checked regularly for accounts of users no longer with the company. The longer you leave old accounts enabled, the greater the risk is for a former employee or an unauthorized user to break into the account. Sometimes the network administrator isn't notified by the human resources department when an employee resigns or is terminated. By checking the login accounts on a regular basis, the administrator can flag any old accounts—especially accounts that aren't recognized—for disabling and deletion.

Intrusion Detection

To be proactive with your network security, special software is available that can help track unauthorized activity on your network, including both your network OSs and network equipment. *Intrusion detection* software can alert you when suspicious activity is recorded on a piece of network equipment or a server. For example, an outside user might have hacked into the administrative account on your company router or firewall. The intrusion detection software can notify you of these occurrences, so you can quickly change the password or disable those accounts. For a network administrator to monitor all the servers and network equipment constantly is next to impossible. Intrusion detection tools can greatly aid the administrator by proactively sending alerts.

CHECKPOINT

✔ **Objective 1.01: Access Control**   Access control is the first line of security for a computer network. Access control methods control how users interact with other resources and computer systems. Users and resources must have their security relationships defined. Use an Access Control List (ACL) to define permissions for users of a resource. Group users into logical units defined by job function, department, or physical location to ease administration of access rights. Start with a default of no access, and then only assign the permissions needed by the user to perform their job.

✔ **Objective 1.02: Authentication**   Once a user is identified, they must be authenticated to use the resources of a computer system or network. Authentication is the act of verifying the user is who he says he is. Create account and password policies to limit abuse of logins and passwords by unauthorized users. Accounts names shouldn't reflect job functions. Accounts should have a maximum number of login attempts set. Passwords should have a minimum length of six to eight characters, and they should be composed of uppercase and lowercase letters, numbers, and symbols. Passwords should be changed on a regular basis. The password database must be protected by access permissions and encryption, and accounts should be audited on a regular basis.

REVIEW QUESTIONS

1. The acronym ACL stands for:
    A. Arbitrary Code Language
    B. Access Control Library
    C. Access Control List
    D. Allowed Computer List

2. What should the default access level rights be?
    A. Full access
    B. No access
    C. Read access
    D. Write access

3. After a user is identified and authenticated to the system, what else must be performed to enable a user to use a resource?

   A. Authorized

   B. Amortize

   C. Encrypted

   D. Enabled

4. Which access right allows you to save a file?

   A. Read

   B. Copy

   C. Modify

   D. Write

5. Which access right allows you to modify the attributes of a file?

   A. Modify

   B. Copy

   C. Change

   D. Edit

6. What access rights should most users be given?

   A. At least read and write access

   B. No access

   C. Enough to perform their job function

   D. Full access

7. What account policy should be set to prevent brute force attacks on user accounts?

   A. Disable unused accounts

   B. Time restrictions

   C. Account expiry dates

   D. Limit logon attempts

8. After a user has been identified, what must happen before they can log in to a computer network?

   A. Authentication with a password

   B. They must enter an encrypted user ID

   C. The access permissions must be set properly

   D. The administrator must enable them to enter

9. The minimum length of a password should be set to:

   A. 12 to15 characters

   B. 3 to 5 characters

   C. 6 to 8 characters

   D. 1 to 3 characters

10. What should be done to the password database to prevent an unauthorized user from cracking the contents?

    A. Remove all access rights

    B. Encrypt the file

    C. Move it offline to a floppy disk

    D. Copy it to a dummy file with a different name

REVIEW ANSWERS

1. **C** The acronym ACL stands for access control list.

2. **B** The default access permission should be no access. Start adding permissions for users on the basis of what they need to accomplish their jobs.

3. **A** Although a user has been given access to log in to the network, they still need to be authorized to use a particular resource.

4. **D** The write permission should be granted to allow a user to save a file.

5. **A** The modify permission should be granted to allow a user to change the attributes of a file.

6. **C** Never give a user more access rights than they need to perform their job.

7. **D** By setting a maximum number of unsuccessful login attempts, the account will be locked out and any further attempts at logging in with that account will be denied.

8. **A** Once a user is identified with their account ID, they must be authenticated by using a password that must be compared to a central password database on the system. If the password matches, then that user is authenticated.

9. **C**   If the number of characters is set higher than six to eight characters, it might be more difficult for users to remember their passwords. If the number of characters is set to less that six to eight characters, it will be easier for a password-cracking program to discover the password.

10. **B**   By encrypting the password file, the contents are protected, even if an unauthorized user gains access to the file.

Attacks, Malicious Code, and Social Engineering

ETA	NEWBIE	SOME EXPERIENCE	EXPERT
	4 hours	2 hours	1 hour

In the past, security of a computing facility was geared toward physical security of the premises and equipment. Only certain people could access the rooms that contained the computer equipment, and the user accounts to access those systems were protected by a login and a password.

With the explosive growth of computer networks and their connections to the public Internet network, a new array of security concerns has arisen. No longer does an unauthorized user need to physically break into a building to access computer terminals. Today, from the comfort of their own home, hackers can access any network connected to the Internet. With a variety of hacking tools, a malicious user can easily bring down an unsecured network with the push of a button.

Attacks can be centered on one specific system, such as a web server, or on an entire network of computers. Malicious code such as viruses, e-mail worms, Trojan horse programs, and logic bombs can wreak havoc on an unsecured network. The need for security to prevent attacks such as these is not only important to a company or organization, but also to its customer base who could rely on their Internet services to perform their daily business.

This chapter explores the dangers and preventive steps to be taken to protect your network and systems from attacks, malicious codes, and social-engineering hacking techniques. The importance of regularly logging security information and auditing it is also stressed.

 **Objective 2.01** Attacks

Security of a network and its systems involves protection against a variety of attacks. These attacks might affect only certain areas of your operations or disrupt them as a whole. Some attacks are an attempt to gain access or damage one particular user account or one server. Other attacks try to disrupt the entire network infrastructure itself or to prevent customers from accessing a public web site.

Attacks are launched for a variety of reasons. A casual hacker might only be testing the security of the system and doing no damage at all. More malicious users could try to damage parts of your system or cause you to lose valuable data. Other unauthorized users might want access to confidential records, which can also be an act of corporate espionage.

The purpose of the attack isn't the main concern. The main concern is how to prevent these attacks from succeeding. By being aware of the various types of attacks, tools, and resources used by malicious users, you're protecting yourself with knowledge. By knowing where and how to expect attacks, you can install preventative measures to protect your systems.

Network-Based Attacks

Of the types of attacks that can assault a network and computer system, many attacks are geared toward specific system accounts, system services, or applications. The most damaging and, obviously, the most popular attacks by hackers involve disrupting the network itself. The *network* is the infrastructure that allows all systems and devices to communicate with each other, so disrupting those communication lines can be the most damaging attack a network can suffer.

The following sections outline some of the more popular types of network-based attacks that have been used to disrupt communications and describes how to prevent them.

Exam Tip	
Be aware of the different types of network-based attacks and how to prevent them.	

Denial of Service

Denial of service (DoS) attacks have been well publicized recently because of their capability to easily deny access to a particular web or Internet site. In a *DoS* attack, a hacker overloads a specific server with data, so it can't process the data fast enough to keep up. System performance slows to a crawl because it simply can't keep up with the flood of data being sent to it. This affects the web site's capability to service legitimate requests because the client won't receive any responses to their queries. This type of attack can also be performed on entire networks, as the DoS attack is targeted at the central router or firewall where all data passes through. The network traffic becomes so high that nothing can get in or out of the network. This type of attack is more common than attacking a single server because the network bandwidth is being attacked, which effectively denies access to all systems on that network rather than only one.

A more organized and devastating attack is a *distributed DoS* attack, where the flood of data originates from multiple hosts at the same time. The combined effects quickly overload any server or network device. As opposed to a single origin of a DoS attack, a network administrator can't pinpoint and deny access by the one host because the attacks will be coming from multiple hosts, distributed throughout the Internet. Usually, these originating hosts aren't willfully engaged in the attack. Hackers can secretly install software on an insecure server somewhere else on the Internet and use that to remotely flood another host with data. This effectively hides the true origin of the attack, especially when the Internet Protocol (IP) addresses are spoofed to show a different originating address than the actual origin of the attack.

The most common form of attack uses simple TCP/IP protocol utilities, such as Packet Internet Groper (ping). *Ping* is a command used to find out if a certain host (classified as the *destination host*) is functioning and communicating with the network. A user sends a ping or query packet to the destination host. The destination host sends back an acknowledgement that it is indeed working and on the network. Used in a DoS attack, a malicious user can send a continuous stream of rapid ping attempts. The host is then overloaded by having to acknowledge every ping, rendering it unable to process legitimate requests.

Another type of DoS attack is the synchronous idle character (SYN) flood. *SYN* is an aspect of the TCP/IP protocol that allows systems to synchronize with each other while communicating. One system sends a SYN packet and this is acknowledged by the other system. This process can be abused by a hacker by sending forged SYN packets to a host, which is unable to reply to the request because the return address is incorrect. This causes the host to halt communications while waiting for the other system to reply. If the host is flooded with a high number of forged SYN packets, it will be overloaded and unable to respond to legitimate requests.

DoS attacks can be difficult to stop and prevent, but some simple configuration changes on the local routers and firewalls can help prevent these types of attacks. The simplest way of protecting against ping flood types of attacks is to disable the Internet Control Message Protocol (ICMP) protocol at the firewall or router level, so the host won't acknowledge any ping attempts from outside the network.

Travel Advisory

Turning off the ICMP protocol can deprive you of important feedback from network troubleshooting tools because commands—such as ping and traceroute—use the ICMP protocol to function and provide important communications information.

Other types of attacks, such as SYN floods, are caused by vulnerabilities in the network protocols themselves. The TCP/IP implementation of your operating system (OS) should be upgraded to the latest version by installing recent service packs and security patches. Some firewalls and other security products also contain the capability to detect network flood attacks, can actively block them, and can try to trace them back to a source.

Back Door

A *back door* traditionally is defined as a way for a software programmer to access a program while bypassing its authentication schemes. The back door is coded in by the programmer during development so, at a later time, they can break into their own program without having to authenticate to the system through normal access methods. This is helpful to programmers because they needn't access the program as they normally would in a typical user mode (where they'd be forced to enter authentication information, such as a user name and password).

In hacking terms, a *back door* is a program secretly installed on an unsuspecting user's computer so the hacker can later access the user's computer bypassing any security authentication systems. The back door program runs as a service on the user's computer and listens on specific network ports not typically used by traditional network services. The hacker runs the client portion of the program on their computer, which then connects to the service on the target computer. Once the connection is established, the hacker can gain full access, including remotely controlling the system. Hackers usually doesn't know what specific systems are running the back door, but their programs can scan a network's IP addresses to see which ones are listening to the specific port for that back door.

Back-door software is typically installed as a Trojan horse as part of some other software package. A user might download a program from the Internet that contains the hidden back-door software. To protect your computer against these programs, antivirus programs can now detect the presence of these back-door programs. Personal firewalls can also detect suspicious incoming and outgoing network traffic from your computer. Port-scanning software can also be used to identify any open ports on your system you don't recognize. The open ports can be cross-referenced with lists of ports used by known back-door programs.

Spoofing

One of the more popular methods for hacking a system is *spoofing* network addresses, which involves modifying the header of a network packet to use the source address of an external or internal host different from the original address. By spoofing the IP address, the destination host could be fooled into thinking the message is from a trusted source. The cause of this problem is that the architecture of Transmission Control Protocol/Internet Protocol (TCP/IP) has no built-in mechanism to verify the source and destination IP address of its network packets. A hacker can spoof the IP address to make it look like it's coming from a different location. It can even be made to look like the IP address of an internal system.

IP spoofing is mainly used by hackers to hide their identity when attacking a network system, especially in a DoS-type attack. By spoofing the IP addresses of the incoming packets, network administrators could have a difficult time determining the real source of the attacks before they can set up a filter to block out that IP address.

Another use for spoofing is the capability to emulate a trusted internal system on the network. For example, if a local server has an IP address of 192.168.17.5, and only accepts connections from that network, a hacker can modify the source address of the packet to mimic an internal address, such as 192.168.17.12. This way, the server thinks the packets are coming from an internal trusted host, not a system external to the network, as shown in Figure 2.1.

To help prevent spoofing attacks, your router or firewall might be able to filter incoming traffic to restrict network traffic coming into the external interface. By configuring the filter to prevent external packets originating from internal addresses, spoofed addresses can't enter the network.

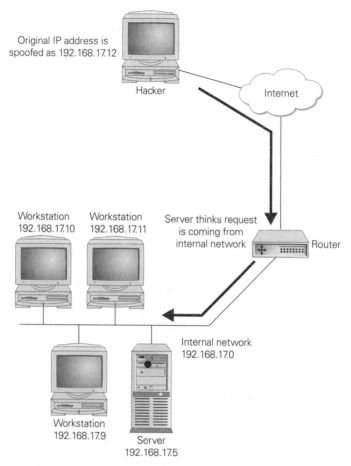

Original IP address is
spoofed as 192.168.17.12

Hacker

Internet

Workstation
192.168.17.10

Workstation
192.168.17.11

Server thinks request
is coming from
internal network

Router

Internal network
192.168.17.0

Workstation
192.168.17.9

Server
192.168.17.5

FIGURE 2.1   A hacker spoofs an internal address to gain access to a server.

Smurf Attack

A *smurf* attack exploits the use of IP broadcast addressing and the Internet Control Message Protocol (ICMP) protocol. *ICMP* is used by networks, and also through administrative utilities, to exchange information about the state of the network. ICMP is used by the ping utility to contact other systems to see if they're operational. The destination system returns an echo message in response to a ping message.

A hacker uses a smurf utility to build a network packet with a spoofed IP address that contains an ICMP ping message addressed to an IP broadcast address. A *broadcast address* is one that includes all nodes of a certain network and messages to that address will be seen by all of them. The ping echo responses are sent back to the target address. The amount of pings and echo responses can flood the network with traffic, causing systems on the network to be unresponsive, as shown in Figure 2.2.

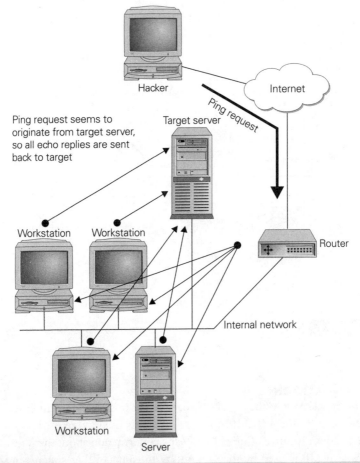

| **FIGURE 2.2** | A target computer is flooded with ping echoes from a smurf attack. |

To prevent smurf attacks, IP broadcast addressing should be disabled on the network router because this broadcast addressing is only used rarely.

TCP/IP Hijacking

Together with spoofing, an unauthorized user can also effectively hijack a network connection of another user. For example, by monitoring a network transmission, a hacker can analyze the source and destination IP addresses of the two computers. Once hackers know the IP address of one of the participants, they can knock them off their connection using a DoS or other type of attack, and then resume communications by spoofing the IP address of the disconnected user. The other user is tricked into thinking they are still communicating with the original person. The only real way to prevent this sort of attack from occurring is having some sort of encryption mechanism, such as Internet Protocol Security (IPSec).

Local Lingo

IPSec   Stands for IP Security, a set of protocols to support secure exchange of packets at the IP layer. IPSec is typically used to secure and encrypt communications on a virtual private network (VPN).

Man-in-the-Middle

A *man-in-the-middle* attack is exactly what the name says: a form of hijack attack. In between the sender and the receiver of a communication, a person in the middle can intercept or listen in to the information being transferred. For example, if a person is talking to someone on the phone and another person listens to the conversation on another phone receiver in the house, this other person is the man-in-the-middle.

These types of attacks usually occur when a network communications line is compromised through the installation of a *network packet sniffer,* which can analyze network communications packet by packet. Many types of communications use plain, clear text and this is easily read by someone using a packet sniffer. During an encrypted communication, a hacker can intercept the authentication phase of a transmission and obtain the public encryption keys of the participants, as shown in Figure 2.3.

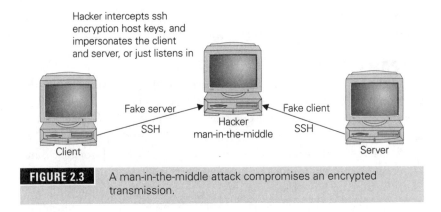

Hacker intercepts ssh
encryption host keys, and
impersonates the client
and server, or just listens in

Fake server
SSH

Hacker
man-in-the-middle

Fake client
SSH

Client

Server

FIGURE 2.3   A man-in-the-middle attack compromises an encrypted transmission.

To prevent man-in-the-middle attacks, a unique server host key can be used to prove its identity to a client as a known host. This has been implemented in newer versions of the Secure Shell (SSH) protocol, which was vulnerable to man-in-the-middle attacks in the past.

Replay

A *replay* attack occurs when an unauthorized user captures an encrypted or password-protected communication, breaks the encryption or password, and then sends the communication to its original destination, acting as the original sender, as shown in Figure 2.4.

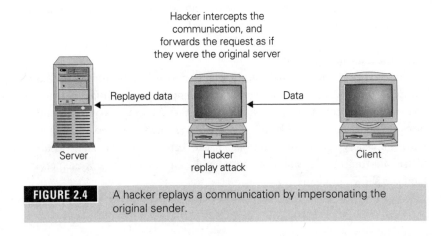

Hacker intercepts the
communication, and
forwards the request as if
they were the original server

Replayed data

Data

Server

Hacker
replay attack

Client

FIGURE 2.4   A hacker replays a communication by impersonating the original sender.

This most often happens with certain types of authentication systems that issue authentication tickets, such as Kerberos. The hacker captures the ticket, breaks the encryption, and then resends the ticket to impersonate the original client.

To prevent reply attacks from succeeding, timestamps or sequence numbers can be implemented. This allows the authentication system to accept only network packets that contain the appropriate stamp or sequence number. If the time stamp is beyond a certain threshold, then the packet is discarded.

Cryptography and Passwords

The increased use of encryption technologies to protect passwords and communications channels has greatly enhanced security for authentication. Unfortunately, early uses of encryption keys have proven somewhat vulnerable because their algorithms are weak and can be broken by today's high-speed processors, which can decipher them fairly quickly. Cryptography continues to evolve and the mathematical algorithms used for encryption are becoming increasingly complex to prevent against cracking. The following sections outline some of the most common attacks on cryptography-based security methods.

Weak Keys and Mathematical Algorithms

Many early types of encryption methods were usable for their time but, with the dramatic increase in processing power, programs were developed that could crack these keys in a short time. Encryption keys have grown in size and complexity, from 40 and 56 bits, which is now considered insecure, to 128 and even 256-bit encryption. The level of protection is also dependent on the public key chosen, especially if it involves a common series of numbers that are easy to guess.

Hackers continually try to break encryption standards. The best practice ˙ to use the strongest encryption and algorithms available, along with sᵗ public keys.

Birthday Attack

A *birthday* attack refers to a statistical, mathematical meth? for you to find encryption key. The basis of the birthday attack is this: it's to find one person two people who have the same birthday, rather than tr̩̍or of the former situa- with a specific birth date. The odds are much more i⸝ people, instead of one. tion and you'll discover the exact birth date ⸍ᵚ⸍ breaking an

In cryptography, this relates to the process of comparing a hashed value of two different encrypted messages. Instead of looking for an exact match for a predetermined hash value, the hacker can analyze data for two hash values that come out as equal. This, in turn, gives the hacker more information on how to break the encryption key algorithm because two values were found that are the same and further investigation can begin to reveal the encryption algorithm.

Obviously, stronger keys using 128-bit or more encryption are less susceptible to such an attack because the processing of all the possible computations could take a long time.

Software Exploitation

Many software and application programs contain bugs that create security vulnerabilities. A *software bug* is a term used to describe an error in a program that hinders or alters its capability to function. There errors, however, can also provide security holes that can be compromised by a malicious user. At risk are not only the applications and programs that run on your computer, but the OS as well. Networking equipment, which runs the backbone of all your communications, also runs on software and firmware that could be vulnerable. If a hacker were to disrupt a network device such as a router, this could disable the entire network.

Application Software

Application-program bugs affect the programs you use daily to perform your job function, such as e-mail, word processing, and Internet access. Security vulnerabilities in these applications can be exploited, so a malicious user can spread viruses more easily into your system and the systems of others. Office productivity programs are especially vulnerable to macro-type viruses, which use their own macro commands that a hacker can use to perform malicious functions. ʾor example, e-mail programs can inadvertently spread viruses and worms to iɪɴe in your address book with only a few lines of macro code. Internet surfof prɪ an insecure web browser can result in the spread of viruses and the loss another ɪᴄause personal information can be sent through the web browser to

By ensurinᴋ
rity vulnerabilitiᴋᴜ application software is current, the new versions fix security. The most recent verₛ bugs so they can't be compromised by malicious users. patches, should be availaᴜ of your software, or any service packs and security from the software vendor's web site.

Operating Systems

OS vulnerabilities can be dangerous if not addressed appropriately. The OS is the brains behind your entire system and, if security vulnerabilities exist in its most critical components, an unauthorized user could exploit them to gain access and cause serious damage to the OS and your sensitive data.

Keeping your OS current with the latest patches and service packs is extremely important, especially those that fix security vulnerabilities and software bugs from previous versions.

Travel Advisory

In an effort to increase application functionality, some OS vendors have tied their applications closely with the OS itself. This caused a large number of serious security vulnerabilities to occur because the application has privileges to OS services and functions. Be aware of the capabilities of your applications and keep them current with the most recent versions and software patches.

Networking Equipment

Networking devices, such as routers, switches, and firewalls, contain *firmware*, which is a type of software that controls their operation. From a networking standpoint, bugs and security vulnerabilities in network device software can result in holes that can be exploited by unauthorized users. If any of these critical network devices are compromised, a malicious user can disrupt or disable communications on the network. This is dangerous because the router is usually the main communications device on your network and, if it's disrupted, you could lose communications for the entire network.

The most recent software and firmware for your device should be installed to ensure any previous software bugs and security vulnerabilities are fixed.

Password Guessing

Most user-account vulnerabilities are caused by insecure or easy-to-guess passwords. Insecure passwords are susceptible to a number of password-cracking techniques that use dictionary names or even personal information in an attempt to guess the password of a login account.

Passwords to any system should have a minimum length between six to eight characters, and should contain both uppercase and lowercase letters, as well as numbers and symbols. Any word that can be found in the dictionary shouldn't be used because password-cracking programs can easily compare your password with words in the entire dictionary in a short time. Personal information—such as birthdates, or names of family members and pets—should never be used because anyone who knows your personal information can use this to try to guess your password.

The following sections outline some of the different methods used when someone tries to access a user account.

Brute Force

A *brute-force* attack is just that—an attempt to break a password or encryption scheme through simple repetition of attempts. A wide variety of utilities can perform these attacks. An actual person trying to log in through repeated use of different passwords could be there for many years before finding the combination. Modern hacking utilities can cycle through thousands of combinations of letters and numbers to guess a password.

To prevent brute-force attacks on user accounts, the simplest and most efficient way is to set the limits on login attempts. For example, if you limit the amount of login attempts to five, the brute-force attack method will only have five chances to guess the password before the account is locked and further login attempts are denied.

Dictionary

A *dictionary* attack is a form of the brute-force attack. By capturing an encrypted password file that contains all the login names and their corresponding passwords, an unauthorized user can run special programs that compare the file with a list of common, dictionary-based passwords. I'm sure you know it's common knowledge that most users tend to use simple, easy passwords, which correspond to everyday words in the dictionary.

By running a comparison of the encrypted password file with the hashed values of the common passwords, many users' login accounts can be unlocked with the revealed passwords.

Social Engineering

The easiest way to discover someone's password often is simply to ask her. *Social engineering* is defined as using and manipulating human behavior to obtain a required result. A user frequently can be easily led to reveal her password or to provide personal information that might reveal her password. For example, someone might call a user on the phone, pretending to be from another department, asking to use the user's password to retrieve a file. The user, thinking she knows who she's talking to, might give him the password without officially authenticating who he is or why he needs this information. Or, the caller might make small talk with the user and trick her into revealing names of family members or her birth date, so he can try out this information as a password to the user's account.

The only way to protect against security abuses because of social engineering is user education, and emphasizing the need to follow security procedures at all times, even when dealing with someone you know within the company.

Objective 2.02 Malicious Code

D*ata security* not only means protecting sensitive information from prying eyes and unauthorized access, but also protecting the integrity and existence of that data from malicious users. The use of malicious code to cause havoc on a network or computer system is a form of digital vandalism, in which not only physical equipment is damaged, but also the files, resources, and bandwidth that make up that network. Previously, most companies used their security resources for prevention against unauthorized physical access to their equipment and facilities. With the advance of the Internet age, companies must now protect themselves from pathways unseen by most users: the computer network.

Damage from virus attacks or unauthorized access because of back-door or Trojan-horse types of programs can be catastrophic. A simple e-mail worm attached to a message can suddenly grind your e-mail and network system to a halt. Other viruses can contain payloads that destroy or damage information, which often can never be replaced.

Travel Advisory

A good backup strategy can go a long way in preventing the damage caused by a virus attack. If a virus manages to infect an entire file server, you'll most likely need to restore all the data from backups.

You must be aware of the different types of malicious code, how they gain entry, and what they do once they infect a system. Proactive protection in the form of knowledge and user education are critical in dealing with these types of attacks.

Viruses

The computing world has been recently rocked by a number of viruses and other types of malicious code, such as the Code Red, Melissa, and I Love You virus. The amount of expense and time needed to clean up and restore operations after a virus attack can be enormous. Some companies take many days, or even weeks, to get back to full operations. For some businesses, this can be fatal.

A *virus* is simply defined as any computer program that replicates itself, even if the program doesn't do any harm to the system. Most computer viruses self-replicate themselves without the knowledge of the user.

Types of Viruses

Viruses can come in a variety of types, with different locations and methods of infection, and severity of payload. The following sections outline some of the more popular forms of virus types.

Boot Sector *Boot sector viruses* infect the boot sector or partition table of a disk. The *boot sector* is used by the computer to determine what OSs are present on the system to boot. The most common way of getting infected with a boot sector virus is by booting a computer system with an infected floppy disk in the floppy drive. By infecting the boot sector, the virus won't allow the system to boot into an OS, rendering the computer useless until the boot sector is repaired.

The best way to remove a boot-sector virus from your system is to boot the system from the floppy drive using an antivirus boot disk. This enables you to start the computer with some basic start-up files on the floppy, bypassing the boot sector, and then running the antivirus program on the disk.

Companion Using the features of the DOS OS, specifically, the 8.3 naming system, which can identify different file types, a *companion* virus disguises itself as a program with the same name, but with a different extension. For example, a virus might name itself program.com, to emulate a file called program.exe. The .com file under DOS is a higher priority than the standard .exe file with the same name, so the virus file program.com will run first. Typically, the virus runs the real program immediately after, so it appears everything is performing normally.

Some viruses simply replace the original file with their own version, which performs the same tasks and includes new, malicious code to run with it.

File Infectors   *File-infector* viruses generally have the extensions of .com or .exe. These viruses can be extremely destructive because they try to replicate and spread further by infecting other executable programs on the system with the same extensions. Sometimes, a file-infector virus destroys the program it infects by overwriting the original code.

Travel Advisory

If your computer is afflicted with a file-infector virus, don't attach it to a network or it could start infecting files on other workstations and file servers.

Macro Viruses   A *macro* is an instruction that carries out program commands automatically within an application. These macros are typically used in popular application programs, like Microsoft Word and Excel. A *macro* virus uses the internal workings of the application to perform malicious operations, such as deleting files or opening other virus-executable programs. Sometimes these viruses also infect program templates that are loaded automatically by the applications. Every time the user creates a file within the default template, the macro virus is copied to the new file.

Memory Resident   When executed, a *memory-resident* virus will stay in memory and infect other files that are run at the same time. For a memory-resident virus to spread, the user has to run an infected program. Once activated, the virus goes into memory, examines each new program as it's run, and, if the program isn't already infected, infects it.

Metamorphic   A *metamorphic* virus is capable of recompiling itself into a new form, so the code keeps changing from generation to generation. A metamorphic virus is similar to a polymorphic virus because both can modify their forms. A metamorphic virus doesn't decrypt itself to a single constant virus body in memory, though, and a polymorphic virus does. A metamorphic virus can also change its virus body code.

Polymorphic *Polymorphic* viruses change themselves with each infection. These types of viruses were created to confuse virus-scanning programs. These viruses are more difficult to detect by scanning because each copy of the virus looks different than the previous copies.

Stealth A *stealth* virus hides itself from virus protection software by encrypting its code. Stealth viruses attempt to cover their trail as they infect their way through a computer. When a stealth virus infects, it takes over the system function that reads files or system sectors. When something attempts to access the corrupted file, the stealth virus reports that the original file is there. In reality, the original information is gone and the stealth virus has taken its place.

Virus Program File Types

Some types of files are most susceptible to virus infections because they're common to certain types of computer systems and applications. The following are a number of the most popular types of program files targeted by viruses:

- **.bat** An *MS-DOS batch* file is a file containing a series of commands for the OS that are executed automatically in sequence.
- **.com** A *.com* file is a MS-DOS command file. These files usually execute with only a command shell interface. Most early computer viruses were created as a .com file because the main DOS program files were in this form.
- **.doc** This is a file extension associated with Microsoft Word. Along with Microsoft Access and Excel files, *.doc* file extensions are susceptible to macro virus infection.
- **.dll** The acronym for dynamic-link library, *DLL* is a library of executable functions or data that can be used by a Windows application. Typically, a DLL provides one or more particular functions and a program accesses these functions.
- **.exe** This is the file extension for an executable file most commonly found on Microsoft MS-DOS and Windows OSs.
- **.html** The filename extension *.html* is for a document written in HTML coding, which can be read by web browsers.

- **.mdb**   This is the file extension associated with a Microsoft Access database. As with Word and Excel files, the *.mdb* file is susceptible to macro virus infection.

- **.scr**   This is the default file extension for Microsoft Windows screen savers. As screen savers are a popular item to copy to other users, *.scr* files were targeted with viruses.

- **.vbs**   Files with the *.vbs* extension are for *Microsoft Visual Basic Scripting*, a subset of the Microsoft Visual Basic programming language. This powerful language can create visual basic scripts, which can perform a wide variety of functions and be used to create malicious code.

- **.xls**   This is the file extension associated with a Microsoft Excel Spreadsheet. As with Microsoft Word and Access files, *.xls* files are susceptible to macro virus infection.

- **.zip**   The *.zip* extension is used for a compressed file that contains one or more other files. Zip files are compressed to save space, and to make grouping files for transport and copying faster and easier. Zip files must also be checked by antivirus software to ensure the files in the archive aren't infected.

Exam Tip

Recognize which types of files are most likely to carry a virus.

Trojan Horses

Trojan horse programs are named from the ancient myth in which Greek warriors invaded the gated city of Troy by hiding in a gigantic wooden horse. Once inside the city, the warriors leapt from the horse and attacked the surprised inhabitants, winning a decisive battle.

Similarly, a Trojan horse program is one that hides on your computer system until called to perform a certain task. A Trojan is usually downloaded through e-mail attachments or from Internet web and chat sites. Trojans are usually disguised as popular programs such as games, pictures, or music. When the program is run, it usually appears as if nothing has happened, but the Trojan has secretly installed itself on your computer. These types of Trojan programs are usually used to run services that allow an external, unauthorized user to access your machine remotely with full privileges. A popular Trojan horse program used by hackers is *NetBUS*, which enables a hacker to take control of a user's computer once the Trojan horse file that contains the NetBUS server is installed.

Travel Advisory
A firewall can detect suspicious incoming and outgoing network traffic from your computer. If you don't recognize the program, it could be a Trojan horse communicating out to the network.

Logic Bombs

A *logic bomb* is a type of malicious program that, although it can be running on a system for a long time, won't activate until a specific trigger, such as a specific date or the number of times a program is started, is set off. Logic bombs can be highly destructive, depending on their payload. The damage done by a logic bomb can range from changing bytes of data on your disk to rendering your entire hard drive unreadable.

Worms

A computer *worm* is a self-contained program or set of programs able to spread full copies or smaller segments of itself to other computer systems. This usually takes place via network connections or e-mail attachments.

The explosive increase in worms within e-mail attachments has caused antivirus program companies and e-mail software companies to reevaluate the functionality of their applications to prevent the spread of e-mail worms. A user might receive an attachment to an e-mail that contains a malicious worm. When the attachment is activated, the worm infects the user's computer, and then replicates itself by sending copies of the same e-mail to everyone in the user's address book. Each user, in turn, sees the e-mail arrive from someone they know and automatically opens the attachment, thinking it's safe. These types of worm infections can spread quickly and can bring down an e-mail server in a matter of minutes.

E-mail application vendors have taken steps to prevent these types of worms from spreading by patching their applications to prevent malicious attachment code from executing.

Antivirus Protection

To protect your network and user systems from being infected by viruses and other types of malicious code, antivirus systems should be installed in all aspects of the network—from desktop computer, to servers and firewalls.

Because viruses can enter into a company in a variety of ways, such as a user bringing in a floppy disk from home, e-mail attachments, and Internet downloads, antivirus protection should be set up for all these different types of access points.

Antivirus protection should be set up on every desktop and laptop, and should include scheduled updates of virus signature files from a central server. This can protect both the computers and the networks they connect to, as well as provide a first level of defense from the user level to prevent viruses from spreading to the network.

Protecting the user systems isn't enough. All servers should also be protected, so any viruses picked up from a desktop system can't spread to any of the server systems. The reverse is also a great concern. If a common file on a server is used by all systems in the company, this can also be infected, simply by accessing the file if it contains a virus.

Most viruses come from e-mail attachments and Internet downloads that come from outside the company. E-mail servers that send and receive mail should be protected with special antivirus software, which can scan incoming mail for attachments with viruses. The virus is either cleaned or the message deleted, and information e-mails are sent to the source and recipient to warn about the existence of the virus.

Travel Advisory

When installing antivirus software on an e-mail server, be certain you install the version of the software that examines incoming mail and attachments. Normal antivirus protection only prevents viruses in normal program files outside the e-mail system.

Many firewalls can be set up with virus protection software that can scan incoming files downloaded from the Internet. With the amount of traffic that goes through a firewall, this type of protection can slow down the network considerably, so be aware and evaluate your needs carefully.

Virus Signature Files

For antivirus software companies to keep up with the new viruses that are created every day, they need to update their software regularly to protect against the latest viruses. Updating the entire software package on everyone's computer would be extremely expensive and impractical. These companies use a virus pattern or signature file to patch user's systems conveniently and quickly.

Each computer virus contains or creates a specific binary code that can be used as a unique identifier. From these binary signatures produced by the virus, the antivirus engineers create a signature file that can be used to identify these viruses when scanning with the antivirus scan engine program. These signature files can contain thousands of known virus types. They can even include special algorithms to detect typical virus behavior that can indicate a new virus. Once the virus is identified, the antivirus software can then use that information to remove the virus from the system.

To make use of these signature files, a user must be diligent in regularly updating their system with the latest file. This usually involves connecting to the antivirus vendor's web site, and downloading and installing the latest signature file. Some antivirus programs can be set up to automate this process, checking for a new signature file on a schedule and automatically updating the file without user intervention.

Objective 2.03 Social Engineering

As mentioned briefly earlier, social engineering involves nontechnical methods of attempting to gain unauthorized access to a system or network. This typically means the hacker tricks a person into bypassing normal security measures to reveal information that can help them access the network. The hacker, in effect, acts much like a con man, who tries to uncover sensitive information through manipulating someone's basic human nature.

A typical example of this type of security breach is if an unauthorized user calls a help desk asking to reset his password. The user pretends he is a high-level manager, who needs access into his account immediately. The help desk operator, if not trained properly, could instantly give this user a new password, without ever properly identifying him. Now the hacker can log in using the account of a high-level person who could have access to sensitive information. Other examples include questioning a network administrator for IP address information of critical network equipment, such as firewalls and routers.

The only way to protect against these types of social-engineering attacks is user education and training. Security processes must always be followed, no matter who is requesting the information. This includes never writing down passwords in conspicuous places, never giving the password to anyone, properly logging off your system before leaving it unattended, and not letting unknown users into a secured area of the workplace.

Objective 2.04 Auditing

No matter how many security procedures you have in place, new ways will always be invented to circumvent them. For security policies and procedures to be fully effective, they must be audited on a regular basis to test and assess their efficiency. *Auditing* also ensures both the users and the network administrators themselves are conforming to security procedures. Auditing can be general in nature, where logs of the most common activities can be analyzed for any suspicious behavior. More advanced and detailed techniques can involve proactive monitoring of as many systems as possible, including right down to the desktop level. Auditing is, ultimately, a way of ensuring accountability.

Creating a Baseline

The goal of any type of auditing is to create a baseline of current activity, and then measure future activity against this baseline for any change from preexisting thresholds. In security, *creating a baseline* involves analyzing user activity, such as physical entrance and exit from the facility, logins to systems, and recording file and application access. The amount of information that can be pulled is daunting and the network administrator must balance the time needed to analyze all this activity versus the security-risk level they represent. The information that can be recorded from user activity can be organized into the following areas:

System-Level Events

These include events specific to a certain system or network of systems, including the following:

- **Login and logout times**   The logs of who entered and exited a system can be helpful in determining who was in the system at the time a security event occurred.

- **Login attempts**   If a user seems to be trying to access an account too many times with the wrong password, this could indicate someone is trying to hack into that account. Many network OSs can limit the logon attempts, so the account will be disabled if too many unsuccessful logins occur.

- **Password and account changes**   By analyzing account and password changes, you can monitor whether a user has suddenly gained privileges they never had before and that weren't entered by the network administrator.

User-Level Events

User-level events can be recorded to monitor activity performed by users. Like application-level events, a large list of activities can be recorded. The most common user-level events that should be recorded are the following:

- **Use of Resources**   The administrator can record what types of resources the user accessed during a login session. These resources can include files, servers, printers, and any other network services.

- **Command and Keystrokes**   At a granular level, the keystrokes and commands used by a user while logged in can be recorded and analyzed for unusual activity. This sort of logging can be the most time-consuming to analyze.

- **Security Violations**   Each time a user attempts to access a resource for which they don't have the necessary privileges, an entry can be written to a log. Too many attempts at accessing something they don't have permissions for is a possible indication of attempted unauthorized activity.

Application-Level Events

These types of events happen at the *application level,* where a user is using an application to view or manipulate data. The amount of information that can be collected with this type of monitoring can be overwhelming, so only certain key elements should be recorded:

- **File Access**   The application logs can record which files were accessed and whether they were modified in any way. This is helpful to monitor what time a certain file was modified from its original form. Monitoring critical system files for this type of activity is especially important.

- **Error Messages**   By recording any error messages that occur during the use of an application, you can analyze whether the user is intentionally trying to use the application in a manner for which it wasn't designed.

- **Security Violations**   Any attempts at using an application to compromise access permissions should be recorded. Repeated security violations of the same resource can indicate suspicious behavior.

Reviewing Audit Information

Simply recording and collecting information isn't going to be helpful, unless the information is reviewed and analyzed. The auditing information can be viewed manually or forwarded by an automatic system but, either way, you must construct meaningful information from the data for it to be of any use.

Having to review all this information can be a daunting task, but many tools and reporting applications can take the raw data and quickly translate it into something coherent and useful. To maximize the efficiency of your reporting procedure, only items perceived to be beyond normal operating thresholds should be included. For example, unless a specific incident occurs, you'd have no need to analyze logs of which users logged in and out at certain times. You might want to see only those users who logged in after normal working hours to look for suspicious activity.

Exam Tip

Know what types of networking and system activity beyond everyday use can be considered suspicious.

Auditing the Administrator

In most corporate environments, the network administrator's job is to analyze and audit network activity. In high-security environments, it might become necessary for an independent auditor to analyze the log information. The network administrators have full access to all systems in the company and it's important also to record and monitor their activity, along with the regular users. High-level functions, such as user account creation, modification, and deletion, as well as changes to system configuration files, should be monitored and analyzed on a regular basis.

CHECKPOINT

✔**Objective 2.01: Attacks**   Network-based attacks include DoS, which can flood a server with network packets or requests, so it can't respond to legitimate requests. IP spoofing and hijacking can be used to disguise the origin of the hacking attacks. Cryptography and encryption can be a powerful way to protect communications, but it should use the latest high-level bit encryption schemes. All software, including applications, OSs, and equipment firmware should be updated to the latest levels to patch security vulnerabilities and software bugs. Passwords should be at least six to eight characters minimum. They should include uppercase and lowercase letters, symbols, and numbers. This should prevent most password-guessing schemes, such as brute-force attacks, dictionary-based attacks, and social engineering.

✔**Objective 2.02: Malicious Code**   Viruses are malicious programs that can replicate themselves. Trojan horse programs are hidden programs on a system that enable unauthorized users remote access. Logic bombs do nothing until an event, such as a certain date, triggers them into activity. A worm is a self-contained program that can replicate itself through network services or e-mail. Install antivirus protection at all levels of the network to protect against viruses. Update virus signature files regularly to prevent damage from new viruses.

✔**Objective 2.03: Social Engineering**   Social engineering involves trickery, based on human nature, to allow an individual to glean personal or confidential information from an unsuspecting user. All security procedures should be followed, no matter who the user is communicating with. All users should be authenticated before giving out any confidential information.

✔**Objective 2.04: Auditing** Security logs should be audited for suspicious behavior. Regular review allows for proactive monitoring of network and system utilities. Create a baseline of normal activity, and then measure all future activity against the baseline. System, user, and application events should be recorded for auditing.

REVIEW QUESTIONS

1. An IP flood by several hosts directed against a web server is an example of what type of attack?
   - **A.** Trojan horse
   - **B.** Worm
   - **C.** IP attack
   - **D.** Distributed DoS

2. During a DoS attack, a network administrator blocks the source IP with the firewall, but the attack continues. What is the most likely cause of the problem?
   - **A.** The DoS worm has already infected locally
   - **B.** The attack is coming from multiple hosts
   - **C.** A firewall can't block DoS attacks
   - **D.** Antivirus software needs to be installed on the target server

3. Which of the following is the best protection against a ping flood DoS attack?
   - **A.** Subnet masking
   - **B.** Installing antivirus protection software
   - **C.** Disabling the web server
   - **D.** Blocking ICMP protocol

4. Which of the following cryptography encryption types is easiest to crack?
   - **A.** 128-bit
   - **B.** 40-bit
   - **C.** 256-bit
   - **D.** 56-bit

5. Which of the following is the best way to protect against security vulnerabilities within OS software?

    A. Install the latest service pack

    B. Reinstall the OS on a regular basis

    C. Back up the system regularly

    D. Shut down the system when it's not in use

6. Which of the following passwords would be the most difficult for a hacker to crack?

    A. password83

    B. reception

    C. !$aLtNb83

    D. LaT3r

7. A user has brought a virus-infected laptop into the facility. It contains no antivirus protection software and hasn't been hooked up to the network yet. What's the best way to fix the laptop?

    A. Get the laptop on the network and download antivirus software from a server

    B. Boot the laptop with an antivirus disk

    C. Get the laptop on the network and download antivirus software from the Internet

    D. Connect the laptop to another PC and clean it up from there

8. Which of the following files is most likely to contain a virus?

    A. database.dat

    B. bigpic.jpeg

    C. note.txt

    D. picture.gif.exe

9. What type of malicious code can be installed with no effect, until a certain trigger activates it?

    A. Worm

    B. Trojan horse

    C. Logic bomb

    D. Stealth virus

10. During an audit of a server system log, which of the following entries would be considered a possible security threat?

   A. Five failed login attempts on a "jsmith" account

   B. Two successful logins with the administrator account

   C. A 500k print job sent to a printer

   D. Three new files saved in the accounting folder by user "finance"

REVIEW ANSWERS

1. **D**   During a distributed DoS attack, a number of hosts will bombard a server with a continuous stream of network packets. The affected server will be unable to reply to legitimate requests.

2. **B**   In a distributed DoS, DoS attacks come from multiple hosts, making it difficult for the network administrator to block them.

3. **D**   By blocking the ICMP protocol, you prevent systems on your network from replying to ping requests from the outside world.

4. **B**   The higher the number of bits in the encryption key, the more computations must be made in trying to crack the algorithm. Smaller keys can be broken by today's fast processors.

5. **A**   To ensure that bugs and security vulnerabilities from previous versions of your OS have been fixed, the latest service packs and patches for your release should be obtained and installed.

6. **C**   The best type of password is one with at least a minimum of six to eight characters, containing a variety of uppercase and lowercase letters, symbols, and numbers.

7. **B**   If you have a virus-infected computer, don't connect it to a network or you run the risk of the laptop infecting other computers and servers. Finding a way to clean the virus off before connecting it to the network is best.

8. **D**   Executable files can contain compiled code for a virus or other malicious program. In this case, a picture file is disguised with the extension .exe, so someone might think it's a picture and open the file.

9. **C** After installation, a logic bomb does nothing until a trigger, such as a specific date, activates it or the program has been opened a certain amount of times.

10. **A** Having a large amount of unsuccessful logins for one user is unusual. Either the user has forgotten their password or someone is trying to guess their password to hack into the account.

PART

II

Communication Security

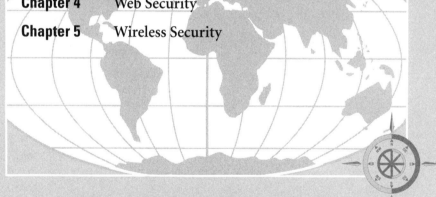

Remote Access

ITINERARY

○ **Objective 3.01**   Remote Access

	NEWBIE	SOME EXPERIENCE	EXPERT
ETA	3 hours	2 hours	1 hour

Objective 3.01 Remote Access

Remote access is an important network feature for companies and organiza- tions that require users to access the resources of their corporate network from home, a hotel, or a location halfway around the world.

With the evolution of telecommunications, a variety of methods are avail- able for a user to access a network remotely. Early methods included attaching a serial cable between two computers via their serial interfaces. The use of modems enabled users to dial-in to a system or network over a common phone line. Modern access methods include complex virtual private networks that enable users to access their corporate network from a public network, such as the Internet. Broadband networking technologies have enabled home users to break free of the bandwidth limitations of modems and phone lines, and create fast, secure communications channels to remote networks.

The most important factor in securing remote communications is the capa- bility both to authenticate a client to a remote network and to encrypt the communications, so they can't be captured. With the explosive growth of high- bandwidth home networks that communicate over the Internet with remote systems, the need for secure communications is critical.

This chapter examines the different types of remote access methods avail- able, and the different types of authentication and encryption protocols that can be used to secure them.

Remote Access Methods

There are many different methods to connect to another system remotely. Each type of communication depends mainly on what type of medium the client user is attempting to use to connect to the remote machine. A user in a hotel in an- other country could be trying to access their corporate LAN by using a modem to dial-in to their remote access server. Another user might be connected to the Internet via a DSL connection, using a virtual private network to communicate with a remote network. A network administrator might use telnet or Secure Shell to log in to a server remotely from home.

Each remote access method must be carefully examined for security vulnera- bilities to ensure users are properly authenticated to use the network's resources and communications are encrypted to prevent someone from tapping into the transmitted information.

Exam Tip
Know the different types of remote access methods and the various security vulnerabilities that affect them.

Dial-Up

For many years, the most common way of accessing remote services to a corporate local area network (LAN) or the Internet was through the use of a dial-up connection using a modem over a common phone line. A modem, short for modulator-demodulator, is used to convert the digital signals of a computer to analog for transmission over an analog phone line. A modem at the receiving end converts the signal back into digital for the remote computer. Many companies don't properly protect their remote access services because they think their regular company firewall will protect them. Unfortunately, the firewall is only protecting traffic that comes in from the Internet.

Travel Advisory
One of the oldest modem-hacking methods is the use of *wardialing*, in which a hacker uses a program to call phone numbers in quick succession to look for those attached to modem. Once one is found, hackers can dial in to the modem and try to break the authentication to gain access.

For remote access to a network, a client machine initiates a call to a remote access server. The remote access server is connected to a modem, or several banks of modems, to provide enough connections for multiple remote users, as shown in Figure 3.1.

Once the client and remote modems are connected, the server typically provides some form of authentication before enabling the client access to the network's resources. This authentication usually takes the form of a user name and password, which is compared to a database of corresponding predefined user accounts. If the credentials match, then the user is granted access. The authentication system could be built into the remote access server itself or be a separate

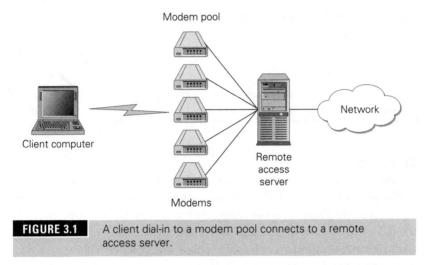

| FIGURE 3.1 | A client dial-in to a modem pool connects to a remote access server. |

service running an authentication protocol, such as TACACS or RADIUS. Additional forms of authentication that can secure communications even further include the use of *security tokens,* which are usually some type of card or token that displays a key code that cycles every few minutes. When synchronized with the server, this token creates another form of authentication that's tied to a user account. Because the sequenced number is cycled with a defined algorithm, the same number can't be used twice within a certain period of time.

Travel Advisory

Security tokens are combined with traditional user names, passwords, and PIN numbers, so if the token card is stolen, the unauthorized user still needs other credentials to gain access.

Another type of dial-in security check that can be performed for dial-in clients is the use of a *call-back feature*: when the client first connects, the remote access server will hang up and try to dial back the client with a preconfigured phone number. Once the client answers, a user name and password can authenticate them for access. This call-back feature ensures the caller is who they say there are and also allows the company to absorb any long-distance charges incurred because of the call.

ISDN

Integrated Services Digital Network (ISDN) technology was created to replace the use of common phone lines for network communications. A special ISDN line must be run to your location, and both your client computer and the remote computer have to use a special ISDN adapter. Unlike a modem, an ISDN adapter doesn't convert signals from digital to analog and back again. ISDN connects digitally between the two adapters over the ISDN line.

Each ISDN connection is divided into channels:

- **B-Channels**   These ISDN channels transmit data, such as voice or computer data communications. The channels can be used individually or combined to create higher bandwidth.

- **D-Channels**   These channels transmit control and signal information for managing the transmission of data.

Three main types of ISDN implementations exist, depending on the level of bandwidth a customer requires:

- **Basic Rate Interface (BRI)**   The *BRI* interface is targeted for lower bandwidth home installations and can run over conventional phone lines. The BRI implementation uses one 16 Kbps D-Channel, and two 64 Kbps B-Channels. The data channels can be combined to provide 128 Kbps communications.

- **Primary Rate Interface (PRI)**   The *PRI* interface is for business customers who have higher bandwidth needs. A PRI implementation contains one 64 Kbps D-channel and 23 64 Kbps B-Channels for data, providing bandwidth up to 1.544 Mbps.

- **Broadband ISDN**   *Broadband* ISDN can handle many different services at the same time and is usually used within a telecommunications carrier backbone. Broadband ISDN is most often used in fiber-optic and radio type networks, such as FDDI, ATM, and SONET.

ISDN has generally been passed over in favor of cable modem and DSL communications. These methods are much less expensive and easier to set up and configure because they use the existing cabling infrastructure in the home.

Cable Modem

Cable modems are one of the most popular ways of connecting home computers to the Internet. Cable modems are misnamed, though, because they don't operate like a typical modem, which translate signals between analog and digital. A *cable modem* is simply a device that enables you to connect to your home's coaxial cable lines, which is then connected by common Ethernet cable to your computer's network interface card (NIC).

The speed of cable-modem communications decreases when more homes are connected to the same cable. For example, in most neighborhoods, several homes are connected to the same segment of a coaxial cable run. If many people are using the Internet at the same time, the bandwidth is shared among them, so the individual connections are slower.

The security risk involved with cable modems is this: unlike dial-up connections, the connection to the Internet is permanent and always on, until the system is turned off or unplugged from the network. As long as a system is connected to the Internet, it's open to attacks from hackers, who continually scan networks for security vulnerabilities in online systems. To secure these connections properly, the use of a firewall is recommended to protect your computer against these intrusions.

Travel Advisory

Hackers make use of programs known as *port scanners* to analyze a bank of IP addresses on a network to look for open service ports and applications that can be compromised. To prevent a port scanner from seeing your system while connected to a cable modem or DSL network, a firewall can be installed, so your system won't reply to such scans.

DSL

A Digital Subscriber Line (DSL), just like cable modem access, is one of the most popular ways of connecting a home computer or small business to the Internet. DSL runs over common copper telephone lines, but requires the connection to be in close proximity to a phone company's access point. The closer you are to the access point, the faster your connection.

DSL can be used for communicating voice and data transmissions over the same phone line. Home users can talk on the phone, while still connected to the Internet. This type of communication was impossible over normal dial-up modem methods. DSL also differs from a typical modem in that it doesn't require modulating the signal from digital to analog and vice versa. DSL uses the entire bandwidth of the phone line for digital transmission.

Like cable modems, a DSL network connection is always on until the system is switched off or unplugged from the network. To protect your system, the use of a firewall is recommended.

Remote Access Utilities

Several software packages are available that provide for or enhance remote access communications. These include simple operating system (OS) utilities that can be used to connect to a remote system, to full-blown graphical remote access solutions that provide a secure application for a client to connect to a remote computer. Most smaller utilities enable access to the command-line console of a system, where programs can be run from the client. More complex graphical-based remote access applications let you communicate as if you were on the console itself, watching the monitor and using the keyboard and mouse input. A user watching the remote system while the client is accessing it might see the actual mouse movements and keyboard strokes as they happen. The following sections outline some of the more popular types of remote access utilities and applications.

Remote Access Applications   *Remote access applications* are specific software used to provide remote access to a machine from a client system. The communication that connects the two systems can be anything from a dial-up modem connection, to a direct cable connection, or over a TCP/IP network.

Typically, these types of applications consist of client and server components. The server software is installed on the system made available for remote access. The server is then either connected to a modem or to a network. Sometimes the client and server computer are connected with a simple network or serial cable. The server software is then configured to accept communications as a host server. If a modem is attached, the program sets it up to answer incoming calls. Once the client connects to the server by dial-up or some other communications medium, it should be authenticated before being granted access. The authentication credentials are usually a user name and a password.

Once connected, the client can remotely control the machine as if they were sitting in front of it on the console. This type of application can create severe security vulnerabilities if it isn't properly secured. This security should include strong authentication methods and, if possible, a call-back function that will call the client back at a specific number to ensure their identity.

> **Travel Advisory**
>
> Be wary of users on your network who hook up modems to their work computers, so they can dial-in from home using a remote access application. They might not set up any authentication or security at all, leaving a large security hole in your network. Remote access standards must be enforced, so users are always communicating using known secure methods.

Telnet   *Telnet* is a text-based terminal emulation utility that's part of the TCP/IP suite of protocols. It allows a system to connect to a remote host to perform commands as if you were on the console of the remote machine. For telnet to work properly, the remote machine must be running a telnet server service, which listens for telnet requests from other hosts. When the client connects, they must authenticate to the remote system using a user name and password specific to that system. Once authenticated, the user can run commands on the remote system as if they were directly on the command console.

> **Exam Tip**
>
> The TCP/IP port used by the telnet service is port 23.

Unfortunately, telnet provides little security other than basic authentication. This means transmissions, including the user name and password, are sent in clear text and can be easily discovered by someone monitoring and capturing the communication. To ensure no one can use telnet to connect to a certain host, the telnet service should be disabled.

Although telnet is a basic utility of TCP/IP communications, its use has been discouraged in favor of more secure methods of remote access, such as SSH.

SSH   Secure Shell (SSH) is a secure form of terminal access to other systems. Like other terminal communications utilities such as telnet, SSH enables a user to log in to a remote machine and execute commands as if they were on the console of that system. Telnet, however, is insecure because its data isn't encrypted when communicated. SSH provides a secure, encrypted tunnel to access another system remotely. SSH is sometimes used as a low-cost alternative to normal virtual private network communications because of its simple installation and delivery of well-encrypted secure communications.

When a client connects to a system using SSH, an initial handshaking process begins and a special session key is exchanged. This begins the session and an encrypted secure channel is created to allow the access.

Vulnerabilities have been discovered in some versions of SSH, so ensure that you are using the latest version. Early versions of SSH were susceptible to man-in-the-middle attacks because a hacker could capture the headers of the handshaking phase to intercept the session key.

Exam Tip

Other utilities that send their information in clear text include remote login (rlogin), file transfer protocol (FTP), and remote shell (rsh). Whenever possible, a secure method, such as SSH, should be used for remote console access and file transfer.

VPN

A virtual private network (VPN) is a secure and private connection over a public network. The connection between the client and the remote network is provided by an encrypted tunnel between the two points, as shown in Figure 3.2.

Aside from remote access, VPNs are also used for connecting two remote routers together to form a secure WAN. For a VPN to work properly, the sender and receiver need to be running the same type of VPN, with the same protocols and encryptions settings.

VPNs grew out of the need for users to access their corporate network remotely from home or on the road, without the need for dialing up over a slow modem connection, especially one that incurs long-distance charges. VPNs can be used over dial-up connections, but the use of high-speed broadband networks has allowed VPN technology to take advantage of the increased performance.

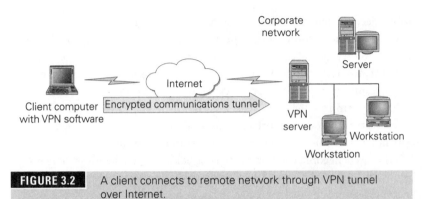

FIGURE 3.2   A client connects to remote network through VPN tunnel over Internet.

The VPN enables the remote user to be connected locally to a public network like the Internet, while also being directly connected to their corporate network through the use of the encrypted VPN tunnel. This connection can be a dial-up through a modem or a direct Internet connection, such as a cable modem or DSL.

The user must first complete their connection to the Internet, using either Point-to-Point Protocol (PPP) over dial-up or connecting with their cable modem or DSL connection. The user then starts their VPN software, which creates a virtual connection to the VPN access server on the corporate network. After the connection is negotiated, clients must authenticate themselves using their user names and passwords before the VPN will let them access the corporate network. A VPN is only as secure as the tunneling and encryption protocols that comprise the VPN connection. Early types of VPNs used older encryption methods, which can be cracked by today's attackers.

Protocols and Encryption

For a remote access communication to work, the data has be transmitted using one or several network protocols. These protocols must be able to travel through different networks and different physical infrastructures. A home user who wants to connect their computer to the Internet has to use a modem to dial-up to and connect with their Internet service provider (ISP) over a phone line. Different protocols, such as Serial Line Internet Protocol or PPP are needed both to facilitate the transmission of digital data over analog phone lines and encapsulate TCP/IP over the serial-line modem communications.

These types of protocols are used by VPNs for tunneling over a public network and to provide encryption for protecting transmitted data.

Exam Tip
Know the advantages and disadvantages of the following protocols, as well as with what type of communications they can be used.

SLIP

Serial Line Internet Protocol (SLIP) is one of the earliest Internet protocols used for encapsulating IP packets for transmission over serial communications, such as a phone line or serial cable. SLIP is considered difficult to configure and not efficient or reliable. SLIP isn't used much anymore and has been replaced by PPP.

PPP

Point-to-Point Protocol (PPP) is used to enable a connection between two computers using a serial interface, usually over a phone line. PPP is the most popular protocol used by an ISP to enable users to dial-in the Internet network from home using a modem attached to their home computer.

The main function of the PPP protocol is to encapsulate IP packets and send them over the Internet. PPP is considered much more reliable and easier to use than SLIP because it contains error checking and the capability to run different types of protocols over a variety of media methods.

PPTP

Point-to-Point Tunneling Protocol (PPTP) is a Microsoft implementation of secure communications over a VPN. Because PPTP is an extension of the PPP protocol, it's become one of the most widely used tunneling protocols that allows network packets to be encapsulated within PPP communications for transfer over another network, such as the Internet through a dial-up connection.

Previous remote access technologies only allowed remote access through a dial-up modem to the corporate network. Depending on where this user is, the long-distance charges could potentially be enormous and, sometimes, a company would need to create its own expensive toll-free 1-800 service for long-distance dial-in access. Tunneling protocols allow a user connected to a public network, such as the Internet—though dial-up or faster cable modem or DSL service—to create their own private connection to their corporate LAN.

PPTP decrypts and encapsulates PPP packets to create the VPN connection. The security mechanisms within PPTP include authentication and encryption of data. One major security problem with PPTP is this: when a connection is negotiated, the communication is transmitted in cleartext. This data can be captured by an unauthorized user who can use the information to try to hack the connection.

L2TP

Layer 2 Tunneling Protocol (L2TP) is another tunneling protocol like PPTP, but combines the best features of PPTP with the L2F protocol created by Cisco Systems. L2TP is most often used with other media technologies, such as Frame Relay.

L2TP consists of two main components:

- **L2TP Access Concentrator (LAC)**   The LAC is responsible for terminating the local network connection and tunneling PPP packets to the LNS.
- **L2TP Network Server (LNS)**   The LNS is situated on the remote end of the connection and terminates the PPP connection originating from the LAC.

Through the use of the LAC and LNS, the connection can be localized because the L2TP components terminate the endpoints of the PPP connection, as shown in Figure 3.3.

The main difference between L2TP and PPTP is that L2PT can run on top of and tunnel through other network protocols, such as IPX and SNA, while PPTP can only run on top of IP networks. L2TP, however, doesn't provide any type

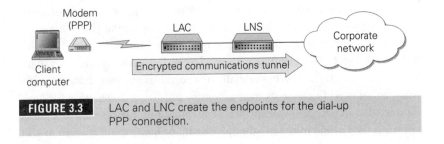

FIGURE 3.3   LAC and LNC create the endpoints for the dial-up PPP connection.

of native encryption, so it must be combined with another encrypted protocol, such as IPSec. Unlike PPTP, L2TP supports TACACS+ and RADIUS for authentication.

IPSec

Internet Protocol Security (IPSec) is a standards-based method of providing privacy, integrity, and authenticity to information transferred across IP networks. IPSec works on the IP layer to encrypt communications between the sender and receiver. IPSec is most often used to secure VPN communications over an open network, such as the Internet.

IPSec uses two types of encryption modes: transport and tunnel. In *Transport* mode, IPSec encrypts only the data portion of each packet, but not the header. This can only be used in host-to-host communications. *Tunnel* mode encrypts both the header and the data of the network packet. This is used to host VPN gateway communications, which is the most common form of VPN. The receiver of the packet uses IPSec to decrypt the message. For IPSec to work, each communicating device needs to be running IPSec and share some form of public key.

Key management is provided by the Internet Key Exchange (IKE), formerly ISAKMP/Oakley. IKE enables the receiver to obtain a public key and authenticate the sender using digital certificates.

Authentication

Just as a user on a wired LAN connection needs to authenticate to the network before accessing its resources, specific authentication mechanisms must be set up for remote access users who connect to the network through other methods, such as dial-up or VPN, over the Internet.

Authenticating remote users requires additional security measures because they're usually communicating over an open line, such as a dial-up modem connection, or using remote access applications over the Internet. This enables an unauthorized user to snoop or perform other network attacks, such as a replay or a man-in-the-middle attack.

A good remote access method needs to secure the password database tables with which the user's credentials are compared and the communication lines with which the client sends their user name and password information.

PAP

Password Authentication Protocol (PAP) is the most basic type of authentication that consists of comparing a set of credentials, such as a user name and a password, to a central table of authentication data. If the credentials match, then the user is granted access. PAP is most often used with dial-up remote access methods using the PPP protocol, such as connecting to an ISP or a remote access server (RAS) that supports PPP.

Although the password tables used by PAP are encrypted, the actual communications are not, allowing the user name and password to be sent over the network in cleartext. This can easily be captured by an unauthorized user monitoring the network. Typically used for dial-up authentication, PAP is also the default authentication protocol within the HTTP protocol. Because of its weaknesses, the Challenge Handshake Authentication Protocol (CHAP) is usually used in place of PAP.

> **Travel Advisory**
>
> Although PAP is built into HTTP for authentication of web communications, it's rarely used because of its lack of encryption. More secure protocols like SSL are used instead.

CHAP

CHAP is much more secure than the PAP protocol. Once the communications link is completed, the authenticating server sends a random value to the client. The client sends back the value combined with the user name and password credentials, plus a predefined secret, calculated using a one-way hash function. The server compares the response against its own calculation of the expected hash value. If the values match, then the client is granted access.

CHAP provides protection against replay attacks, which are used by hackers to capture data, and then resend it again. To prevent this type of attack, CHAP uses an incrementally changing identifier and a variable challenge value. The authentication can be repeated any time while the connection is open.

> **Travel Advisory**
>
> Microsoft has its own version of CHAP called MS-CHAP, which extends the functionality of CHAP for Microsoft networks.

RADIUS

Remote Authentication Dial-in User Service (RADIUS) is an authentication protocol that's the most common Internet standard used for authenticating clients in a client/server environment, especially dial-in users. A typical remote access solution for a company includes a pool of modems a user can dial into from a remote location. When communicating through the modem with the remote access server, the user is authenticated to the network by the RADIUS server, which compares their login and password credentials against those of the server's authentication database. If the credentials match, then the user is granted access to the rest of the network. The client's credentials that are sent to the RADIUS server are encrypted to prevent someone from capturing the transmission. RADIUS servers also include accounting and reporting functions that can monitor and log data on each connection, such as packet and protocol types, as well as length of time connected. Figure 3.4 shows an example of how a RADIUS server authenticates a remote access client.

TACACS

Terminal Access Controller Access Control System (TACACS) is an older type of authentication protocol, similar to RADIUS. A remote access user dials into a network with a modem and is authenticated by the TACACS server before being allowed access to the network's resources. Three versions of TACACS have been used: the original TACACS, XTACACS, and TACACS+.

- **TACACS**   The original protocol, which performs both authentication and authorization.
- **XTACACS**   Extended TACACS, which builds on TACACS by separating the functions of authentication, authorization, and accounting.

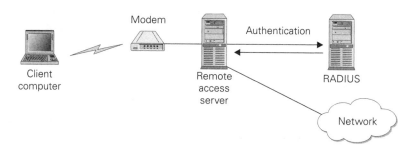

FIGURE 3.4   RADIUS server authenticating dial-in remote access clients

- **TACACS+**   This added the use of both a user name and password for authentication or other authentication methods, such as Kerberos or dynamic passwords through security tokens. All communications are also encrypted.

Local Lingo

Kerberos   An authentication system that uses a special key ticket assigned to the user, which is embedded in all their network data to identify the sender.

Unfortunately, the TACACS protocols have been known to have several security vulnerabilities, including a weak encryption algorithm. This has decreased its use in favor of the standards-based RADIUS authentication protocol.

802.1X

The *IEEE 802.1X* standard is an authentication mechanism for wireless networks. Its goal is to provide a centralized authentication framework for wireless LANs, which include both wireless clients and the access points that connect them to the network. In most current wireless LANs, a client automatically connects to the closest access point, and then authenticates to the network by directly communicating with the network's native authentication. Unfortunately, unless the LAN is protected with a strong encryption method, this still enables a client to perform certain network functions without authentication, such as networking functions like ping.

Using 802.1X, when a client connects to an access point, the client port is set to an unauthorized state, so it can't perform any network functions, which includes receiving an IP address from a DHCP server. The access point then asks the client for authentication credentials, such as a user name and password. Once received, this data is forwarded to an authentication server running a service such as RADIUS. If the client is accepted as an authorized user, then the client port on the access point is switched to an authorized state and normal communications can commence.

802.1X can be helpful in allowing wireless LANs to scale upward in size easily, while maintaining a centralized authentication system. This authentication, however, should be coupled with a strong communications-encryption mechanism to provide full security.

CHECKPOINT

✔**Objective 2.01: Remote Access**   Access methods include modem dial-up, remote access applications, TCP/IP utilities such as telnet and SSH, and VPN. SLIP and PPP protocols provide communications for IP over a serial or dial-up connection. Protocols such as PPTP, L2TP, and IPSec are used to provide an encrypted tunnel over public networks to enable the use of secure VPNs. Authentication can be provided by separate services and protocols such as TACACS+, RADIUS, and 802.1X for wireless networks.

REVIEW QUESTIONS

1. Which method of remote access communication is typically connected to the Internet all the time, creating an increased security risk because it's constantly open for attack?

   A. Cable modem
   B. Dial-up
   C. Wireless
   D. SSH

2. What security feature can be used for a dial-up remote access client on top of using a user name and password?

   A. Encrypted phone number
   B. Modem string check
   C. Call-display
   D. Call-back

3. Which of the following command-line utilities is a more secure method of remote access than telnet?

   A. SSL
   B. SSH
   C. IPSec
   D. VPN

4. Which of the following tunneling protocols only works on IP networks?
   A. SLIP
   B. IPX
   C. L2TP
   D. PPTP

5. The purpose of a RADIUS server is
   A. Packet sniffing
   B. Encryption
   C. Authentication
   D. Negotiating connection speed

6. Which of the following authentication protocols is geared toward wireless networks?
   A. 802.1X
   B. 802.11b
   C. 802.11a
   D. 803.1

7. Which of the following protocols works on the IP layer to secure IP traffic on a network?
   A. IPX
   B. IPSec
   C. SSH
   D. TACACS+

8. A LAC and an LNS are components of what tunneling protocol?
   A. IPSec
   B. PPP
   C. PPTP
   D. L2TP

9. The most common type of protocol for dial-up access to a remote server is
   A. SLIP
   B. PPP
   C. RAS
   D. Telnet

10. Which technology is used for secure communication over an unsecured network?

    A. Telnet
    B. SLIP
    C. VPN
    D. PPP

REVIEW ANSWERS

1. **A** Cable modems and DSL connections that connect home users with the Internet are typically on all the time, unless the system is shut down or the network cable is unplugged.

2. **D** A remote access server can be set to call back a client immediately after the client connects to authenticate the origin of the call.

3. **B** Secure Shell is more secure than telnet because it encrypts all communications, while telnet transmits data in cleartext.

4. **D** Point-to-Point Tunneling protocol only works on IP networks, while other protocols, such as L2TP, work on other networks, such as IPX or SNA.

5. **C** The purpose of a RADIUS server is to authenticate the credentials, such as user name and password, of a user before granting access to a remote network.

6. **A** This authentication protocol allows wireless access points on a wireless LAN to have clients authenticated to the network before being able to transmit and receive information on the access point.

7. **B** The IPSec protocol is used to secure VPN communications on the IP layer.

8. **D** The LAC (L2TP Access Concentrator) and the LNS (L2TP Network Server) are components of the L2TP protocol. The LAC is responsible for terminating the local connection and tunneling PPP packets to the LNS. The LNS is situated on the remote end of the connection and terminates the PPP connection originating from the LAC.

9. **B**   Point-to-Point Protocol is the most widely used protocol for dial-up access to a remote access server.

10. **C**   A virtual private network is a secure and private connection created over a public network, such as the Internet. Through the use of encryption and tunneling protocols, the VPN can connect a user on the Internet to their corporate LAN in a safe and efficient manner.

Web Security

ETA

NEWBIE	SOME EXPERIENCE	EXPERT
4 hours	2 hours	1 hour

As nearly everyone knows, the Internet was originally created by academic and military organizations to exchange information among their various departments. The few tools and utilities originally available performed tasks primarily for e-mail and file-transfer capabilities. Now, with the explosive growth of the Internet among home and corporate users, a wide variety of applications and functions have been created to increase functionality of Internet communications.

This growth in functionality and use has also required the need for increased security within all aspects of the Internet—from its infrastructure and transport systems to applications and user education. As the Internet is used increasingly for more confidential transactions, such as banking and shopping, the need for security becomes a paramount concern.

Objective 4.01   Web Security

The World Wide Web grew out of the need for people on the Internet to share information with one another. Originally, web pages only contained text and a few graphics because modem data-transfer speeds were slow. Today, with high-bandwidth home-cable modem access and high-speed corporate networks, users can download multimedia video and music over the Internet in seconds.

Web site functionality has also changed, with the static web pages of years ago being replaced by dynamic, media-intensive sites with greater user interaction and online shopping and banking becoming routine daily tasks. With this increased functionality, especially where the transfer of confidential information is concerned, the need for security for web communications has become a top priority. Users must now be authenticated to use secure areas of a web site, and the communications channel between the client and the web server needs to be encrypted, so unauthorized users can't capture the data.

The following sections outline some of the various web-security protocols and the types of attacks that might compromise your Internet servers.

SSL/TLS

Although the data on a server might be secured from unauthorized access, the communications pathways between the server and client systems might not. Secure Sockets Layer (SSL) is a protocol that enables communication between systems to be encrypted, as shown in Figure 4.1.

FIGURE 4.1 SSL encrypts the communications channel over the Internet.

Many web sites have both secured and unsecured areas. The secured areas might provide access to a financial bank account or a database of personal information. This secured area of the web site usually requires authentication to proceed further. To increase security when switching from the unsecured public part of a web site to a secured area, SSL encryption is invoked. SSL must be supported by both the web server and the client browser to function.

In an SSL communication, a process known as a *digital handshake* occurs. The handshaking phase begins when the server sends a message to the client indicating a secure session must be set up. The client then sends its security information and encryption key to the server, which compares the credentials with its own to find the right match. Next, the server sends authentication information, so the client knows the web server they're communicating with is the correct one. This is important because it's possible, through redirection or other methods, not to be on the web site where you originally thought you were. If you enter your user name and password, you might be entering the information into a bogus web site that collects this information to perform unauthorized activity with your accounts. This handshake confirms not only are you who you say you are, but the site you're contacting is what you think it is.

When this handshaking is complete, the client and server then establish encrypted communications throughout the duration of the session. When the client moves to another web site, the encrypted session is closed.

Transport Layer Security (TLS) is the next generation of the SSL protocol. *TLS* builds on the strong security of SSL with more enhanced encryption and authentication techniques. Unfortunately, TLS and SSL aren't compatible because a TLS-secured communication can't interoperate with an SSL communication.

HTTP/HTTPS

Hypertext Transfer Protocol (HTTP) is the protocol used by the World Wide Web. *HTTP* runs on the Internet's networking protocol TCP/IP and forms the communications protocols that allow web browsers to connect to and retrieve content from web servers. When a user clicks on a web hyperlink, it tries to connect with the associated Uniform Resource Locator (URL). The browser sends an HTTP request to the corresponding web server hosting that URL. The web server returns the content of the web site to the browser through HTTP. HTTP is a *stateless protocol,* meaning that with each communication, the link between the browser and the server is created, and then it's broken when the communication is finished.

Hypertext Transfer Protocol Secure (HTTPS) is a secure means of communicating HTTP data between a web browser and web server. HTTPS protects the communication channel by using SSL to provide encrypted and protected communications. When connecting to a web site that uses a secured channel, the URL begins with https instead of http, such as https://secure.website.com. This is typically used in banking and online shopping transactions, where the transfer of credit card and personal information must be encrypted to prevent an unauthorized user from stealing the information. The capability to perform HTTPS communications is usually built into the web server software itself and the web page is simply created in a special directory. When a client connects to the secure site, SSL is activated between the server and client, if the client supports it. In many web browsers, a secure site is indicated by a small padlock icon in the application task bar.

Exam Tip	
HTTP uses TCP/IP port 80, while HTTPS uses port 443.	

Web Application Vulnerabilities

As programmers add increased functionality to web sites and web browsers, the potential for security vulnerabilities increases. The biggest danger is the tendency toward integrating the web browser functionality with other computer applications and even the operating system (OS) itself. This means if a web-browser security vulnerability is exploited, an unauthorized user has access to the core system files and data of someone's computer. The following sections outline some of the more popular web-application components and the security vulnerabilities they might create.

JavaScript

JavaScript is a scripting language created by Netscape, but it isn't related to the Java programming language. JavaScript's code isn't compiled; instead, it's interpreted by the web browser. JavaScript can interact with HTML source code, enabling web authors to create web sites with dynamic content.

Since the introduction of JavaScript, the language has been plagued with security issues. The problems originate from the nature of JavaScript, which allows executable content to be embedded in web pages. These vulnerabilities include the capability for hackers to read files on a user's hard drive, and to monitor and intercept a user's web activities. Security precautions are required to prevent malicious code from entering, executing, and retrieving data from the underlying system.

The insecurities of web browsers that implement JavaScript, rather than its language, are the source of the vulnerabilities. Most security problems discovered in JavaScript implementations require the installation of software patches from the web browser vendor. JavaScript can also be disabled on your web browser as an option. Check your web-browser options to disable or enable the use of JavaScript for web sites you access.

Java

Java is an object-oriented, platform-independent programming language created by Sun Microsystems. Java is typically used on Internet web sites to provide small programs called *applets,* which can be downloaded to a user's web browser. Because Java is platform-independent and can run on any type of machine or OS, it requires the use of a Java Virtual Machine (JVM) to convert the program to the code understood by the local machine or OS. Java programs run in their own special area, called a *sandbox,* which restricts the applets' access to certain parts of the computer system. This prevents malicious or buggy software from accessing critical parts of your system. Hackers, however, are able to program applets that can bypass the security features of the sandbox and access the data on user's hard drives. For added security, most web browsers can be configured to allow only certain access privileges to Java programs.

Signed Applets

Signed Java applets are programs that are authenticated through the use of a digital signature that provides information on where the applet originated. The web browser reads this signature and checks to see if it comes from a known, trusted source. This allows an applet to have less restrictions put on its operations, as would a normal unsigned applet. An authenticated signed applet is usually given more access over OS functions to perform an application.

ActiveX

ActiveX is a technology created by Microsoft to create reusable components across Windows applications. This includes increasing the functionality of Internet applications. Similar to components created with Java, ActiveX components can be downloaded to the computer through the web browser. Unlike Java, which has software controls that only allow programs to run in a certain area of memory and influence, ActiveX functions are controlled by the users themselves. This requires the need for greater security controls because a malicious ActiveX component can be downloaded that could compromise the security of your system. Users must be more careful when configuring their web browsers to control ActiveX programs.

> **Exam Tip**
>
> ActiveX controls run with the same permissions as the user currently logged in.

For web-browsing security, ActiveX uses a form of authentication control based on security levels. The user's web browser can be configured to set a certain security level at which ActiveX controls can operate. The lowest level allows all ActiveX components to be downloaded automatically. Increased levels provide warning dialog boxes to alert you of an ActiveX element and enable you to download it or not. ActiveX relies on digital certificates and trusting certificate authorities to authenticate the origin of ActiveX controls.

As always, your web browser should be updated to the latest version, so the most recent security controls are in place and any previous security vulnerabilities are removed.

> **Travel Advisory**
>
> Many people, in the interest of higher security, disable some of the advanced web-browser functions, such as downloading ActiveX and running Java applets. Unfortunately, many web sites require these to perform even the most basic functions and you might be unable to access the site. A balance must be maintained between convenience and security.

Buffer Overflows

Buffer overflow is a programming term used to describe when input data exceeds the limits recognized by a program. For example, a program might only be expecting a certain amount of characters in an input dialog box. If the amount of characters exceeds this limit, the added information might also be processed. This extra code could be malicious in nature and cause the program or even the entire system to crash.

Travel Advisory

A number of Denial of Service (DoS) attacks are in the form of buffer overflows.

For Internet web applications, this buffer overflow vulnerability is a common security concern for web servers and web browsers. A malicious web server set up by a hacker can crash the systems of the users connecting to that web site by sending various HTTP buffer overflow data streams to the client. Similarly, a hacker using a simple web browser can send certain HTTP data to a web server that overflows its software buffers and crashes the web site.

Buffer overflows are mainly caused by bad programming, which allows illegal data to be entered into the application. Software, especially Internet applications, should be carefully programmed to accept only certain types of data. Buffer overflows are typically fixed by patches issued by the software company. You should ensure that all your software is current with the latest software patches and service packs to prevent these types of errors. Patches can be downloaded from the software vendor's web site and installed onto your computer to fix the application.

Travel Advisory

Buffer overflows have often been a thorn in the side of companies that create web-server and web-browser software. These vulnerabilities are easy to exploit and can significantly affect the performance of a system, which includes crashing it. The only way to protect yourself is to ensure you have the latest versions and patches for the software you're using.

Cookies

Cookies are special text files saved on your computer when you visit a web site. A cookie is used to save information particular to that web site. Cookies are typically used by web sites for tracking demographic or user-specific information pertaining to that site. This information can be used by the web sites themselves or for advertising purposes. For example, the first time you visit a web site, you could be required to register by filling out a web form. Some information from this form is saved on your system as a cookie. If you specified your age and gender, this information is read from the cookie the next time you visit that site and the advertising is altered accordingly for your demographic group.

Most cookies contain relatively harmless information, but some of them could contain user names or passwords for certain Internet and web site accounts. Cookies of this nature are usually encrypted by the distributing site, but those that aren't are vulnerable to unauthorized users accessing this information.

Most web browsers let you customize the capability to use cookies or enable more strict controls on their use. Cookies can be disabled completely, but this could cause certain web sites not to work at all in your web browser.

Travel Advisory

To protect your privacy even further and to avoid sending demographic information to web sites, most web browsers enable you to disable cookies and to delete any existing ones on exiting the program. Unfortunately, many web sites require cookies to be enabled to function properly.

CGI

Common Gateway Interface (CGI) scripts are programs designed to accept and return data that conforms to the CGI specification. The programs are typically written in scripting languages, such as PERL, and are the most common way for Web servers to interact dynamically with users. Web pages that contain forms typically use a CGI program to process the form's data once it's submitted.

A security concern with CGI is this: each time a CGI script is executed, a new process is started. For some web sites, multiple CGI requests can noticeably slow the server. CGI scripts also are vulnerable to programming bugs, so they should be written with the same care and attention as any software application.

Poorly programmed CGI scripts can intentionally or unintentionally provide information about the host system that can aid hackers in accessing the web server. Scripts that utilize user input from web forms can be used against the client machine. For example, on a server system, a subverted CGI script can be used to run malicious code as a privileged user and provide unauthorized access to any part of the system, including sensitive user data, as well as logins and passwords. Another concern of CGI scripting is the capability of the user to input data that can be used to attack the web server through buffer overflows and malformed requests.

Objective 4.02 # E-mail Security

The capability to send electronic mail from one computer to another over a network is one of the original main uses of the Internet. Even today, e-mail is the most important communications tool used by corporate institutions and the public.

Security has become increasingly important regarding e-mail communications. The most publicized abuse of e-mail is the use of malicious viruses and worms that can quickly spread from user to user, and envelop hundreds of networks in a matter of minutes. These viruses take advantage of security weaknesses within e-mail programs to use their intended mechanisms of sending and receiving e-mail to spread malicious program code instantly to a large number of people.

Other security concerns include the use of *spoofing* e-mail addresses, where someone replaces the original FROM field of the e-mail with a different source address. This technique is most often used by *spammers,* who send unsolicited advertisements to users, while hiding behind a fake originating e-mail address.

E-mail security can be increased through the use of encryption to protect information from being stolen by unauthorized users. The user must also be educated on the proper ways of sending and receiving e-mail attachments. Finally, a good antivirus program should be installed to scan e-mails and their attachments for viruses and other malicious code.

Encryption

As a default setting, the mail server usually doesn't encrypt e-mail messages. This means anyone who might have access to your account or who has hacked the system can read your private e-mail messages. E-mail messages, once sent, can relay among a large number of e-mail servers until they get to their destination. If any one of these servers is insecure, your e-mail could be captured and viewed. Users can protect themselves by using encryption products, such as Pretty Good Privacy (PGP), or through the use of digital certificates. Once the e-mail is encrypted, there's no way for an unauthorized user to view the contents of the e-mail. The destination user must also have the matching encryption key, so they can unlock the message when it arrives.

> **Local Lingo**
>
> **PGP**   Pretty Good Privacy, a tool for encrypting messages, is one of the most common ways to protect messages on the Internet because it's both easy to use and effective. PGP uses a public-key encryption method with two keys. One is a public key you give to anyone who you share messages with. The other is a private key you use to decrypt messages you receive.

Mail Attachments

E-mail messages themselves typically consist of only text characters, which can do little to harm your computer. The attachments sent along with e-mails can potentially cause the most damage if they happen to contain malicious program code or viruses. The following sections outline some of the tools and protocols used when sending and receiving attachments.

MIME

Multipurpose Internet Mail Extension (MIME) is a specification for transferring multimedia and attachments through e-mail. This specification ensures a standard way exists for all mail clients and mail transfer systems to handle certain types of attachments. For example, if a user sends an audio clip to another user through e-mail, the MIME header will include information on the attachment. When the audio clip reaches the destination user, their computer will understand what type of file it is and what application can be used to open it.

The uses of MIME, however, also extend beyond e-mail. For example, when a user downloads a graphic from a web site, the header for the request usually contains information on what type of file it is, such as a GIF format graphic. When the file is saved on the user's computer, it can easily identify what type of file it is and automatically open the corresponding application to use it.

S/MIME

Secure MIME (S/MIME) is an extension of the MIME standard, and is used for digitally signing and encrypting e-mail. *S/MIME* is used for sending confidential e-mails that need to be secured so other users can't capture the message and read its contents. By encrypting the e-mail, an unauthorized user will be unable to decipher the contents of the e-mail and its attachments.

Antivirus Protection

E-mail attachments can potentially contain harmful viruses, worms, or Trojan horse programs that can allow an unauthorized user access to your computer. Viruses and worms can replicate themselves quickly to the files of your computer and those of other users. Trojan horse programs install and hide themselves on your computer and perform activities that allow remote users to acccss your system. The first rule is never to click or activate an attachment from a source you're unsure of. Many e-mail worms and viruses can infect your e-mail application itself, however, so it will forward the malicious program to users in your address book whether or not you open an attachment. Because the user recognizes your name, they might feel it's safe to click on the attachment, and then become infected. The virus then goes through that person's address book, sends out infected e-mail, and so on.

Travel Advisory

These types of e-mail worm viruses spread so fast that e-mail servers can be overloaded within minutes as the virus automatically propagates itself to people in the e-mail program's address book.

Many users have been tricked into activating a virus-infected file or running a malicious program, often in the guise of an antivirus product or software update, which can give an unauthorized user access to another's computer. Sometimes, a user might receive a seemingly innocent file, such as a .jpg picture file, but the extension .exe has been added to the end, meaning, in reality, this is an application file. Assuming that picture files can't carry viruses, the file is opened, and the malicious executable program is started.

To protect your computer fully from e-mail viruses, you should have an antivirus program installed that supports scanning e-mail attachments. As an e-mail is downloaded into your mailbox, the antivirus scanner examines it for any known viruses, and then quarantines or deletes the attachment before it can be activated. Your virus signature files must be kept current, so any new viruses can be detected.

Some e-mail applications, such as Microsoft Outlook, can inform the user if another program is trying to access your address book or attempting to send you an e-mail.

Local Lingo

Virus Signature File A special virus signature and definition file that an antivirus program uses as a database of known virus types. Files can be scanned for evidence of any of the signatures of known viruses.

Spam and Hoaxes

One of the most annoying e-mail problems is that of spam and hoaxes. *Spam* is a deliberate attempt to mass e-mail a large number of users with unsolicited advertisements. Any time you enter your e-mail address on a public web site or a newsgroup, you open yourself to the possibility of having your e-mail address added to spam mailing lists. These mailing lists are shared among Internet spam advertisers and, sometimes, you can receive multiple junk e-mails every day. This annoys not only users, but also networking administrators because of the amount of space and bandwidth these mass mailings can consume. Many Internet service providers (ISPs) and corporate networks use antispam mail filters that can block incoming spam e-mail from reaching the mailboxes of your users.

Hoaxes can be just as annoying as spam, but they're caused more by social engineering than maliciousness. A hoax is typically some kind of urban legend users pass on to others because they feel it's of interest to them. The most common types of these e-mails usually tell the user to forward the e-mail to ten of their friends to bring the user good luck. Others claim to be collecting e-mails for a sick person. Of course, all this does is consume network and computer resources as the number of e-mails grows exponentially as users send them to all their friends, and so on. The only cure for the spreading of hoax e-mails is user education.

Exam Tip
Know how to spot an e-mail hoax and how to handle it properly. The best solution is to delete it immediately and do nothing more at all.

Authentication

All Post Office Protocol 3 (POP3) and Internet Message Access Protocol (IMAP)-type e-mail servers are usually configured to protect user's mailboxes by requiring them to authenticate to the account. If the user login or password isn't valid, they won't be able to access the contents of the mailbox.

POP3 is an Internet protocol that provides a way for users to retrieve mail from their mailboxes using a POP-enabled client like Outlook Express or Eudora. The e-mail messages are stored on the server until the user connects to it and downloads their message to the e-mail client using POP. Most POP accounts are set to delete the messages once they're retrieved.

IMAP is similar to POP, in that it's used to provide a mechanism for receiving messages from a user's mailbox. IMAP has more functionality than POP, however because it gives the user more control on what messages they download and how it stores them online.

> **Exam Tip**
>
> POP uses TCP/IP port 110 and IMAP uses port 143.

On the other hand, the capability to send e-mail from a mail server often isn't protected at all. This enables any user to send an e-mail that originates from that mail server. This is most often exploited by spammers who use unprotected e-mail servers to send large quantities of junk e-mail. The receiver will see the source of the e-mail was that server, even though the e-mail didn't originate from that company or institution. By also authenticating the sending process, this ensures that only authorized users are allowed to send mail from that server.

SMTP Relay

Simple Mail Transfer Protocol (SMTP) is the e-mail message-exchange standard of the Internet. While POP and IMAP are used to read e-mail, SMTP is the Internet protocol for delivering e-mail. SMTP operates on the main networking protocol—TCP/IP—to navigate an e-mail to its destination server. Mail servers that run SMTP have a relay agent that sends a message from one mail server to another. Because mail servers, as per their function, need to accept and send data through an organization's routers and firewalls, this relay agent can be abused by unauthorized users who relay mail through that server. These e-mails are usually sent by spammers sending out unsolicited e-mails and advertisements, while hiding the original sending location of the e-mails. The need for e-mail server security becomes even more important when these users send malicious e-mails with attachments that contain computer viruses.

To protect the mail server from this type of abuse, the SMTP relay agent should be configured only to send mail originating from its own network domain.

> **Exam Tip**
>
> SMTP uses TCP/IP port 25 for communication.

Instant Messaging

One of the most popular Internet services today is *instant messaging,* which enables users to send messages to each other via their personal computers. Unlike e-mail, in which a delay occurs between the time a user sends an e-mail and when another user receives that e-mail, the messages are received immediately.

For instant messaging to work, both users must be online at the same time, using the same type of instant messaging software, and both parties must be willing to accept instant messages. An attempt to send a message to someone who isn't on-line or who rejects the message results in notification that the message couldn't be sent. On the recipient's computer, a window and sound will indicate a message has arrived and the recipient can choose to accept or reject the incoming message. Files and Short Message Service (SMS) text messages can also be exchanged between instant messaging users.

Local Lingo
SMS   Similar to paging, Short Message Service is used for sending short text messages to mobile phones, computers, and hand-held devices.

Unlike e-mail, which can be protected by authentication and encryption tools, instant messaging applications reside on a user's hard drive and are usually not protected by a firewall by default. This is even more critical in corporate environments, where instant-messaging program used by employees makes the corporate network vulnerable to attack because these programs bypass traditional network security. To prevent users from using messaging programs in the workplace, the administrator can configure the firewall to block those specific ports. The following sections outline some of the security vulnerabilities specific to instant messaging programs.

File Transfer Vulnerabilities

Like any service or application that's Internet-based, vulnerabilities occur that make running instant messaging programs a security risk to your computer. Just like e-mail, instant messaging can be used to send files to another user. As with e-mail, the same risks associated with attachments exist, such as receiving virus-infected files.

When receiving a message with an option to download the file, you must always establish the identity of the sender before replying or downloading the file. The best practice is simply to ignore the message unless you have no doubt about its origin. Some instant messaging programs enable you to create a list of users whose messages will be automatically rejected. This is helpful if the unknown user continues to send you messages even after being ignored the first time.

Packet Sniffing

Like e-mail, instant messages must travel from a source to the destination user and, along the way, might travel through a number of servers and network equipment. An effective hacking technology that's been used to capture data along these routes is packet sniffing. *Packet sniffing* refers to using a hardware device or software program to tap into a network connection and record the network packet information that passes through. Most instant messaging programs send their data unencrypted, so if a user sends sensitive data such as logins, passwords, or banking information, it could be recorded by the packet sniffer and used by the hacker.

Some instant messaging programs have the option to encrypt their communications. This option should be used if you're transferring confidential messages, conducting business conferences, and transferring files with your instant messenger program. The packet sniffer will still record the data, but the hacker won't be able to read it because the data is encrypted.

Privacy

Care must be taken when using instant messaging programs not to reveal personal information, especially to strangers. If you don't recognize the person you're communicating with and they begin to ask for personal details, such as addresses, phone numbers, or credit card information, end the connection immediately.

Instant messaging runs on the Internet networking protocol TCP/IP. This means messages are transferred back and forth using the IP addresses of the source and destination computer. If a malicious user knows your IP address, they can run all kinds of special hacking software that probes your computer for vulnerabilities, and then exploit them. Some instant messaging programs can hide your IP address, so it can't be discovered by the person you're messaging. When this option is available, you should activate it.

Travel Advisory

Many hacking tools can now reveal your IP address, even though you have it disabled within the messaging system itself. To protect your computer fully, you should use a personal firewall program that can block scans and attacks that use your IP address.

Instant messaging programs can store information about you that can be used as part of a messaging directory, much like a telephone or the White Pages, or for demographic advertising purpose. Carefully check these settings to ensure you aren't providing information about yourself that invades your privacy, such as addresses or phone numbers.

 **Objective 4.03** Directory Security

A network *directory service* identifies all resources on a network and makes them accessible to users and applications. These resources can include anything from e-mail addresses to computers and peripheral devices, such as printers. Some directory services also manage network authentication. The primary purpose of a directory service is to make the physical network and its various parts transparent to the individual user, who only needs to see a listing of the resources they can access. For example, a user might want to see a directory of company e-mail addresses or a list of all printers on a certain floor of the building.

A number of directory services are used widely for various purposes. Lightweight Directory Access Protocol is the standard protocol used for searching directories. OS-based services such as Netware Directory Service (NDS) are used to manage the entire network's resources and can also take advantage of the LDAP protocol.

LDAP

Lightweight Directory Access Protocol (LDAP) is a protocol that can be used to look up information in a database for other users and network resources. A *directory* is a database that's often compared to the telephone White Pages or the Yellow Pages because the information can be searched and quickly found within the indexed database. The directory database itself can consist of a wide variety of information, including not only basic user contact information, such as e-mail addresses or phone numbers, but also objects, such as printers and computers. Some directory services are used to configure and control access to every single network resource object on the entire network or to contain a centralized database of logins and passwords. With such a critical collection of network data, security is of prime important when using directory access protocols such as LDAP.

All LDAP servers have some security controls in place for allowing read and update access to the directory database. Typically, all users can read a majority of the information held in the database, but only a few users have the access to update it. Large directories usually have multiple information administrators who have access to update only information pertaining to their departments or regions.

For a client to access an LDAP server, it must first be authenticated, unless the server allows anonymous connections. This type of access control allows the LDAP server to decide exactly what that client can access and what information it can update.

Many LDAP servers support the use of encrypted secure channels to communicate with clients, especially when transferring information like user names, passwords, and other sensitive data. LDAP servers use the SSL protocol for this purpose.

Exam Tip

LDAP uses TCP/IP port 389. LDAP over SSL uses port 689. LDAP over TLS uses 636.

Objective 4.04   File Transfer Security

Another popular function used by Internet users is file transfer. Any file can be transferred over the Internet from a computer to a server or between two computers in a peer-to-peer fashion. The most popular Internet utility for file transfer is File Transfer Protocol, which runs on the Internet's underlying network protocol, TCP/IP. Another increasingly popular method of transferring files over the Internet is through the use of peer-to-peer connectivity.

FTP and S/FTP

The File Transfer Protocol (FTP) is one of the oldest Internet applications. *FTP* is the protocol used to upload files from a workstation to a FTP server or to download files from a FTP server to a workstation. By using an FTP application, files can be transferred from one Internet system to another. To start an FTP session, you must connect to another system running an FTP service, and then log in with a user name and password. Once authenticated, you can upload and download files.

Exam Tip

FTP uses TCP/IP port 20 for data transfer and port 21 for connection control information.

The main security vulnerability of FTP is this: any information passed is in clear, unencrypted text, including the logon information. This means a hacker monitoring the system with some type of packet sniffer can clearly read your login user name and password. Secure FTP (SFTP) is a program that uses Secure Shell (SSH) to transfer files. Unlike the original FTP, it can encrypt both commands and data, so it can't be captured by a packet sniffer.

> ### Local Lingo
>
> **Secure Shell (SSH)** Secure Shell is a program that enables you to log into another computer over a network, to execute commands, and to move files from one machine to another. SSH provides authentication and secure communications over insecure channels.

Blind FTP

Blind FTP is a method of enabling certain users to download files, which are sensitive in nature or unavailable to the general public, from an FTP site. When logging in to a Blind FTP site, no files appear to be in the FTP directory. The directory does contain files, but their names are hidden from view. To download the files, you need to know their exact names beforehand to initiate a download through the FTP command-line prompt. This information needs to be communicated to the user in some other way beforehand, such as by e-mail or a phone call. If anyone were to hack into the FTP server with a user's account, they wouldn't be able to see the files in the directories and they couldn't download the files unless they knew their exact names.

Anonymous FTP

A new FTP server is usually installed by default with an anonymous or ftp user. This account isn't protected with a password and it's most often used in public web sites as a general account to log in and download files. Most anonymous accounts have no permissions to upload files. If you're setting up an FTP site to be secured with logins and passwords for users, you must ensure this anonymous account is disabled. The account could provide a doorway for an unauthorized user to examine the system and exploit any vulnerabilities.

File Sharing

While utilities such as FTP provide an application-based way to transfer files, the proliferation of Internet file-sharing utilities has greatly reduced FTP use and has renewed concern for proper file sharing and transfer security.

Internet file-sharing is much like sharing files on a local area network (LAN). For example, in a corporate network, users might access file servers with network shares from their own computers. In Internet file sharing, most connections are peer-to-peer (P2P).

Local Lingo

Peer-to-Peer   As opposed to a client/server architecture—where many clients connect to a central server for their services and applications—peer-to-peer networking involves two computers connecting to each other directly, rather than through an intermediary server.

The most popular application of P2P Internet file sharing has been the trading of music or videos, such as MP3 files. Unfortunately, many of these programs contain a number of security vulnerabilities that can give an unauthorized user access to your system. The P2P application enables you to configure a specific directory on your hard drive that can be accessed by other users. The P2P servers can scan the contents of these directories to create a master database that can be searched by users of the service. Once the user finds the file they're looking for, they connect directly to your computer to download the file.

The biggest problem with P2P sharing is the files you download might be disguised viruses or Trojan horse programs. The open nature of this type of networking and file sharing means little control exists over what files are offered for download. When using these types of P2P file-sharing programs, you must ensure your computer is fully protected by a current antivirus program and a personal firewall.

Exam Tip

Know the various ways of transferring files over the Internet and how to protect these communications properly.

CHECKPOINT

✔ **Objective 4.01: Web Security**   Use SSL and TSL to encrypt HTTP communications for confidential and secure web communications. Configure your web browser to prevent unknown or malicious Java applets and ActiveX components from being downloaded by the browser. Keep your web software current with the latest versions and patches to prevent unauthorized access from current security vulnerabilities. Control the use of cookies on your system to protect your privacy. Protect yourself when using instant messaging programs by not downloading files from unknown users.

✔**Objective 4.02: E-mail Security**   Encrypt confidential e-mails with encryption programs, such as PGP. Configure your antivirus scanner to scan e-mail attachments as they're downloaded to your mailbox. Be aware of hoax e-mails and simply ignore them or delete them when received. Don't send them to other people because you're simply clogging e-mail systems and slowing network communications. Disable or restrict SMTP relay to prevent unauthorized users from sending e-mail from your mail server.

✔**Objective 4.03: Directory Security**   Maintain proper access controls on directory service systems, so only certain users can make changes to the central directory database, while the rest of the users only have read access. Access permissions can be used to control what information can be read by users.

✔**Objective 4.04: File Transfer Security**   Use secure FTP methods to encrypt file transfer communications. Regular FTP logins and password are sent as cleartext. Disable the anonymous account to prevent unauthorized guest access to your system.

REVIEW QUESTIONS

1. Which of the following protocols is the next generation of SSL?
   A. SFTP
   B. S/MIME
   C. HTTPS
   D. TLS

2. What should be done if your web browser prompts to download an ActiveX control whose source you don't recognize?
   A. Accept the download
   B. Download the ActiveX component and scan for viruses
   C. Cancel the download
   D. Try to download in another browser window

3. What is the primary purpose of a cookie?
   A. Stores user information particular to that web site
   B. Encrypts web file-transfer communications

C. Provides for online banking transactions

D. Stores and caches web-site graphics

4. Why should SMTP relay be disabled or restricted on an e-mail server?

A. SMTP is only used for file transfer

B. You don't need it if you run antivirus software

C. To prevent unauthorized users from checking their e-mail

D. To prevent unauthorized users from sending mail through your server

5. After you receive a file in an e-mail attachment, you can't open it and the file itself has no identifying extension. What is the most likely problem?

A. The file is probably a virus

B. No MIME type set exists for the file

C. The e-mail is spam

D. SMTP relay isn't working

6. You receive an e-mail stating it should be forwarded to 20 of your friends or else you'll receive a virus that will damage your system. What should you do?

A. Check the e-mail's MIME type

B. Forward it to ten of your friends to see the result

C. Delete the e-mail—it's a hoax

D. Forward the e-mail to 20 friends to be safe

7. While chatting in an instant messaging session, an unknown user wants to send you a picture file named lookatme.jpg.exe. What should you do?

A. Ignore it and don't download the file

B. Download the file and run it from a safe location

C. Download the file and check it with an antivirus program

D. Accept the file, and then forward it to friend to check it

8. You need to send a credit card number immediately to a family member through an instant messaging program. What should you do?

A. Send the number in a message right away

B. Encrypt the message

C. Send the first half of your credit card number in one message and the second half in another message

D. You can't send a credit card number through instant messaging

9. As a network administrator, you need to set up a file transfer service for customers, so they can retrieve confidential files from your servers. What service should you set up?

   A. SFTP

   B. FTP

   C. Windows File Sharing

   D. P2P sharing

10. When you set up a new FTP server, what should you do first when creating accounts for your FTP users?

    A. Enable file sharing on the server

    B. Set up an ftp account with no password

    C. Create a blind FTP directory

    D. Disable the anonymous account

REVIEW ANSWERS

1. **D** Transport Layer Security is the next generation of Secure Sockets Layer (SSL), which is a protocol used to encrypt communications over the Internet. For web sites, TLS provides a method for defining secured and unsecured areas of a web site, especially if part of the web site performs financial and shopping transactions.

2. **C** If you don't recognize the source of the ActiveX control, according to its digital signature, don't download it. This could be a malicious virus or another destructive program.

3. **A** A cookie is a small text file that resides on a user's computer. It contains information on a particular web site, such as customization details and demographic advertising data.

4. **D** If your SMTP relay agent is left wide open, users from other networks can send e-mail through your server. This is most often used by spam advertisers who want to hide the identity of the source of the e-mail. By disabling or restricting the SMTP relay, only users who reside in your network should be able to send e-mail.

5. **B** Multipurpose Internet Mail Extension (MIME) is a specification for identifying and transferring attachments through e-mail. A MIME type identifies the type of file and which application is used to open it.

6. **C**   The purpose behind these hoax e-mails is to use social engineering to make users forward multiple copies of these e-mails to other people. The chain reaction of these e-mails can cause network and e-mail server performance problems.

7. **A**   Although the user appears to be trying to send you a harmless graphic or picture file, this is an executable file with the .exe extension. This is most likely a virus or a Trojan horse program that will damage or provide access to your system. Never accept files from users you don't know.

8. **B**   If no other way exists of sending the information, then you should encrypt the instant message if this option is available in your program. Sending unencrypted confidential information through instant messaging is dangerous because hackers can use network packet sniffers to record information as it passes along a network.

9. **A**   By using Secure FTP, you provide a way to transfer files over an encrypted communications channel. SFTP uses Secure Shell (SSH) to provide this function.

10. **D**   Most FTP programs automatically configure an anonymous or ftp user login that doesn't require a password to log in. This is most often used in public FTP servers, so logins for the hundreds or thousands of people that visit the site needn't be created. If you're setting up logins for accounts, this should be disabled to prevent unauthorized guest access.

Wireless Security

	NEWBIE	SOME EXPERIENCE	EXPERT
ETA	2 hours	1 hour	0.5 hour

One of the greatest changes in networking technology is the phenomenal growth of wireless communications. Wireless networks use radio frequency technology to transmit data through the air, effectively bridging the gap between data connectivity and user mobility. Wireless networks allow the mobile world to reach the Internet, not only with laptop computers, but also with other telecommunication devices, such as wireless phones, personal digital assistants (PDAs), and pagers.

Wireless connectivity enables a user to perform their daily computing functions, such as checking e-mail, voice mail, and calendars without physically plugging into a network. Wireless applications also extend into the business world, where inventories are taken by handheld devices and entire floors of a building are set up with wireless networks to enable mobile users to move their laptops from room to room without the encumbrance of wires.

The popularity and explosive growth of wireless networks, however, have also brought up increased concerns for the security of wireless data. If steps aren't taken to protect the wireless network properly, the data being sent through the air by radio frequencies can easily be captured by an unauthorized user. With wireless networks, much of the typical physical security that prevents someone from plugging into a network is gone. Anyone within the vicinity of a wireless LAN can connect to it easily with the use of a laptop or other wireless-equipped device. More so than traditional wired networks, wireless security heavily involves the use of encryption technologies, coupled with traditional security mechanisms, such as access control and authentication.

Exam Tip

Many corporate wireless LANs are set up and configured with no encryption or access control. Hackers have been known to roam neighborhoods with a large corporate presence, using simple laptops with wireless connectivity to connect to unprotected local area networks (LANs) and access their resources. This is called *war driving*.

Objective 5.01 **Wireless**

Wireless security is dependent on the different types of wireless network configurations available and the type of devices that will connect to them. The following sections introduce the various wireless network configurations, as well as the protocols, hardware, and software that make them work.

WLAN (Wireless LAN)

Wireless LANs use electromagnetic airwaves to transfer information from one point to another without the need for a physical connection. To communicate these signals, the sender and receiver need to be tuned into the same radio frequency. The receiver tunes in one radio frequency, while rejecting all others.

Wireless LAN Technology

Wireless LANs can comprise a range of technologies, each with its own set of strengths and limitations.

Narrowband Technology   A *narrowband* system transmits and receives data only on a specific radio frequency. The signal frequency is kept as narrow as possible—large enough to communicate only the required information. Crossover between communications streams is prevented through the use of separate channel frequencies. The radio receiver filters out other radio signals, except the ones on its designated frequency. The disadvantage of narrowband technology is that a Federal Communications Commission (FCC) license must be issued for each site where it's employed.

Spread Spectrum Technology   Most wireless LAN systems use spread-spectrum technology to transmit their information. *Spread-spectrum* technology is a wideband radio-frequency technique used to ensure reliable and secure communications systems. More bandwidth is consumed than in a narrowband transmission, but spread-spectrum technology produces a stronger signal. Two types of spread-spectrum radio exist—frequency hopping and direct sequence:

- FHSS   *Frequency-hopping spread-spectrum* uses a narrowband carrier that changes frequency in a pattern known to both the transmitter and the receiver. When synchronized, a single logical channel is maintained. FHSS uses a lower data rate (3 Mbps) than DSSS systems, but can be installed into virtually any location without fear of interference interrupting its operation. FHSS is used by the 802.11 wireless networking standard.

- DSSS   *Direct-sequence spread-spectrum* generates a redundant bit pattern for each bit to be transmitted. Through the use of these bit patterns, transmissions can be easily recovered if interfered with or damaged, without the need for retransmission. DSSS delivers higher speeds (11 Mbps) than FHSS and is used by the 802.11b wireless standard.

Infrared Technology   Infrared (IR) systems use high frequencies, just below visible light in the electromagnetic spectrum, to carry data. Like light, infrared transmissions can't go through solid objects and its application is mostly for short, line-of-sight communications between devices. Infrared technology is rarely used in wireless network applications. Instead, it's geared more toward implementing fixed subnetworks or allowing devices like PDAs to communicate with each other when in line-of-sight of their infrared ports.

Wireless Access

In a typical wireless LAN setup, a device called an *access point* is connected to a wired network from a fixed location using standard LAN cabling. The access point acts as a gateway, connecting the wireless and the wired LAN together. A single access point can support a small group of users and can function within a range of less than one hundred to several hundred feet. The access point is usually mounted at the top of a wall or ceiling to provide maximum coverage for the wireless area. The access point, and any wireless device, usually contains an antenna that can be extended to aid in signal reception.

To access the wireless LAN, the end user can use a regular PC with a special wireless-LAN adapter, a notebook computer with a wireless PC card, or even a hand-held device, such as a PDA or other device. The wireless adapter appears to the operating system (OS) of the computer or device as a typical network adapter.

Site Surveys

An initial site survey should be performed before the installation of the wireless network to ensure the environment will be conducive to wireless communications. The survey can also help determine the best placement and coverage for your wireless access points. The following are some important issues to remember for the site survey:

- **Antenna type and placement**   Proper antenna placement is a large factor in maximizing radio range. As a general rule, range increases in proportion to antenna or access point height.
- **Physical environment**   Clear or open areas provide better radio range than closed or filled areas.
- **Obstructions**   Metal physical obstruction can hinder the performance of wireless devices. Avoid placing these devices in a location where a metal barrier is located between the sending and receiving antennas.
- **Building materials**   Radio penetration is affected by the building materials used in construction. Drywall construction allows greater range than concrete blocks, while metal construction can hinder and block radio signals.

Wireless LAN Topologies

Wireless LANs can be as small and simple as two PCs or laptops networked to-gether through their wireless interfaces. This type of peer-to-peer networking would require little configuration and administration, and the wireless devices would only have to be within range of each other to communicate. No interme-diary access points or servers are on this type of network. Each client would only have access to the resources of the other client, as illustrated in Figure 5.1.

More complex networks can encompass a large number of access points, connected with many different wireless PCs, notebooks, or hand-held devices. Installing an access point can extend the range of a small wireless network, effec-tively doubling the range at which the devices can communicate. The access point is directly connected to a wired network, so any wireless clients accessing that access point can communicate with the resources of the wired LAN through the access point. Resources on the wired network that wireless clients might access include file servers, mail servers, and the Internet. Figure 5.2 shows an example of a typical wireless LAN access-point setup.

An access point can accommodate many clients, depending on the number and the type of bandwidth transmission required. Typical access points can handle up to approximately 50 client devices. The disadvantage is this: the more users that connect to the access point, the less bandwidth is available to each client.

Exam Tip

Whether the network is peer-to-peer or through wireless access points, access security must be carefully planned and implemented, no matter what kind of architecture is used.

Access points are limited by range—ranging from 100 meters indoors to 500 meters outdoors—depending on the physical environment. In large wireless en-vironments, multiple access points are needed to provide a wide coverage area for the clients. The access point ranges must overlap, so network connectivity will not be lost roaming from one access point to another.

Laptop computer

Laptop computer

FIGURE 5.1   A wireless peer-to-peer network

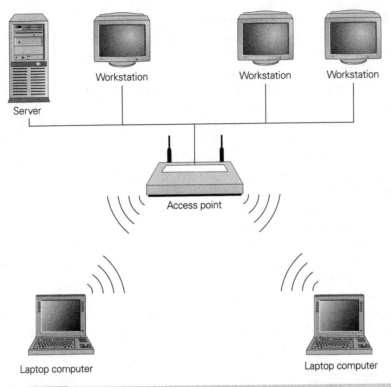

| FIGURE 5.2 | Access point connecting a wireless LAN to a wired LAN |

Wireless Protocols

Just like regular networked LANs, wireless LANs run on specific networking protocols optimized for use with wireless communications. As wireless networks began to proliferate, a number of competing wireless protocols were released that weren't always compatible with each other. A wireless device using one type of protocol might be unable to access a wireless LAN using an entirely different protocol. The industry has settled down somewhat and the most popular protocol for wireless devices currently in use is the Institute of Electrical and Electronics Engineers (IEEE) standard, 802.11b. The following sections outline some of the various protocols.

WAP

Wireless Access Protocol (WAP) is a specification that provides the delivery mechanisms for transmitting information to wireless devices. WAP supports the use of Wireless Markup Language (WML) instead of HTML to send web data to wireless devices, such as handhelds, and cell phones. Through the use of WML, web sites can tailor their content so it can be handled by WAP browsers embedded into wireless devices. Wireless devices typically have small memory and processors, so the web content must be stripped down to work on these types of devices.

Security for WAP is handled through the use of Wireless Transaction Layer Security (WTLS), which provides authentication and encryption functionality similar to the Secure Sockets Layer (SSL) in typical web networking. The wireless client and the server must be authenticated for wireless transactions to remain secure and to provide encryption. WTLS resembles SSL in that both rely on certificates on the client and server to verify the identity of the participants involved.

Local Lingo

Secure Sockets Layer A protocol developed for transmitting private documents via the Internet. SSL works by using a public key to encrypt data that's transferred over the SSL connection. Most popular web browsers and web sites support the use of the protocol to obtain confidential user information, such as credit card numbers. By convention, URLs that require an SSL connection start with https: instead of http:.

Unfortunately, WAP hasn't caught on as strongly as other wireless protocols and architectures because it's limited to smaller, hand-held devices and restricts its usefulness with higher bandwidth wireless solutions.

Bluetooth

Bluetooth wireless technology is designed to enable and simplify wireless communication between small, mobile devices. In an effort to implement wireless methods that eliminate the need for proprietary cables, Bluetooth is an attempt to allow connectivity between any device, including peripherals such as cameras and scanners. For example, no need exists for cables to transfer digital photographs between a camera and a PC because the communications can be performed using wireless. Bluetooth has low-power consumption and transmits via common radio frequencies (2.4 Ghz). Configuration is usually performed dynamically in the background, allowing seamless communications between Bluetooth wireless devices.

Bluetooth also enables devices to form small, wireless networks called *piconets*, which are established using a radio transceiver embedded within each Bluetooth device. This is designed to operate in a noisy radio environment and to provide a fast, robust, and secure connection between devices. The range for

Bluetooth, however, is much smaller than typical wireless networks, allowing for a link range between ten centimeters and ten meters because typical Bluetooth connectivity is between one device and another. Figure 5.3 illustrates how a Bluetooth network works.

For security, Bluetooth defines three security modes: nonsecure, service-level security, and link-level security.

- **Nonsecure mode**   There is no type of security at all.
- **Service-level security mode**   Application security policies are used, where the actual applications on the wireless device are responsible for security.
- **Link-level security mode**   The most secure of the three modes authenticates the actual communications link before data transmission can begin. Data encryption can also be performed in this mode, once

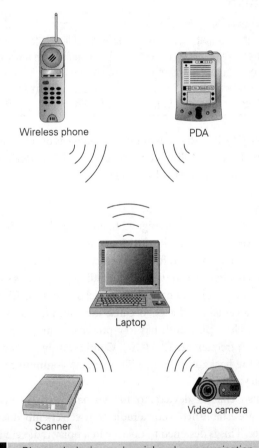

Wireless phone

PDA

Laptop

Scanner

Video camera

FIGURE 5.3   Bluetooth device and peripheral communication

the link is authenticated. Authentication allows the devices to decide if a connection will be formed based on available identification at the hardware level. Once the link is established, additional security might be applied to the data transmission using encryption. Stronger encryption can also be enabled at the software level, if needed.

Travel Advisory

Bluetooth standards and technology, much like the WAP architecture, have only slowly penetrated the market. This is because of Bluetooth's narrow application to smaller, hand-held devices, such as PDAs and wireless phones.

802.11

802.11 refers to a family of specifications developed by the IEEE for wireless LAN technology. 802.11 specifies an over-the-air interface between a wireless client and a base station, or between two wireless clients. The IEEE accepted the specification in 1997.

Several specifications are in the 802.11 family:

- **802.11**   Applies to wireless LANs and provides 1 or 2 Mbps transmission in the 2.4 GHz band using either frequency hopping spread spectrum (FHSS) or direct sequence spread spectrum (DSSS).

- **802.11a**   An extension to 802.11 that applies to wireless LANs and provides up to 54 Mbps in the 5GHz band. *802.11a* uses an orthogonal frequency division multiplexing encoding scheme, rather than FHSS or DSSS.

- **802.11b** (also referred to as 802.11 High Rate or Wi-Fi)   An extension to 802.11 that applies to wireless LANS and provides 11 Mbps transmission (with a fallback to 5.5, 2, and 1 Mbps) in the 2.4 GHz band. *802.11b* uses only DSSS. 802.11b was a 1999 ratification to the original 802.11 standard, allowing wireless functionality to give a performance comparable to the Ethernet 10baseT standard, which runs at 10 Mbps.

- **802.11g**   Applies to wireless LANs and provides 20+ Mbps in the 2.4 GHz band.

Currently, the 802.11b standard is the most popular for home and business wireless users. The characteristics that have allowed it to become so popular include its fast speed of 11Mbps, reliability, long range, and capability to be easily integrated into an existing, wired Ethernet network. As the most common standard, for 802.11b has a wide variety of hardware and software solutions, with many companies creating wireless PCI cards for PCs, PCMCIA cards for laptops, and wireless network infrastructure products, such as wireless access points, switches, and routers.

The popularity of 802.11b, however, has created the need for even better security for wireless LANs at home and in the workplace. Without any type of security mechanisms, wireless LANs can be easily compromised. All an unauthorized user needs is to bring their own wireless laptop or wireless device into the range of the LAN and they instantly have access. This is because no mechanisms for authentication or encryption are configured.

Travel Advisory

With the proliferation of home networks with high-speed Internet connections, many users have also added wireless systems to their home networks. Broadband companies are worried that because of the lack of security on these home wireless networks, unauthorized users nearby can access a neighbor's network without subscribing to the service.

Securing a wireless LAN with as many layers of security as possible is extremely important. The following methods, individually and collectively, can be used to secure access to 802.11 networks:

- Network Identifier
- MAC (Media Access Control) address filtering
- WEP (Wired Equivalent Privacy)
- VPN (virtual private network)
- Personal Firewall

Network Identifier   The most simple wireless network access control is the use of a network password or name, known as a Service Set Identifier (SSID). This network identifier can be set up on one or a group of wireless access points. The identifier provides a way to segment a wireless network into multiple networks serviced by one or more access points. This is helpful in companies that are separated by departments or physical floor locations. To access a particular network, client computers must be configured with the correct identifier. For roaming users, multiple identifiers can be enabled on their wireless device, enabling them access to different networks as required. This type of security is minimal, however, because it's simply a network password, which could easily be compromised by word of mouth or through access points that broadcast the network name.

Travel Advisory

Many access points advertise their SSID by default. For security reasons, check the settings of all your access points to disable this feature.

MAC Address Filtering   Access points can be identified with network names and passwords, but a client computer can be identified by the unique MAC address of its 802.11 network card. Access points can be configured with a list of MAC addresses associated with the client computers allowed to access the wireless network. If a wireless client's MAC address isn't included in this list, the wireless client isn't allowed to connect with the access point and the network. This is a much better solution than using network identifiers alone, but maintaining the list of client MAC addresses can quickly become a daunting task with larger networks. In addition, each access point must be configured individually, so each node contains the same list of addresses. This type of security is best suited to small networks because the administrative overhead quickly limits its scalability.

Exam Tip

Enable MAC Address filtering on access points to configure what clients can access the network.

WEP Security   The 802.11 standard defines the *WEP* security protocol to provide encrypted communication between the wireless clients and access points. WEP uses a key encryption algorithm to encrypt communications between devices. Each client and access point on the wireless LAN must use the same encryption key. The key is manually configured on each access point and each client before they can access the network. WEP specifies the use of a 40-bit encryption key, but there are also implementations that can support 64- or 128-bit keys. Recently, 40-bit WEP encryption has been proven to be vulnerable to attack because of a weak algorithm. Using 128-bit WEP encryption—in conjunction with the MAC address filtering and network identifier methods described previously—is highly recommended to fully secure the wireless network.

Exam Tip

You should use the highest level of encryption. Older levels of encryption, such as 40 bit, have been shown to be vulnerable.

VPN   For larger networks with high security requirements, a VPN wireless access solution is a preferable alternative or addition to the other solutions previously discussed. VPN solutions are already widely deployed to provide remote workers with secure access to the network via the Internet. The *VPN* provides a secure, dedicated path or tunnel through a public network like the Internet. Various tunneling protocols are used in conjunction with standard, centralized authentication solutions using a login and password. The same VPN technology can also be used for secure wireless access. In this application, the public network is the wireless network itself. Wireless access is isolated from the rest of the network by a VPN server and, for extra security, an intermediary firewall. Authentication and full encryption over the wireless network are provided through the VPN server. The VPN-based solution is scalable to a large number of users. Figure 5.4 illustrates the architecture of a VPN-based wireless network.

Personal Firewall   In addition to the overall wireless network security, all 802.11 client systems should be equipped with personal firewall software protection. Similar to home computers with permanent cable modem and DSL Internet access connections, 802.11 clients can be vulnerable to attacks by unauthorized users accessing the same network. The personal firewall software can be used to protect the roaming user's confidential local data against many types of possible attacks.

Exam Tip

Be aware of the advantages and disadvantages of all the wireless access security solutions. Depending on the type of network and the scope of security required, some of the detailed security solutions won't be acceptable or they'll need to be augmented by other methods.

CHECKPOINT

✔**Objective 5.01: Wireless**   Wireless clients access a network by communicating through radio frequencies from peer-to-peer or through wireless access points that connect to a wired LAN. The most popular protocols and standards include 802.11, WAP, and Bluetooth, with 802.11b currently as the most popular. Ensuring access security on a wireless network is crucial because of its open nature. Access control methods include network security

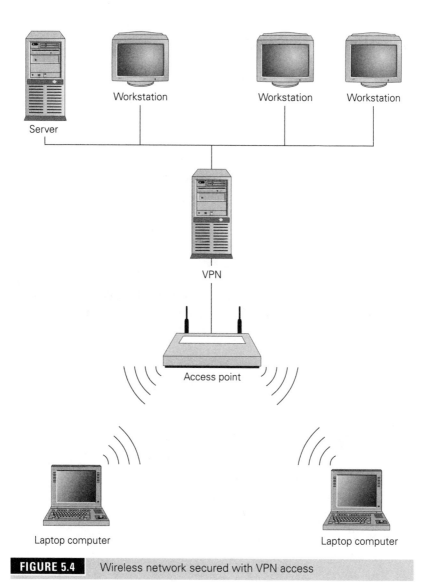

| FIGURE 5.4 | Wireless network secured with VPN access |

identifiers, MAC address filtering, WEP encryption, VPNs, and firewalls. Network identifiers and MAC address filtering aren't recommended for larger networks because of administrative overhead. WEP encryption should be at least 128-bit and should be coupled with a VPN to provide the most secure access.

REVIEW QUESTIONS

1. Which of the following devices can be enabled for wireless networking?
    A. Desktop computer
    B. Laptop computer
    C. PDA
    D. All of the above

2. What device should be installed to allow wireless clients to access a wired LAN?
    A. 802.11b
    B. Firewall
    C. Wireless access point
    D. VPN

3. Which of the following wireless protocol standards delivers Wireless Markup Language (WML) content to web applications on hand-held devices?
    A. WAP
    B. WEP
    C. 802.11g
    D. SSL

4. Bluetooth link-level security is defined as:
    A. Implementation of application-based security policies
    B. Authentication before the link is established
    C. Access control through a login and password
    D. Authentication after the link is established

5. Which of the following IEEE wireless protocol standards is the most popular?
    A. 803.11b
    B. 802.11g
    C. 802.11a
    D. 802.11b

6. What WEP encryption level should be set on an 802.11b network?
    A. 128-bit
    B. 40-bit
    C. 28-bit
    D. 16-bit

7. Which of the following wireless security mechanisms is the least secure?

    A. VPN

    B. WEP 40-bit encryption

    C. Network security identifier

    D. WEP 128-bit encryption

8. MAC Address filtering is defined as:

    A. Allowing access to only specified MAC addresses

    B. Preventing access from only specified MAC addresses

    C. Encryption of wireless device MAC addresses

    D. Personal firewall

9. The most secure and efficient method of access control for wireless security is

    A. WEP 40-bit encryption

    B. VPN

    C. MAC Address filtering

    D. Network security identifier

10. What security mechanism is used with the WAP wireless standard?

    A. WTLS

    B. SSL

    C. HTTPS

    D. WEP encryption

REVIEW ANSWERS

1. **D** All of the above items can be enabled for wireless access. A desktop or laptop computer can use a wireless LAN and PC cards, respectively, while many current PDAs have wireless access built-in.

2. **C** A wireless access point acts as a gateway to enable clients from the wireless network to access the resources on a wired LAN. The access point has a physical connection to the wired LAN.

3. **A** The Wireless Application Protocol is a protocol for delivering WML content for display on smaller hand-held devices, such as wireless phones and PDAs.

4. **B** Link-level security authenticates a wireless client before the actual communications link is established, preventing any communication on the wireless network before authentication can take place.

5. **D** This protocol has emerged as the most popular wireless protocol because of its reliability, high bandwidth, and variety of applicable security methods.

6. **A** Weaknesses in the WEP encryption algorithm have made 40-bit encryption a security weakness because an unauthorized user can break the encryption with relative simplicity.

7. **C** All clients who access the wireless network need to be configured with a network identifier. The identifier, however, can be easily spread by word-of-mouth or discovered by monitoring the access point network name broadcasts.

8. **A** A list of authorized client MAC addresses must be configured on each access point for the network. If any client tries to communicate with the access point and its MAC address isn't in its list, it will be denied access.

9. **B** Through the use of an existing Virtual Private Network (VPN), the wireless communications can be authorized and encrypted just like any other type of remote user.

10. **A** The Wireless Transaction Layer Security (WTLS) provides authentication and encryption similar to SSL security used by Internet web sites. WTLS is used by the WAP standard, while WEP is used by the 802.11b standard.

Infrastructure Security

Devices and
Media Security

	NEWBIE	SOME EXPERIENCE	EXPERT
ETA	4 hours	2 hours	1 hour

Device and media security is often thought of as just the physical protection of your company's computing assets, such as servers, desktops, and laptops. Although property theft is a big security concern, it's overshadowed by the possibility of someone using these devices to access your network and cause damage or data theft.

Device security must also include the methods and communications technologies that enable your regular users to access the network's resources. Network devices such as routers, switches, and firewalls—which can be compromised—can potentially cause much more damage than the simple theft of a laptop computer. Communications channels such as wireless LANs, remote access systems, and Internet access must be secured from unauthorized intrusion.

Media security involves the protection of the ways in which you store and transfer information. The price of lost data, whether because of damage or corporate espionage, can ultimately put a company out of business. The media you use to store information, such as tapes, hard drives, or memory cards, must also be protected from damage, theft, and unauthorized access, just like any other aspect of your network.

By enacting security policies to cover your computer network's devices and media, you're preventing unauthorized access to your company's computer resources and the valuable data they contain.

 **Objective 6.01** Device Security

Device security is the protection of your network's assets from theft, damage, and unauthorized access. Any device that's configured to connect to your network is a potential access point for unauthorized users to gain entry to your system. The following are the three main categories of potential access to a network:

- **Networking Communications** The pathways of communication among all devices on your network. These devices connect all the resources of your network together and connect them to public networks, such as the Internet.
- **Remote Access** Users who like to work from home or on the road need to access the resources of the network remotely.

- **Servers and Clients**   The network servers and client computers, such as desktops and laptops, provide direct communications to the network.

Networking Equipment

Device security begins with the protection of the backbone of your network communications. If an unauthorized individual were able to tap in to any part of your network, that person would have access to virtually everything connected to that network. With the advent of the Internet, a hacker needn't be onsite at a physical computer console. The hacker can be far away in another country, trying to log in to your mail server from a home computer. Several key devices within your network can be configured to increase security against unauthorized intrusion. This is your first line of defense against incoming network attacks, and it's vital that these devices be secured and all security holes fixed. The main networking equipment includes the firewall, routers, switches, and wireless access points.

Firewalls

A *firewall* is used to separate a private network from a public network, such as the Internet. A firewall provides a barrier that protects the internal network from outside communications by filtering packets according to a set of predefined rules. A company, however, might have some servers, such as a web or FTP server that needs to accept connections from the outside world. The firewall usually splits off these servers into their own network, called a Demilitarized Zone (DMZ). The *DMZ* is simply a place where more generous access from Internet users can be configured. Figure 6.1 shows an example of how a firewall is positioned within a local area network (LAN).

The firewall can also act as a proxy for internal users trying to use Internet services. The internal networks usually have their own IP addressing scheme, which won't work on the public Internet. The proxy forwards their requests and acts as a point of contact for the particular service being used, such as web browsing. The firewall will use network address translation (NAT) to masquerade the internal Internet Protocol (IP) of a client with a real, public Internet address.

To configure the firewall, an administrator must set up a number of rules to use each time on incoming and outgoing network communications. These rules can be general or specific. For example, a firewall can be configured with a rule that states that any HTTP traffic can come and go on a specific network. It can also be much more detailed and state that a SMTP packet destined for a particu-

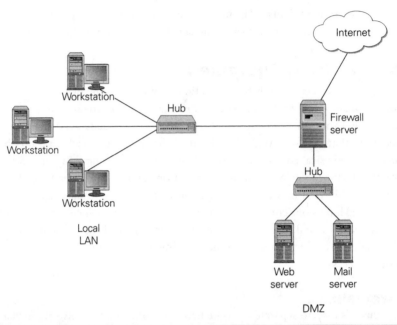

FIGURE 6.1   A firewall protecting the local LAN from the Internet

lar mail server can only come from a specific host. The best practice to use when configuring a firewall for the first time is to deny everything by default, and then create rules to allow the access you need. This ensures you're starting off with the most secure model and working backward to configure the firewall to accept certain types of communications.

A firewall can be an independent hardware device, or a software application running on a normal computer or server. In either case, the firewall software should always be kept current with the latest versions and patches. This will ensure you're using the most recent software that doesn't contain previous software bugs and security vulnerabilities.

See Chapter 7 for more details on firewalls.

Travel Advisory

Documenting all the rules applied to the firewall and why you're implementing them is important. When auditing them at a later date, you might find you're allowing access to services that don't exist anymore and the rules can be removed.

Routers

A *router* is a network device that connects several networks together and relays data between them, as shown in Figure 6.2. A router usually contains a number

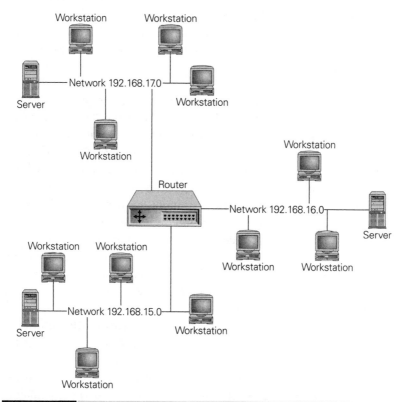

FIGURE 6.2   A router connecting three different networks together

of network interfaces that each represents a different network. Smaller companies generally only have one main router, while larger companies could have several routers to relay information from all their networks.

Router software contains a lot of the same protection found in firewalls, including packet filtering and access control lists. These enable you to control more carefully the protocols, services, ports, and source and destination of the information that flows through the router. For example, you can configure the router only to accept FTP communications to a certain network. Other security features of routers include the capability to protect against spoofing and denial of service (DoS) attacks.

Router software can be complex and it's practically an operating system (OS) in itself. Just like any other piece of software, router software can contain a number of bugs and security vulnerabilities. Always ensure you have the latest software and patches for your system that can fix any bugs or security issues.

Switches

A *switch* is a network device used to segment networks into smaller, more manageable sections and relays packets between the segments. Switches are used more for load balancing and performance reasons than security. You can, however, configure the switch to accept only data from certain MAC address ranges. These ranges can be spoofed by a hacker, though, so they can access the switch and usually mount some form of DoS attack by flooding the switch with packets.

Most attacks are usually directed at the administrative console of the switch, which is used for configuration. Many administrators don't change the default account password and this provides easy access to an unauthorized user who knows the default passwords used by the vendor of the switch. If possible, remote access methods, such as the use of telnet to connect to the switch, should be disabled. This will prevent users from accessing the device, unless they're physically attached to it with a cable.

The use of the Simple Network Management Protocol (SNMP) on switches enables you to use network monitoring programs to analyze information on the switch. But SNMP has been known to contain a number of security vulnerabilities, so disabling its use is best. SNMP also makes use of a type of password system called *community strings*. Most administrators leave the default community string "public" as is, which provides a vulnerability because anyone knowing the community string can connect to the SNMP-enabled device. SNMP passwords should be immediately changed from the default if set up on the switch.

Exam Tip

The default "public" community name string should be changed when SNMP is installed.

Wireless

Wireless communications, with their recent introduction into corporate networks, have created many security vulnerabilities that administrators are unaware of. Unlike *LAN networks*, where an unauthorized individual has to gain access to a physical connection, or connect remotely to a system on the network, a *wireless LAN* creates a network with a varied boundary that can provide access for anyone with a wireless device, even if they aren't in the facility. Wireless security creates a number of new issues that must be added to your current security procedures.

Wireless clients access a regular LAN through the use of wireless access points, which accept connections from wireless clients and connect those wireless clients to the LAN. The access point usually has its own wired network connection to the network. Without proper protection, unauthorized clients can use these access points to gain entry to the network. The following are some of the more important security configurations that should be enabled on a wireless LAN.

See Chapter 5 for more information on wireless networks.

MAC Address Filtering   The access point can be configured to accept connections from only certain hardware MAC addresses. This way, you can create a list of all devices that use the wireless LAN, and then add them to the filter on the access point. Any other device trying to connect that isn't on the list of known addresses is denied access. This is an excellent, but impractical, procedure for larger wireless networks because the amount of administration in keeping the list of addresses and uploading them to each access point would be daunting.

Security Identifier   A special network name or *security identifier* can be configured on the wireless LAN, so only clients that have configured their system to use that identifier are granted access. This is a simple scheme, much like using a public password, and it can be easily compromised if someone finds out the name. Some access points broadcast this name in cleartext, which can be picked up by a network packet sniffer.

Encryption   The best protection for a wireless LAN is the use of encryption to secure network communications. *Encryption* is used to convert clear, plain text communications into secure ciphertext. If the communication is captured, the data cannot be read unless it is decrypted with the corresponding encryption key. The client must be configured with the same type of encryption and also the correct public encryption key. This prevents unauthorized users from capturing network transmissions that contain confidential data. Some earlier forms of encryption, like 40-bit, are weak and can be cracked by a hacker. Using larger bit key systems—such as 128-bit and higher—is best because they're much less likely to be compromised.

Remote Access and Communications

In today's corporate environments, many employees need to access the resources of the computer and phone networks when they aren't physically in the building. This requires the use of modems to connect to a network using a phone line and more advanced methods, such as encrypted virtual private network (VPN) access over the Internet. These *remote access methods* offer opportunities for hackers to compromise these systems that don't install proper security mechanisms. Through a modem or the Internet, an unauthorized user needn't physically be at a console inside the location. That user can be halfway across the world in another country, merely using a simple dial-up Internet connection. To protect these communications from unauthorized access, a security policy must be put in place to provide authentication measures and data encryption.

To ensure communications security, the use of network monitoring and intrusion detection tools can aid in proactively monitoring the network for suspicious and unauthorized activity.

Modems

For remote access in the days before the Internet, the modem was, and still is, an important tool for remote communications. A *modem* allows two computer systems to communicate over an analog phone line. While this is a much slower method than modern VPN and remote access solutions that use broadband Internet access, modems are still in use today as secondary methods of contact, especially for mobile laptop users who must be able to call in from a hotel or an airport.

At minimum, any type of modem access to a network should require authentication before the session can begin. Adding other types of security is ideal, especially if the laptop is stolen. An important feature to implement is the *call-back security*, which requires this: after the user connects to the system, the system dials them back and lets their modem answer to continue the connection.

In corporate networks, some users install modems to their work systems so that they can dial in and access it from home, bypassing any security that was set up by the administrator, such as a firewall or VPN system. Unfortunately, most users do not properly configure their modem to authenticate when someone calls, meaning that any unauthorized user can gain access to the corporate network if they know the right phone number. The administrator must be vigilant in not allowing any type of modem access that bypasses normal security measures.

Remote Access Services

Remote Access Services (RAS) typically refers to the service provided with Microsoft Windows servers to allow remote access to a network through a specific system equipped with a modem. When a user dials in to the server, the RAS handles the procedure of authenticating the client, and allowing them access to the rest of the network through that server.

There are a number of authentication protocols that can be used with the RAS server, including PAP (Password Authentication Protocol), and CHAP (Challenge Handshake Authentication protocol). CHAP is considered to be more secure than PAP and its variants because it does not need the transfer of a password, encrypted or not, between the client and the server.

The system should also be configured with the ability to allow only certain protocols that are used on the network. For example, in a TCP/IP network, communication using other protocols such as IPX/SPX or AppleTalk should be restricted.

RAS servers also support client call-back, which requires the server to call the client computer back to ensure authentication and the origin of the communication.

See Chapter 3 for more details on remote access security.

VPN

A virtual private network is a special, encrypted communications tunnel between one system and another. VPNs are used to secure remote access in most modern networks, as shown in Figure 6.3.

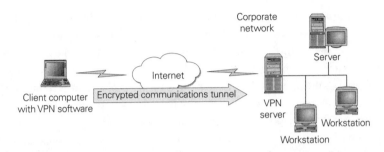

FIGURE 6.3   VPN secures access across the Internet to a remote network.

One of the problems with RAS is users had to use a modem to call a RAS across a great distance, which created an expensive long distance call. One of the benefits of VPN is users can make a local call to their Internet service provider (ISP) to get their Internet connection, and then call their VPN server across the Internet at no additional cost. After connecting to the VPN server, users have a secure channel between them and the network to which the VPN server is attached, enabling them access to network resources.

With the growth of the Internet, users can now access their corporate networks from any Internet connection, whether this is over a modem or a fast broadband connection. To protect these communications and to reduce the possibility of any Internet user gaining access to a corporate network, most companies use a VPN.

The VPN creates an encrypted communications tunnel between your computer and the corporate system through the Internet. Users are authenticated with a login and a password. The use of special encryption keys is used to provide added security. Another added feature of VPN is the use of *protocol encapsulation,* which enables a client to communicate using an internal network protocol, such as IPX. IPX is then encapsulated into a TCP/IP packet for travel over the Internet.

Another way to protect VPN communications is to allow the VPN to assign IP addresses as the user connects and to allow only these blocks of IP addresses to access the network.

Telecommunications

In most organizations, phone services also come under the Information Technology (IT) banner because they're just as much a part of the everyday communications of the company as the computer network.

Instead of assigning a direct line for each user, which can be expensive, most large companies prefer to use a phone switch system, such as a Private Branch Exchange (PBX). The PBX allows the company to maintain a certain number of internal and external lines. For example, a company of 200 people could only have 50 incoming lines and 20 outgoing lines. Internal users also have the capability to call each other using only three- or four-digit extensions. A centralized voice mail system is also usually a part of the entire phone network. This can generally be accessed from an outside line, in case someone wants to check their voice mail when they're at home or traveling.

Security for phone systems, however, has traditionally been lax compared to computer networks. If an unauthorized user were to gain access to the PBX, they might be able to make expensive long-distance phone calls, all charged to the company. Unauthorized voice mail access can invade the privacy of your individual users and it can also be used to glean information for corporate espionage. Important to note is that most phone PBX systems are equipped with a modem to allow remote access for the service technicians from the system vendor. If this modem isn't secured with proper authentication systems, anyone might be able to call that number and access the phone system. A good practice is to unplug this modem when it isn't in use and plug it in when a technician needs access to the system.

The voice mail system should be configured to allow only secure passwords for user voice mail boxes, with a minimum of six to eight characters, composed of uppercase and lowercase letters, numbers, and symbols. The same rules should also be applied to the PBX administrator account.

Intrusion Detection

Intrusion Detection Systems (IDS) are used as a way to detect suspicious activity on a system or network. IDS can be compared to a home security system, which watches your doors and windows for unauthorized entry, and sounds alarms and alerts authorities if they're opened. Similarly, the IDS can monitor common network and system entry points for suspicious activity. For example, you can configure the IDS to inform you when someone logs into a router with an administrator account. If you're the only one who should be accessing it, this can alert you if someone manages to compromise the account.

IDS vary greatly among vendors and each one must be carefully analyzed to ensure it covers the types of security you need. Some systems can detect IP spoofing or if someone is attempting to use a port scanner on your network. The best types of IDS systems can spot a potential attack, such as someone logging in to the system in the middle of the night or repeated attempts at logging in to a certain user account.

Intrusion detection also relies on the capability to be proactive and send alarms to administrators on detection. IDS should be able to send notification using e-mail, phone, and pagers because a serious intrusion must be dealt with immediately before the intruder can access further into the system. The system should also contain a good logging function, so suspicious activity can be fully logged and analyzed later if the intruder leaves before the administrator can lock them out.

> **Travel Advisory**
>
> IDS must be carefully configured to discourage alerts for "false-positives." If an administrator receives too many bogus alerts, they could begin to ignore any alerts, including legitimate intrusions.

Network Monitoring Tools

A variety of tools are available that can monitor your network traffic for problems and suspicious activity. The most popular of these types of tools is the network analyzer or "sniffer." The *sniffer* utility can monitor network traffic right down to the packet and frame level. Typically, the sniffer software includes hardware monitoring devices that are distributed to key areas of the network. The devices forward the information to the sniffer, which then analyzes the data in real time. The main sniffer console can provide the administrator with a wide range of information, and the use of filters and reports can be used to provide the information in an easy to analyze form. For example, the network administrator can set the sniffer software to show only TCP/IP statistics on the network or traffic between two specific computers.

Some network analyzers can be proactive and monitor network traffic in real time and alert you of any error conditions, such as sending an alarm if overall network traffic load is greater than a certain predefined threshold. In this case, the administrator can see if a certain device on the network is flooding the network with traffic and narrow it down to the MAC address of a system. This is helpful in troubleshooting a willful or accidental DoS type of situation, where the network is so saturated, devices can't respond to legitimate requests. Network floods are often caused by devices with faulty network cards that flood the network with garbage information.

Other monitoring and diagnostic utilities can be run to specifically find security weaknesses on your network. For example, a port scanner can be run to analyze all your network devices and service for open TCP/IP service ports that might create security vulnerabilities. If the service and port aren't used, then they should be disabled to close the potential security breach.

Another popular monitoring tool is the use of SNMP, which is a management protocol built-in to many hardware devices and operating system (OS) programs and applications. SNMP is a standard protocol for collecting network information about a certain system. It can provide data on hardware settings, network traffic to and from the system, and software settings and configurations, plus a wide variety of other system information.

Unfortunately, SNMP has been shown to have a number of security vulnerabilities and, if not configured properly, can enable unauthorized access into the system or device for an attacker. If using SNMP, ensure you have the most recent software and firmware revisions for your system. SNMP also uses a form of password called *community strings,* which are typically left as the default "public", and never changed to another value. Any user can use the protocol with the default password and access information about the unsecured system. Another security problem with SNMP is its messages are sent in cleartext, including the community string names. To secure an SNMP implementation fully, its communications should be encrypted with something like IPSec. Finally, if you aren't using SNMP, it should be disabled.

Servers and Clients

Once communications among your various systems are established and secured, the next step in your security plan is to implement security policies and procedures on your internal servers and clients. The servers are the heart of your operations, and they provide most of your centralized processing power and storage. The servers need to be protected from both external and internal users, to prevent the main resources of your network from being compromised. Security issues with servers include access from the Internet, open unused service ports, physical access to the server, and authenticating and granting access to its resources.

The workstation and mobile computers in your organization are what enable your employees to perform their daily work, and to connect to the resources and services offered by your network servers. Protecting the client systems from unauthorized use is another extremely critical aspect of network security. Anyone who can gain access to an unsecured client system might have access to the resources of the entire network. Client security issues include Internet access, remote access to clients, application and workstation privileges, and the security and data protection of mobile devices.

Servers

Your network servers are responsible for providing access to data and services used by all the users on your network. They are your central resources on the network, and a high level of security must be maintained to secure your data and services from unauthorized individuals. The following sections outline the most common security concerns for servers.

Internet Servers   Servers on your network that connect to, or are accessed by, the Internet are prime candidates for hacking attempts. To increase security and protect your private network from your publicly accessible Internet servers, a firewall should be installed. Internet servers that you run, such as HTTP web servers and FTP systems, should be running on their own network off the firewall. If an unauthorized user hacked into your FTP server and it was part of your internal private LAN, the hacker might be able to access any system on that network. With the firewall in place, the hacker can only see the servers on the Internet portion of the firewall, which effectively hides the internal network from external users.

Services and Ports   Many server OSs are installed by default with a number of different Internet services, such as web, telnet, and ftp, which enable outside users to access the server remotely. These services can contain security vulnerabilities that can be exploited by unauthorized users to gain access to the system. Network ports operating without your knowledge can also provide access holes into your server.

To ensure that you're only running what the server needs, you should examine the services and open network ports running on a system and disable any that aren't in use. This is especially necessary for Internet servers, which can be accessed by anyone on the network or Internet and are vulnerable to network scanners that look for and exploit open ports. Some of the most common programs installed by default on an Internet server include HTTP server software, FTP, SMTP, and telnet. These services should be turned off if they aren't used.

Travel Advisory

Auditing your system regularly and removing access to services and ports that might no longer be in use is important.

Physical Access   Access to the servers should be restricted to authorized individuals, such as the network administrator. Servers should be stored in a locked room or, at the very least, be locked in some type of cage or rack to prevent passersby from accessing the console or the server equipment itself.

The server console should be password-protected, so anyone physically accessing the server or attempting access through a network connection, can't gain access unless they're authenticated.

Authentication and Access Permissions   The data and services offered by your network services need to be secured from unauthorized access. The most common form of security employed is the use of authentication and access permissions.

Authentication is used to identify an individual user through the use of a login and a password. By verifying the user's credentials, the server can authenticate that person as an authorized user of the network resources.

Access permissions work on a more granular level and provide security for specific areas on the servers, such as directories, files, and printers. For example, for someone accessing a file server that contains user data directories, that user can be authenticated to use the server, but might only have permissions to access their own specific directory of data. They could also have permissions for other common directories, such as a departmental repository of information.

Workstations

The *workstations* of a company are the desktop computers with which the users perform their daily job functions. A mid-size to large company can have hundreds or thousands of computer workstations, all wired together on a network. Trying to control the security of all these computers can be a nightmare, but within a well-planned network, it can be made fairly easy.

When dealing with so many workstations, properly structuring the network is important, so user data is stored on centralized file servers. This enables you to control access to these resources easily through the use of authentication and file access permissions. Each user should be required to authenticate to the network with a user name and password before they can access any network resources. The real problems begin after a user is authenticated to the network. The following sections outline the security concerns for workstation users.

Internet Access   In today's corporate networks, most users have access to the Internet to send and receive e-mail, and to access the World Wide Web (WWW) for information. Although most networks are secured from outside intrusion through the use of routers and firewalls, several security vulnerabilities can be created by the users inside.

End users often download and install other applications that shouldn't be operating on the company network. These applications include chat programs, file sharing, and music-swapping programs. Because the administrator doesn't have direct control over these applications, they might contain known security vulnerabilities that can provide access to an unauthorized user. These programs provide their services on unique service ports that the firewall might not be blocking. On top of the security vulnerabilities, user interaction with Internet users can result in the downloading of viruses or Trojan horse programs, which allow backdoor access to a user's computer. To protect against the use of these programs, the network administrator should block the service ports used by these programs on the firewall, so they can't communicate with the Internet. The administrator can also assign rights to users on their computers that deny them the capability to install any type of software that isn't already on the system.

Another legal problem companies have run into is the capability for users to download questionable content from the Internet, such as pornographic material or other objectionable content. Many companies have been sued because they allowed such access. To prevent this activity, network administrators can install special web filter programs that can block access to these sites. These filters use a list of known objectionable sites, which is compared to the web sites users try to access through their web browsers.

Remote Access   Some users might install remote access tools or a modem on their work computer, so they can access it from home. This creates many security vulnerabilities because a modem line creates a direct connection to the company network if an unauthorized user tries to connect to that system using a phone line. If the user didn't set up any proper authentication schemes, a hacker can simply call that modem with their own computer and instantly access the corporate network.

Remote control access software can be installed so the user can connect to their work computer from home over the Internet. This creates a worse situation than a general modem because anyone on the Internet can access that. If the user didn't set up any proper authentication, then anyone connecting to that computer remotely can effectively have access to the network.

Network administrators must be aware of all remote access devices connected to the computers on the network. They should be removed if no critical business reason exists why they should be installed. If user must have a modem or needs remote access to their computers, the administrator should ensure that proper authentication and encryption schemes are set up to protect the line of communication from unauthorized users.

Locking the Workstation   When the workstation is to be left unattended for a long period of time, such as a lunch break or the end of the workday, the user should either log off or lock the computer with a password. This prevents users who pass by from accessing the systems of others and gaining access to other network resources.

Software Access and Privileges   All software on the workstation should be kept current with the most recent patches and upgrades to remove any security vulnerabilities from previous versions. Also important is to ensure that users only have enough access to their computers as they need to perform their job functions. For example, any system functions that enable you to change the network address of a computer, or any other type of system change, should be disabled to the regular user and only accessible by the administrator. Regular users shouldn't be able to access any application or configuration program other than what they need to use. The most efficient way of preventing certain system functions from user abuse is to use network-wide system policies that are automatically set for each workstation on the network. This can save considerable time over having to visit each workstation and block out items one by one.

Mobile Devices

Mobile computing has always been thought of as only involving portable laptop computers but, in today's world, this also includes devices such as cellular phones, personal organizers and personal digital assistants (PDAs), and wireless devices. Security concerns for mobile devices derive from the nature of their portability, which makes them more susceptible to theft, vandalism, and unauthorized access. The following are some of the most common security concerns that affect mobile devices.

Physical Security   The portable nature of mobile devices means they're much easier to steal without observation. A PDA lying on a desk can be swiped up into a coat pocket within a few seconds, while unattended laptops have been known to disappear quickly even within a company's own offices. Mobile devices should never be left unattended and small items, such as a phone or PDA, should be safely secured on the owner in a pocket or belt holder. Larger items, such as laptops, can be secured to a desk or workstation by using a special lockable cable.

Authentication   If your mobile device is stolen, a simple authentication scheme can deter the unauthorized user from accessing any sensitive information on the laptop or device. The reason for the theft could be simply for the hardware, but devices that contain confidential information might be stolen for their content, as in industrial espionage. A login and password can be set on everything from entry into the OS, on a single file or directory, to the unit itself.

Travel Advisory

A password can be set on the hard drive or basic input/output system (BIOS) of a laptop system. With this authentication, the unit will turn on, but won't load the OS until the correct password is entered.

Data Protection   Beyond authentication, critical data can be protected through the use of encryption. By encrypting the contents of a flashcard or hard drive, unauthorized users are unable to read the data unless they have the corresponding encryption key. This is useful for password files that people sometimes keep on their PDAs or flash memory cards.

Objective 6.02   Media Security

M *edia* in computer network terms can be described as the ways in which you store and transfer information from one point to another. This can include a desktop computer transferring a file from its hard drive to that of another computer using a floppy disk or a digital camera downloading picture files on to a laptop using a memory card. Tape media is used to perform backup and storage of critical network data, while hard drives store all your information on a computer. Media can be part of a computer system itself or a portable version of the same media type, so it can be connected to another system.

Another consideration is the media of your network itself. This is the physical cabling that allows information from one system on a network to transfer data to another system that's physically connected to another part of the network.

Computer media can contain critical and confidential data that must be protected from unauthorized access, or from physical damage or destruction. The portable nature of many types of computer media means they might be less secure and provide more opportunities for an unauthorized user to obtain or damage the information they hold. The following sections detail the most common types of computer media and network cabling, as well as the security concerns they create.

Exam Tip

Be aware of which cabling types are more secure and which are more suited for a particular environment.

Cabling

Media security not only concerns portable and main storage subsystems, but also the communications media uses to transfer information on a network from one point to another. The physical *cabling* is a critical part of your infrastructure because your entire network operation wouldn't run without it.

Although many companies don't consider cabling a security priority, your physical network cabling offers an easy opportunity for an unauthorized individual to tap directly into your network to perform malicious functions.

Several types of network cabling are in use today, each with its own advantages and disadvantages, especially in the area of security. Cabling security not only includes intrusion protection, but protection against the physical environment as well.

Coaxial

Coaxial cable consists of a copper core surrounded by layers of insulation and protective shielding, and, finally, an outer jacket. This type of cabling is used most often with Ethernet networks, in both thin and thick versions. Each end of the coaxial network must be terminated with a resistor and each cable segment is connected to the other using several types of connectors, such as a T, barrel, or bayonet-Neill-Concelman (BNC) connector. ThinNet, or 10Base2, is much easier to work with than ThickNet and is used for smaller distance runs. ThickNet, or 10Base5, is used for longer distances, up to 300 meters. Connecting workstations to ThickNet is also more complicated because it requires the use of transceivers and "vampire" tap connectors, which pierce the cable.

Local Lingo

Vampire Tap A special connector used in coaxial cabling that uses a number of sharp metal teeth to clamp down on a cable and pierce into it to connect to the core copper wire.

Although it's not as popular as twisted-pair cable, coaxial cable is most often used in manufacturing environments, where the dangerous environment demands a cable that can withstand the physical and electromagnetic environment.

The disadvantage of coaxial cabling is if one segment is disconnected without being properly terminated or broken, that segment will disconnect the entire network. In fact, all you need to do to disable a coaxial network is unplug one of the end terminators. Overall, coaxial networks are less reliable than other cabling options, such as twisted-pair or fiber-optic cables.

A security concern with coaxial networks is the capability for an unauthorized user to access the cable and tap into the connection with their own "vampire" tap or, in the case of ThinNet, to add on another segment to the network, and then add a new computer or device.

UTP/STP

Twisted-pair cabling is the most popular type of network cabling today and it's also used for virtually all phone-system cabling. Twisted-pair cabling typically consists of four to eight copper wires, surrounded by an outer, protective jacket. The wires are twisted together, which prevents signal crossover interference among the wires.

Two basic types of twisted-pair cabling exist: unshielded twisted pair (UTP) and shielded twisted pair (STP). These are essentially the same, except STP provides an extra foil-shielded layer to provide extra protection against electromagnetic interference (EMI).

Disadvantages of twisted-pair wiring include its susceptibility to EMI, especially in the case of UTP, and attenuation, which means the signal becomes weaker over greater distances.

Twisted-pair cabling is considered the least secure of network cabling because someone can easily connect it by simply connecting their computer or network device to an existing cable from a wall jack or to a central hub. Twisted-pair cabling is also easy to damage physically.

Exam Tip	
Twisted-pair cabling is the least secure of network cabling types.	

Fiber-Optic

Fiber-optic cabling, as opposed to other cabling that uses electrical signals over copper wire, uses light as the medium to transfer information. Fiber cabling consists of a central glass core, surrounded by protective layers of cladding. Fiber can transfer information quickly and over greater distances than conventional copper wire cabling. And fiber cabling is also immune to EMI and it doesn't emit or radiate signals that can interfere with other cables.

Fiber-optic cabling, however, is expensive compared to other forms of wiring and is typically used as a main network backbone. Copper wiring is used to break off into smaller networks, right down to the desktop computer.

With the added performance advantage of fiber-optics comes the security of knowing unauthorized users can't tap into a fiber cable to snoop network traffic, as they can with a copper-based cable. The main disadvantage of a fiber-optic cable is the expense and knowing if a cable is damaged or severed, it can't be easily repaired. Often, a new fiber-optic cable must be run to replace the damaged one.

Exam Tip	
Fiber-optic is the most secure type of network cabling.	

Removable Media

The capability to transfer information easily from one computer device to another has been made easier with the introduction of several types of removable media. The most common forms of data storage in previous years were the use of hard drives, floppy disks, and tapes. New technologies, such as removable hard drives, flash cards, smart cards, and CD-ROMS, enable users much more flexibility with moving information from one system to another. This has also provided ways to transfer data from small devices, such as digital cameras, PDAs, MP3 music players, and video game console systems.

With the introduction of any new media type, security must be a priority to protect the confidentially and integrity of data, especially when this information is being physically moved from one place to another. This involves the use of encryption and authentication to secure access to the data, as well as physical and environmental protection of the removable media themselves.

Tape

Tape media is the most popular for backup use among large and small companies. Tape backups can provide a large storage capacity for an inexpensive price. Tapes can hold as much as 80GB or more of data, providing an excellent way to back up data on large file or database servers.

Tape media, like any other magnetic type of media, is susceptible to magnetic interference, which can corrupt or delete the data on the tape. Care must be taken in labeling tapes properly, so important information isn't overwritten the next time the tape is used. Like floppy disks, tapes have write-protect mechanisms that can be enabled, so a tape can't be written to.

Tapes are also prone to wear and tear, so you need to refresh your media supply constantly with new tapes. This is because continued use of a tape slowly wears down the integrity of its recordable areas. The best practice is to pull tapes out of rotation after about a year of constant use.

Many companies send their tapes to an offsite storage facility so, in case a disaster destroys the main company site, a recent backup of data will still be available at the facility. Ensure the facility has proper environmental controls because tapes can be damaged from prolonged exposure to extreme hot or cold temperatures, or to humidity.

To ensure completely secure data integrity, your backups should be tested regularly by performing weekly restores. Even though your backup program states a backup was successful, mechanical problems such as misaligned head, can cause corrupted data to be written to the tapes. Only by regularly testing the restore process can you ensure your backups are working properly.

Travel Advisory

When storing your tapes for long periods of time, ensure you also have available the backup application software used to write the data to the tapes. Many companies continually upgrade their software or switch to a different vendor. Many applications can't read the data of another and you could be in a position where you can't read the contents of a tape because you don't have the application with which it was recorded.

CD-ROM

The use of CD-ROM disks to store and back up information has become increasingly popular. As the prices of recordable CD-ROM drives have become more affordable, this can be a preferred solution to using expensive digital linear tape (DLT) or digital audio tape (DAT) and the corresponding tape drives. CD-ROMs use optical technology to record information on a disk. Each disk can hold approximately 650MB of data. This is a good size for personal home use, but impractical for large companies that need to back up several gigabytes of data.

Two main types of CD-ROM media exist: CD-R (CD Recordable) and CD-RW (Rewritable). CD-R media can be written to only once, while CD-RW can be erased and new information rewritten to them.

CD-ROMs, although resistant to many kinds of physical abuse such as dropping, can be damaged by scratches on the surface of the CD. Some have argued that the chemical composition of CD-ROMs can break down over time, anywhere from 20 to 100 years depending on the type of CD. Because of these disadvantages, using CD-ROM technology is suitable for short-term backups or archival of data but, for increased protection, other media, such as tape, should be considered.

When discarding CDs, a good security practice is either to break the disk or damage its surface before throwing it away. This can prevent someone from retrieving the discarded disk and accessing the information stored on it.

Travel Advisory

A simple way to make CD-ROM disks unreadable is to take a sharp object and scratch part of the reflective layer of the CD.

Hard Drives

Desktop, laptop, and server hard drives are the most common form of general magnetic storage for information. While desktops and laptops typically only have one hard drive per machine, servers can have several hard drives to provide a large amount of storage space and fault redundancy.

An increasingly popular new technology is the use of removable hard drives. By installing a special removable drive bay in your computer, the hard drive can be removed and installed in a removable drive bay on another system. This technology, however, doesn't include the capability, such as SCSI-based RAID storage systems, of hot swap technology. The system must be shut down before a removable hard drive can be removed. To protect the information on this type of hard drive, it should be encrypted. To store the removable hard drive safely, it should be stored in a secured or locked area.

Hard drives aren't considered safe for data integrity and long-time storage. Because of their mechanical and magnetic nature, hard drives are susceptible to magnetic interference or physical shock because of the sensitivity of the magnetic heads that read the data. Simply dropping a hard drive on the ground might render it useless. Hard drives are also more prone to failure than other storage media because the constant heating and cooling of the components causes expansion and retraction, which shortens the life of its usability.

Unlike diskettes, hard drives can't easily be write-protected and a simple error entering a command can possibly delete the entire contents of the hard drive. If you don't have backups of the data on your hard drives and you suffer from a mechanical or user error that deletes or corrupts data, you might have to send the device to a special data-recovery lab. These labs can attempt to extract the information from the damaged hard drive, but the costs can be expensive.

To prevent someone from examining the contents of a hard drive after it's been given to someone else—or disposed of—special "shredder" type programs exist that can write "garbage" data to the drive to overwrite the previous data. Simply erasing or formatting the drive doesn't always overwrite the data on the hard drive. These utilities only erase the data from the hard-drive directory sector, while the data remains where it is until it's overwritten. This is for disaster recovery purposes, so a user can "unerase" or unformat data. For security reasons, however, to prevent any sort of data recovery, the data should be overwritten.

Diskettes

For many years, the floppy diskette, or the "floppy," was the storage and backup medium of choice for most personal computer users. Until storage capacities for disk and hard drive media began to grow enormously, the typical 3.5-inch 1.44MB floppy disk was used to transfer information from one computer to another or to store backups of data. The use of networks has replaced the use of floppy disks as a mode to transfer information from one computer to another and, because of storage requirements, 1.44MB was far too small to store anything of importance. Diskettes are still in use, however, usually to distribute patch files for computer applications, OSs, and firmware updates for hardware devices.

For security, the most anyone can do to protect information on a floppy disk is to write-protect it. All floppy disks have a write-protect tab in the top right-hand corner of the disk. When the tab is set in the open position—where you can see through the hole—the disk is write-protected, and nothing can be saved to the disk. This is important for ensuring viruses don't get transferred from a personal computer to the disk because the virus won't be able to replicate itself to the write-protected disk. These types of viruses typically install in the boot sector of the diskette. If the floppy disk is then used to boot another computer, it will transfer itself to the boot sector of the computer's hard drive.

Floppy disks, like any other type of magnetic media, are susceptible to magnetic interference, which can corrupt or erase their contents.

Flash Cards

A *flash card*, sometimes also referred to as a memory card, is a popular device that can be used for a variety of applications, including console game systems, MP3 music players, and digital cameras. The flash card contains information in its memory and doesn't provide any sort of processing capability, as seen in smart cards. The memory is similar to RAM on a personal computer, except the information is stored there indefinitely—until the information is updated, or deleted, and replaced with new information. This allows data to be extracted from a device or computer, and then carried around on the flash card to another device to transfer the information. For example, users can save the current information of a game they're playing on a console system and take the flash card to another user's house to transfer the information to that system and continue playing. Digital cameras can save photographs on the card, which can then be attached to a desktop computer where the user can manipulate or print the pictures as they want. PDA users could save confidential information from their organizer on their flash cards, such as login and password information they use frequently.

Travel Advisory
Storing confidential information on devices that don't use encryption to protect their contents isn't recommended.

Unfortunately, many types of these cards don't contain any inherent security mechanisms, and the information is usually unencrypted and easily accessible. Some software programs can be used to encrypt the contents of flash cards if desired. This is important if the information is considered confidential because these small cards can easily be lost or stolen.

Smart Cards

A *smart card* is a small device resembling a credit card, which contains its own memory and CPU unit. A smart card is similar to a memory or a flash card, but it provides even more functionality because of its capability to process information like a computer. The amount of memory on a smart card is just enough for it to retain information and run its programs. The smart card can store a wide variety of information, such as authentication data, and personal financial or biometric data.

To use the smart card, the user must swipe or insert the card into a card reader. Typically, to access the information on the smart card, the user must enter a personal identification number (PIN) before the card reader will authenticate. This allows a dual authentication security mechanism, where the user must authenticate as the owner of the card, while the card reader authenticates the credentials on the card itself. These security protections greatly reduce the risk of someone gaining unauthorized access with a stolen card or trying to access the information stored on the smart card. The contents of the card are usually encrypted with one of the current encryption standards, such as RSA or MD5.

Exam Tip
Smart cards are usually encrypted with a standard like RSA or MD5.

CHECKPOINT

✔**Objective 6.01: Device Security** Device security from a networking standpoint includes networking devices such as firewalls, routers, and switches. Remote access methods must be secured, such as modems, RAS servers, and VPN solutions, using strong authentication and encryption. Server and client computers need to be protected from unauthorized access from users passing by the console and networked users exploiting security vulnerabilities on a client system.

✔**Objective 6.02: Media Security** Fiber-optic cabling is the most secure of cabling types compared to coaxial and twisted-pair cabling because it's immune to EMI and attenuation, and can't be easily tapped into. Removable media must be protected from theft and damage. Data can be protected by encryption and authentication methods.

REVIEW QUESTIONS

1. What type of device uses packet filtering and access rules to control access to private networks from public networks, such as the Internet?
   A. Wireless access point
   B. Router
   C. Firewall
   D. Switch

2. What communications product enables you to connect to a company LAN over the Internet through a secure, encrypted channel?
   A. VPN
   B. WEP
   C. Modem
   D. Telnet

3. What networking application can be used to analyze and inspect network traffic?
   A. IDS
   B. FTP
   C. Router
   D. Sniffer

4. Which of the following is the default community string for SNMP?

   A. Public

   B. Private

   C. Default

   D. Admin

5. What can be done to protect the data on a laptop if it's stolen?

   A. Lock the floppy drive

   B. Enable a login and a password on the operating system

   C. Regularly archive it to CD-ROM

   D. Encrypt the data

6. What can be done to prevent someone from accidentally overwriting data on a magnetic tape?

   A. Rub it with a magnet

   B. Label it carefully

   C. Set the write-protect tab

   D. Store it offsite

7. Which of the following media would *not* be susceptible to magnetic interference?

   A. Floppy disk

   B. CD-ROM

   C. Flash card

   D. Tape

8. What should be used in conjunction with a smart card for authentication?

   A. PIN

   B. Retina scan

   C. Encryption key

   D. Memory card

9. Which of the following media is *not* a removable device?

   A. Floppy diskette

   B. CD-ROM drive

   C. Smart card

   D. Tape

10. Which of the following security applications or devices would be used to track and proactively alert administrators about unauthorized access?

    A. Antivirus program

    B. Switch

    C. Intrusion detection system

    D. Network analyzer

REVIEW ANSWERS

1. **C**   By creating access lists and packet filtering rules, a firewall can protect incoming and outgoing communications between a private and a public network. A firewall is most often used to protect an internal network from the Internet.

2. **A**   Virtual private networking enables a user to connect to a corporate network from a remote location over the Internet. To provide protection, the VPN uses encryption and authentication to provide a secure, private tunnel through the Internet to its destination.

3. **D**   Also referred to as a network analyzer, a sniffer can capture and analyze network traffic right down to the frame level. The sniffer can give you information on the protocols and MAC addresses of the computers and devices communicating on the network.

4. **A**   Using SNMP, the community string is a simple, password-based security scheme to authenticate SNMP communications. When first setting up SNMP, the default community string should be changed to something more secure to prevent unauthorized access.

5. **D**   By encrypting the data on the laptop, you're ensuring that if it's ever stolen, the confidential information contained on it can't be read.

6. **C**   By setting the write-protect tab on your tape, this will prevent someone else from overwriting the data stored on it. The person can only read the data currently on the tape and can't write to it.

7. **B**   The CD-ROM doesn't consist of any components that would be affected by magnetic interference.

8. **A**   When using a smart card, a PIN number should also be required to authenticate the person using the card. This prevents an unauthorized user from using a stolen smart card. Without the PIN number, the card is useless.

9. **B** Although the CD-ROM discs themselves can be removed, the CD-ROM drive itself is usually mounted inside the computer and can only be removed by taking the computer apart.

10. **C** An IDS system can detect suspicious activity, send alerts to the administrator, and begin logging the actions of the intruder.

Security Topologies
and Intrusion Detection

	NEWBIE	SOME EXPERIENCE	EXPERT
ETA	3 hours	1.5 hours	1 hour

The security of an entire network is placed in the hands of a few network administrators who must ensure that all aspects of the network—from the internal system, to Internet servers, and to communications with public networks such as the Internet—are secure from unauthorized access and intrusion attacks.

Most networks consist of a variety of different hosts, systems, devices, and network protocols compounded with the need for them to interface with public networks such as the Internet or the networks of other organizations. Security for such a wide array of systems can be a daunting task, but a number of security procedures and mechanisms can be installed to help the administrator in proactively monitoring and configuring network security.

A network can be split into smaller, more manageable pieces through the use of firewalls, routers, and switches that create logical networks comprised of systems with common security needs. By creating security topologies within a physical network, the capability to secure the pathways between each section is simplified, while retaining a high level of access security.

To make the procedure of monitoring network security even more proactive, an intrusion detection system can be installed to scan automatically for and detect network intrusions, and then notify the administrator or take immediate actions on its own by reconfiguring the system to remove the threat.

The use of security topologies and intrusion detection systems can enable network administrators to secure and monitor a network for attacks and intrusions proactively without the need for constant physical monitoring. A network administrator can't be everywhere at once, but the use of these security procedures and services can come close to achieving that goal.

Objective 7.01 Security Topologies

Security of your network can be a daunting task for a network administrator. Depending on the size and complexity of the network, the administrator must examine the security implications of several different types of systems and communications, from the networking equipment, such as routers, firewalls, and switches, to the protection of the internal hosts who communicate through the Internet with the outside world.

Compounding the problem are the several types of Internet services that most companies and organizations need to run their business: web services, e-mail, and file transfer servers. These types of applications require special attention regarding security. At the same time, you need to protect your internal network hosts and servers from unauthorized access from the public Internet.

To provide maximum security with the least amount of administrative overhead, the use of security zones is recommended. *Security zones* are created when parts of your network are divided into special zones where similar systems and servers reside. By putting all your Internet servers in one zone and your internal network in another zone, you create a protective wall to regulate access between them. This type of topology is created through the use of a *firewall*, which controls access to the various zones through a rules-based access system.

Other network protection schemes, including the use of network address translation (NAT), virtual local area networks (VLANs), and tunneling protocols, can help you divide the network into more manageable zones to secure access.

Security Zones

Dividing your network into various security zones lets you create physical and logical barriers between the different areas of your network. These zones enable you to allocate different types of security, depending on the sensitivity of the data and network equipment within that zone. This is the equivalent of setting up fences or walls between different buildings in a facility, which prevent users of one building from entering another building for which they aren't authorized. A firewall is used to set up these zones on the network. A *firewall* is a special server or network device used to regulate network traffic and to prevent access to the private network from a public network, such as the Internet. The firewall uses a special set of rules to admit or deny network access, as appropriate, such as only allowing FTP traffic to a specific server. By setting up the firewall to split the network into different zones, creating firewall rules to allow access to servers in those zones is much easier.

The three main zones into which networks are commonly divided are the external public network, the internal private network, and a demilitarized zone (DMZ), as shown in Figure 7.1.

DMZ

The *DMZ* is an area of the network where a high number of publicly accessed Internet systems should be located. The DMZ, in an overall network security

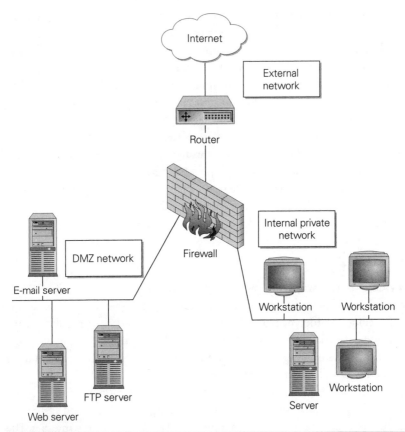

FIGURE 7.1   A network divided into security zones using a firewall

topology, is situated between the public and protected zones (private network), as shown in Figure 7.2.

The DMZ provides a buffer zone between your external network devices, such as a router, and the internal network that comprises your servers and user workstations. The DMZ usually contains popular Internet services—web servers, mail servers, and FTP servers. These services need to be accessed by those on the public network, the Internet. Your company might use a web site that hosts certain services and information for current clients and potential clients. A public FTP server on the DMZ might serve files to all users or only to certain clients. Your mail server needs to allow a connection from the Internet to let e-mail be relayed to and from your site, and also to provide mail access for your own users who might be using the system remotely.

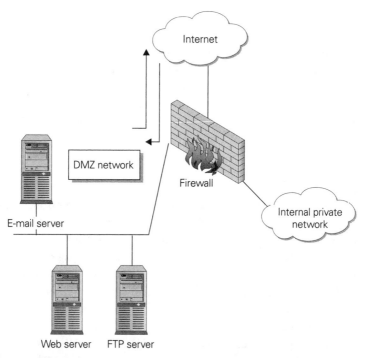

FIGURE 7.2 The DMZ sits between the public and the protected zones of your network.

Exam Tip

Know the purpose of the DMZ and how a firewall can be configured to split these Internet servers away from the internal network.

These Internet services, however, should be separated from your internal LAN. If you were to host a web server on your internal LAN that's accessible from the Internet, you would create vulnerabilities in your network because an unauthorized user might be able to compromise the web server, and then have full access to your local LAN. If the web server is on your DMZ and it's somehow compromised, the hacker could only get as far as the DMZ because the internal LAN is on another network, protected by the firewall.

> **Travel Advisory**
>
> Many web servers act as a front-end for access to database servers, which need to be located on the internal LAN. Care must be taken to ensure that only those ports needed for access to the database are opened by the firewall and that access can only be granted from that web server. If a hacker were to compromise the security of the web server, they might be able to use that as a jumping point to get to the database server on the internal LAN.

Intranet

An *intranet* is a locally available web network that is not accessible from the public Internet. The prefix "intra" specifies this is an internal network. Many companies provide web services that are only relevant to their internal employees and not to the public or the company's customers. These web pages usually contain such services as a directory of contact information for everyone in the company, web pages dedicated to specific departments (for example, human resources or engineering), or finance web pages dealing with the company's stock and financial plans. Web-enabled applications for internal use can also be created, giving employees access to internal services via a web browser.

The intranet only lets internal employees have access to these web pages because the information they provide can be confidential and shouldn't be accessed by the public, especially rival companies. The web servers that host intranet services are located on the private internal LAN in the overall security zone model to prevent access from both the public and DMZ zones. As part of the internal network security zone, the network is configured to use Internet Protocol (IP) address ranges that are set aside as private addresses. These standard private addresses can be used by any internal network and can't be routed on the Internet. The following are the private address ranges that can be used.

- Class A Network   10.0.0.0
- Class B Network   172.16.0.0 - 172.31.255.255
- Class C Network   192.168.0.0 - 192.168.255.255

> **Exam Tip**
>
> Know the standard nonroutable private address ranges for different classes of networks.

Extranet

An *extranet* is an extension of your private network or intranet. An extranet extends outside the body of your local network to enable other companies or networks to share information. For example, an automobile manufacturing company could have an extranet that connects selected business partners, so they can access and share specific information on availability and inventories between the networks. These are often referred to as business-to-business (B2B) communications or networks because one company uses the internal resources and services of another.

Extranets can open security vulnerabilities in your network unless they're configured properly. Older types of extranets used dedicated communications links between the companies, which are much more difficult for an unauthorized user to penetrate. Nowadays, extranets use virtual private network (VPN) tunnels over the Internet to communicate, which makes it more susceptible to intrusion. To ensure extranet communications are secure, your VPN, encryption, and firewall configuration must be carefully planned to limit the access of an intruder.

Networking Security

Beyond physically dividing the network into zones to secure network communications, several software-based network configurations can aid in securing your network from unauthorized intruders. These enable you to reconfigure the network logically, instead of physically, which reduces administrative overhead and removes the need to purchase additional expensive networking equipment.

NAT

NAT is a service that allows private IP addresses on your internal network to be translated into a routable address for communication on the Internet. NAT was initially created to solve the problem of the lack of IP addresses available for private networks to use on the Internet. The number of remaining IP address ranges were scarce, so an alternate method of using already existing addresses was needed. Private networks can make use of special private IP address ranges internally and, when they communicate with the Internet, they can use an external address. Most companies only have a certain amount of external Internet IP addresses to use. To work around the problem, a NAT service can be installed, so when an internal client wants to communicate with the outside world, it's assigned an external IP address for that communication. From the outside world, any communications from that internal network seem to come from one external IP address. The NAT service takes care of handling what requests go back to which clients on the internal network, as shown in Figure 7.3.

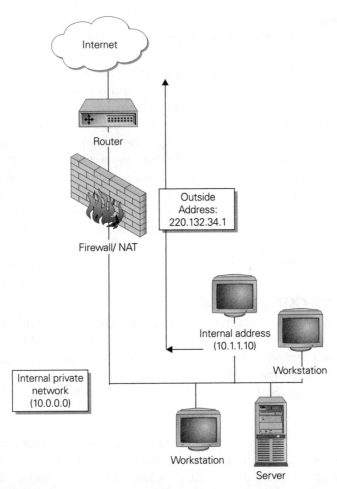

| FIGURE 7.3 | Network using NAT to hide and translate internal network addresses |

NAT is also important for security because the internal address of the client can't be accessed from anyone in the outside world on the Internet. If an unauthorized user tries to see what's in that network, they can only get as far as the external router or firewall. Most routers and firewalls have the NAT service built in to provide this functionality.

One hacking method that's been used to try and compromise a network using a firewall is to "spoof" the IP address to make it look like the request is coming from the internal network. The NAT service helps prevent these attacks because the addresses of the internal private network are hidden.

Tunneling Protocols

To connect two networks together or to let users remotely access local network servers, the use of VPNs has increasingly become the communications technology of choice. Previously, to connect the networks of two companies together or to connect two offices of the same company in different locations, an expensive communications link needed to be run. With the growth of extranets that connect the internal networks of different companies and organizations over the Internet, VPNs allow the existing Internet to be used to link them together. VPNs are much more secure and less expensive to install and maintain than running expensive WAN links between offices.

A VPN makes use of tunneling protocols to connect networks together. A tunneling protocol allows an existing internal protocol, such as IPX or a network with private IP addressing, to be encapsulated and relayed over the Internet to its destination. This VPN link is encrypted to provide secure access to a private network over the public Internet. The VPN link should be protected with strong encryption and authentication mechanisms to ensure its security.

VLAN

A virtual LAN (VLAN) is a type of logical network that exists as a subset of a larger physical network. In smaller networks, the network can be divided into segments fairly easily, with little administrative overhead. Splitting the network into segments allows network data and broadcast traffic to stay on the local segment, without broadcasting data to the entire network as a whole. Segmentation of LANs also provides extra security because a user on one LAN won't have access to another one without special permission.

Unfortunately, segmenting a larger network into smaller networks can be tedious and might involve the purchase of extra networking equipment, such as switches and routers, and extra cabling to separate them. This is where VLANs can help because the network segmentation is performed through software, rather than hardware. VLANs have the capability to isolate network traffic on specific segments, and even provide crossover functionality to enable certain VLANs to overlap and allow access between them.

Exam Tip
Know how VLANs can increase security and performance in a network, as well as the different ways they can be implemented.

The capability to create VLANs is dependent on the capabilities of your network equipment. Most modern switches and routers support the use of VLANs, which can be enabled simply through changing the configuration of the network device. Three basic types of VLANs exist.

- **Port-based VLAN**   The *port-based VLAN* uses the specific port of a network switch to configure VLANs. Each port is configured as part of a particular VLAN. To assign a client workstation to that VLAN, they need to be plugged into that port.
- **MAC Address-based VLAN**   The *MAC address-based VLAN* tracks clients and their respective VLAN memberships through the MAC address of their network card. The switches maintain a list of MAC addresses and VLAN membership, and they route the network packets to their destination, as appropriate. The advantage of MAC address-based VLANs is if their VLAN membership changes, they needn't be physically moved to another port. One drawback of this method is that being part of multiple VLANs can cause confusion with the switch's MAC address tables. This model is recommended for single VLAN memberships.
- **Protocol-based VLAN**   A *protocol-based VLAN* is the most flexible and logical type of VLAN. It uses the addresses of the IP layer to assign VLAN settings, so an entire IP subnet can be assigned a certain VLAN membership.

Figure 7.4 shows an example of a typical VLAN configuration. This network is divided by network subnets, configured as part of a certain VLAN. The switches are using a port-based VLAN configuration across two floors of a building.

Objective 7.02 Intrusion Detection

Although several protection mechanisms can be put in place to prevent malicious attacks and unauthorized access to your network, they usually aren't proactive in nature and, after an incident, security must be reviewed and stronger new techniques must be created to prevent further attacks.

As a first line of defense for your network security, the implementation of an intrusion detection system greatly enhances the security of your network. An *intrusion detection system* can monitor your network and host systems for suspicious behavior that can indicate if someone is trying to break in or damage your

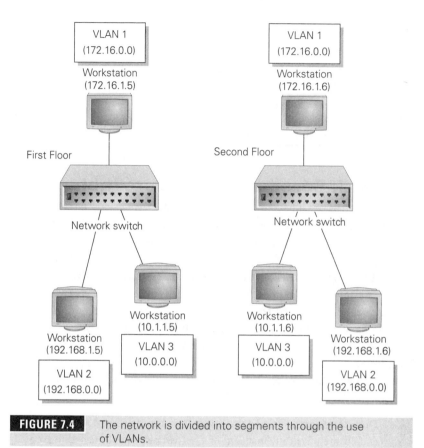

FIGURE 7.4   The network is divided into segments through the use of VLANs.

system. By proactively monitoring the system, the detection system can immediately notify an administrator through paging or an e-mail of the intrusion. Some detection systems can self-repair the problem and either disconnect suspicious network connections or turn off network services that are being attacked.

Two main types of intrusion detection systems exist.

- **Network-based**   A *network-based system* analyzes network traffic going in and out of your network. It can detect suspicious behavior that can indicate unauthorized access or network attacks against network hosts.

- **Host-based**   A *host-based system* protects one specific host or device. By analyzing incoming and outgoing network activity, and logging user logins and access, it can detect any possible attempts to compromise security.

Intrusion detection systems can also be either active or passive. In an *active detection system*, intrusion attempts are dealt with immediately by shutting down network connections or services that are being attacked. A *passive detection system* relies on notification to alert administrators of an intrusion.

> **Exam Tip**
>
> Ensure you know the difference between network and host-based intrusion detection systems, as well as the difference between active and passive versions of these systems.

Network-Based Intrusion Detection

To prevent intrusions into your network systems, a *network-based intrusion detection system* can be installed to monitor incoming and outgoing traffic in your network. A network-based intrusion detection system analyzes network activity and the data packets themselves for suspicious activity against hosts on the network.

A network-based intrusion detection system can examine network patterns, such as an unusual amount of requests destined for a particular server or service, such as an FTP server. The headers of network packets can be analyzed for possible spoofing attempts or suspicious code that indicates a malformed packet. Corrupted packets and malformed data can bring down a web server that's vulnerable to such attacks.

A network intrusion detection system typically consists of the following components, as shown in Figure 7.5:

- **Detector Agent** The *detection agents* of an intrusion detection system usually are physically installed in a network and are attached to core network devices, such as routers, firewalls, and switches. Detection agents can also be software agents that use network management protocols, such as Simple Network Management Protocol (SNMP). They simply collect the data passing through the network and send it on to the network monitor for analyzing.

- **Monitor** The *network monitor* is fed information from the detection units and analyzes the network activity for suspicious behavior. This is the heart of the intrusion detection system, which collects information from the network, analyzes it, and then uses the notification system to warn of any problems.

- **Notification System** The *notification system* is used for notification and alarms, which are sent to the administrator. Once the network monitor recognizes a threat, it writes to a log file and uses the notification system to send an alert, such as an e-mail or a page to an administrator. The notification system is usually configurable, to allow for a variety of methods of communication.

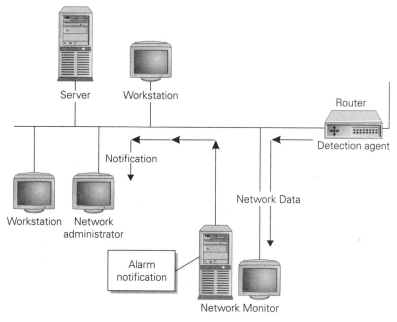

Server   Workstation

Router

Detection agent

Notification

Network Data

Workstation   Network administrator

Alarm notification

Network Monitor

FIGURE 7.5   The components of a network-based intrusion detection system

To protect the entire network, the intrusion detection system is usually located at a central point, such as a main router, switch, or firewall system. A detection system can only monitor what it sees, so placing it further down in the system lessens the chance of finding intrusions, especially because your firewall and routers are the entry points to the network. This characteristic makes a network-based system much more important than a host-based system because of its capability to detect intrusions at the entrance to the network. The disadvantage of a network-based system is it can rarely detect intrusions originating from the internal network. This is where also using host-based intrusion detection systems in your overall security model is important.

Travel Advisory

Network-based intrusion systems also aren't effective in monitoring encrypted communications, such as a VPN.

When an intrusion is detected, the system works in either an active or a passive way to alert an administrator of the problem. A passive system will only send warnings and alarms through log files, or e-mail and paging. An active system tries to fix the problem through shutting off certain services or preventing connections from a suspicious host.

Active Detection

A network-based intrusion detection system that uses active detection methods can take immediate steps to halt an intrusion. The advantage of this method is it can attempt to prevent the intrusion from continuing. Active detection prevents the suspicious activity from ballooning into actual damage or data loss. This is a great advantage over passive-based detection systems, which merely log the incident or send an e-mail to the administrator who might not see the message for many hours before they can perform any preventative actions. By then, it could be too late.

Network-based active detection systems can automatically reconfigure logical network topologies to reroute network traffic in case of some form of network attack, such as a denial of service (DoS) attack. They can also detect suspicious activity on a network connection and terminate it, logging the IP address to prevent any further connections from that origin. The detection system can also sense attacks on certain ports or services, such as an SNMP port on a router, and shut it down to prevent any more attacks on that service port.

The disadvantage of active detection systems is the occurrence of false alarms can cause the system to shut down services or network connections for legitimate requests.

Passive Detection

Passive detection by network-based intrusion detection systems involves alerting an administrator of the intrusion, so they can take the necessary actions to stop it. The system won't take any active steps to prevent the detected intrusion from continuing. The disadvantage of a passive system is this: the administrator might not get the alert immediately, especially if they are offsite and not carrying a pager. By the time they get to the system, the damage of the intrusion could have already been done.

Passive methods of detection usually consist of some form of logging utility that logs events as they happen and stores them for later examination or notifies the administrator through e-mail or a paging device of high-level warnings and errors. If no type of messaging alert function is configured, the administrator must make certain to scan the log files regularly for suspicious behavior.

Host-Based Intrusion Detection

Host-based intrusion detection systems differ from network-based systems because they monitor a specific host or device for suspicious behavior that could indicate someone is trying to break into the system. Host-based intrusion detection systems monitor inbound and outbound network activity, networking service ports, system log files, as well as the time stamps and content of data and configuration files to ensure they haven't changed.

A host-based system needs to be installed on a specific system or network device. This differs from networking intrusion detection, which only needs to install monitors at certain points on the network. The host-based system can only monitor the system it's installed on and should only be used for critical server systems, rather than user workstations.

The advantages of a host-based system is it can detect attacks that occur from someone physically on the system console, rather that over the network. They might be trying to access an administrator account or trying to copy files to or from the system. The intrusion detection system is able to alert the administrator if someone has tried to log into an account unsuccessfully too many times.

Like network-based intrusion detection systems, a host-based system can provide both active and passive protection.

Active Detection

A host-based intrusion detection system using active methods of detection can take immediate steps to halt an intrusion. This is the most preferable method because it prevents the suspicious activity from continuing. Passive methods merely log the incident or send an e-mail to the administrator who might not see the message for many hours before they can do something about it. An active detection system can terminate network connections from clients who seem to be performing some type of suspicious activity. The system can prevent any further connection from that particular network address. Another method of preventing an intrusion is shutting down the network service that's under attack. For example, a web server can immediately stop accepting HTTP requests to prevent the attack from continuing.

If the intrusion is detected as coming from the system console, the system can shut down and disable that user account. This type of detection is used by most network operating systems (OSs) that disable accounts if a predefined number of unsuccessful logins occurs.

The disadvantage of active detection is in case of a false positive detection, the system might automatically shut down services when no attack is occurring, which can cause unnecessary and often costly downtime.

Passive Detection

Passive detection methods are those that don't take active steps to prevent an intrusion from continuing if it's detected. Passive methods typically include logging events to a system log, which can be viewed by an administrator at a later time or, if configured to do so, to forward the log entries through a pager or e-mail systems. The latter method is preferable because it enables the administrator to be notified as the intrusion is happening. This gives the administrator a chance to catch the unauthorized user in the act and to prevent any damage or data theft. If the administrator isn't immediately notified, they must ensure to audit system log files regularly for critical warnings and errors that indicate suspicious activity.

Honey Pots

A *honey pot* is the name given to a device or a server used to attract and lure attackers into trying to access it, thereby removing attention from actual critical systems. The name refers to using a pot of honey to attract bees who are, in this case, the hackers. The honey pot server is usually situated in the DMZ zone of the network and it runs popular Internet services that are vulnerable to attack, such as web or FTP services. The server doesn't have any basic protections and it freely advertises open Internet ports that can be picked up by hackers' port scanners, as shown in Figure 7.6.

A slight danger exists if the honey pot isn't configured correctly—if an unauthorized user hacks into the server—that the hacker might be able to attack other systems on the DMZ. To prevent this scenario, some honey pot systems can emulate services, instead of running them.

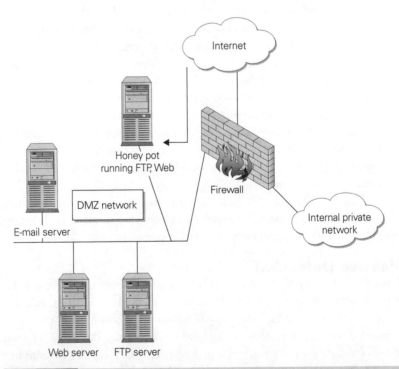

FIGURE 7.6 The honey pot system lures attackers away from production servers.

Travel Advisory

To ensure your honey pot system doesn't allow an intruder to attack other machines, use service emulation, rather than running the full services.

Honey pots can simply be used as a decoy device, distracting attention from real production servers or they can be used by a network administrator to find out the identity of the hackers through logging and auditing. By keeping accurate logs of the IP addresses being used by the attacker, the administrator might be able either to track them down or pass information on to legal authorities. From a legal standpoint, however, this can be tricky, especially if the server advertises files for downloading or viewing because this is considered entrapment and is illegal.

Honey pot systems are best suited for understanding the different types of attacks that can happen to your network. You can log when and what types of attacks are occurring, and then use that information to secure your network even further by including protection against attacks that weren't included in the original security plan.

Exam Tip

A honey pot is the name given to a device or server used to attract and lure attackers into trying to access it, removing attention from actual critical systems.

Incident Response

As part of your organization's overall security policy, preparations must be made to ensure a proper procedure for responding to a security intrusion is in place. Quite often, as in any stressful situation, panic can take over and you might cause even more damage than the original attacker intended. If a web server were suddenly disabled because of a DoS attack, many people would instantly pull the plug on their Internet connections to stop the attack. But this would take down your organization's entire communications to the outside world, causing your entire network to lose contact with the Internet. The result of this type of response is to aggravate the problem, which originally was only affecting one server, but now affects the entire network. By following a prepared incident response plan, the origin and effect of the incident can be identified and neutralized.

Your incident response plan should include the following procedures:

- **Identification** The initial step is to identify the source, type, and effect of the attack quickly. This includes studying the symptoms of the attack, such as scanning log entries, and what services or specific servers the attack is affecting. This is probably the most difficult procedure of an incident response because it might take some time to identify the type and source of the attack, especially if the hacker is using spoofing to hide their source IP address. In many cases, the attack could have already come and gone, and time will be spent performing a forensic examination of your systems to identify exactly what happened.

- **Containment** Once the attack and its source are identified, measures must be taken to contain the attack so it doesn't spread to other systems on the network. This greatly depends on the nature of the server or device that's suffering from the attack. If this is a web site that hundreds of clients connect to every hour, depending on the nature of the attack, it might not be feasible to take down the web site. Pulling the plug on your network connection will probably cause more damage than the original attack. The target of the attack should at least be isolated from other machines on the network to prevent a virus or malicious user from taking its attack to other systems.

- **Neutralization** Once the attack is identified and contained, the next step is to neutralize and stop it. If your server is infected with a virus, worm, Trojan, or any type of malicious code, it's likely you might need to install the server from scratch, and then restore any data from backup. Some viruses can infect so far into a system that it's beyond simple repair. If the attack is network-based, the possibility exists that you can reconfigure the firewall or routers to stop the attack using rules or access control lists.

- **Recovery** In the aftermath of an attack, your next step is to recover your systems as quickly as possible and get them back to regular operation. This could involve recovering lost files from backup, cleaning them of viruses, or reconnecting them to the network. You must ensure you've neutralized the source of the attack first or else your system, once reconnected, will be under attack again from the same source.

- **Reassessment and Documentation** Your final step, after you've identified, contained, and neutralized the attack, and then recovered your system to full operation, is to document the vulnerabilities that caused the attack in the first place. System configuration, log and audit files, and security procedures should be examined for the vulnerabilities, and then steps should be taken to remove them. By learning from the attack, you can protect your systems by adding security procedures to prevent future attacks.

CHECKPOINT

✔**Objective 7.01: Security Topologies** Networks can be split into security zones to manage the security of the network more efficiently. Internet services should be separated from the internal LAN in a DMZ zone using a firewall. An intranet is an internal company web network, while an extranet extends to include the networks of other companies with which you do business. Use network address translation (NAT) to hide internal IP addressing schemes from outside users. VPNs and tunneling protocols can be used to secure communications between two sites over a public network like the Internet. Use VLANs to subdivide your network into smaller, more manageable networks for performance and security.

✔**Objective 7.02: Intrusion Detection** Intrusion detection systems can proactively monitor networks and host machines for suspicious behavior. Network-based systems are installed to monitor network activity, and host-based systems are installed to protect a specific host system. Active detection systems can reconfigure systems automatically to prevent further attacks, while passive detection systems make use of notification to warn administrators of intrusion incidents. Use honey pot servers running Internet services and open ports to lure hackers away from production servers. Incident response should include identification, containment, neutralization, recovery, and follow-up reassessment and documentation.

REVIEW QUESTIONS

1. Which zone of a network security topology should contain your Internet servers, such as web, FTP, and e-mail servers?

   A. DMZ

   B. VLAN

   C. VPN

   D. Intranet

2. Which type of network describes a configuration where the internal network of one company is available to another for business-to-business (B2B) transactions?

   A. VLAN

   B. Intranet

   C. Extranet

   D. VPN

3. Which network service allows internal addresses to be hidden from outside networks and allows several internal hosts to use the same external address?

   A. NAT

   B. VPN

   C. VLAN

   D. IP spoofing

4. What networking technology would be used to divide an internal network into smaller, more manageable, logical subnets?

   A. NAT

   B. Tunneling

   C. VPN

   D. VLAN

5. When using a port-based VLAN system, what would be the best way to move a host from one VLAN to another?

   A. Move the host to the department where that VLAN works

   B. Install another network card on the host and connect it to the new VLAN

   C. Configure the host's switch port to use the new VLAN

   D. There's no way to move a host between VLANs in a port-based system

6. Other than using a dedicated link, what would be the best method for connecting two networks located in geographically distant offices?

   A. VLAN

   B. Firewall

   C. DMZ

   D. VPN

7. After trying to log in to a workstation for a third time, a user finds they're locked out of the system and can't make any more attempts. What's the most likely problem?

   A. The network port is disabled

   B. The firewall disabled access to the host

   C. The user forgot their password

   D. The host's intrusion detection system disabled the user account

8. The network administrator is configuring the network intrusion system for notification while they're away for the weekend. Which of the following would be the best notification method for the situation?

   A. Notification by e-mail

   B. Notification by pager

   C. Notification by instant messaging program

   D. Notification by SNMP trap

9. When installing a network-based intrusion detection system, where would the best place be to locate the detector agents?

   A. Connect to each host on the network

   B. Connect to every network switch and hub

   C. Connect to your VPN

   D. Connect to the main router

10. A network intrusion detection system has detected an IP flood attack from an external IP address. To stop the threat, the system blocks any further data from that IP address. What type of intrusion detection system is being used?

    A. Active

    B. Passive

    C. Host-based

    D. Instant notification

REVIEW ANSWERS

1. **A** The demilitarized zone (DMZ) is a network that contains Internet servers and services that are accessible from the outside world. The DMZ ensures incoming connections for these services don't reach the internal LAN.

2. **C** An extranet is a network that spans across multiple companies, so they can access the resources of each other's network. They are usually connected with an encrypted VPN tunnel.

3. **A** Network address translation (NAT) allows an internal host with nonroutable Internet addresses to access the Internet using an external address. NAT also hides the IP information of the internal network from the outside world.

4. **D** A virtual LAN (VLAN) is used to segment a network into smaller logical units to aid in security and performance.

5. **C** In a port-based VLAN system, each network port on a switch is configured as part of a specific VLAN. To change which VLAN the host is on, the port needs to be reconfigured with the new VLAN.

6. **D** Running a dedicated link between geographically distant networks can be expensive. A virtual private network (VPN) offers a way to create a secure, encrypted tunnel over a public network, such as the Internet, between the two networks.

7. **D** To prevent an unauthorized user from hacking into an account on a specific host, an intrusion detection system can limit the amount of unsuccessful attempts at trying to log in with a specific account. Once the limit is reached, the account is disabled and can only be enabled by an administrator.

8. **B** Because the network administrator is out of the office, the only method of notification that would reach them in a timely manner would be a pager.

9. **D** The network-based intrusion detection system can only analyze what it sees, so the detector agents should be connected to a central network device, such as a router, where all network traffic passes through.

10. **A** An active intrusion detection system automatically tries to identify and neutralize the threat by reconfiguring networking settings to stop the attack. A passive intrusion detection is only used for notification of an intrusion and doesn't actively try to stop the intrusion or attack.

Understanding
Security Baselines

	NEWBIE	SOME EXPERIENCE	EXPERT
ETA	3 hours	1.5 hours	1 hour

Objective 8.01 # Security Baselines

Establishing security baselines is a procedure to ensure all aspects of your network and its computer systems are running at a certain level of security. A *security baseline* is a minimum standard that each system and network device must follow to ensure protection against security vulnerabilities.

These minimum security standards need to be established in all areas of a network and its systems—from the network infrastructure, which includes firewalls, routers, and switches, to the operating systems (OSs) and applications that run on your servers and desktop computers.

To establish initial baselines, information can be gathered from industry security standards, associations, and organizations of systems administrators; specific security requirements of your environment; and a history of past security vulnerabilities in your network. When these baselines have been compiled and specifically configured for your environment, they must be implemented and updated regularly to ensure maximum security efficiency.

Security baselines must be established in three main areas:

- Network Devices
- Operating System
- Application Software

Network Hardening

One of the most important steps in securing your network and systems is to ensure the devices that form the infrastructure of your network are examined for security vulnerabilities. Several aspects of networking devices can create a number of security holes, if not properly examined or configured. These include the following:

- **Firmware** The software that controls how the hardware functions. This is the OS of the network device.
- **Configuration** The configuration settings of your device that affect the way it handles network traffic, such as interface settings on a router.

- **Services and protocols**   The types of protocols and services the device offers.

- **Access Control Lists**   The special rules that define what type of network traffic can pass through the network device.

Firmware Updates

The *firmware* of a network device is the software that controls the functions of the hardware. Essentially, firmware is the OS of the network device. The firmware of a device is typically encoded in flash memory. The firmware can be updated just like any other software application, by obtaining a newer version of the release, and then installing it into the device's flash memory.

Like any other OS or application software, the system should be running the most recent versions with the latest security and bug-fix patches installed. This ensures that any security vulnerabilities and software bugs since the last version have been fixed. Some firmware updates also include added security functionality that weren't in previous versions. For network devices such as firewalls and routers, which form the first line of defense for the security of a network, regularly updating the firmware is critical for maintaining maximum security.

Configuration Settings

Each of your software applications and services contain its own configuration settings that control how they operate. It's important for the administrator to examine these configuration settings after installation to ensure the default configuration is suitable for the security needs of the network.

Typically, the default configurations of most programs only provide the least amount of security needed. For example, a web application might be set up by default not to use encryption to protect the privacy of communications. Authentication methods might only use the least secure option available.

When examining the configuration of application or service settings, the administrator must ensure the most secure settings are enabled and any options that aren't needed by the current setup are disabled. Leaving optional services enabled might create additional security vulnerabilities that can be exploited by unauthorized users. In many network devices, Simple Network Management Protocol (SNMP) is enabled by default to allow the device to be examined by network monitoring equipment. Unfortunately, SNMP has many security vulnerabilities that can be compromised by an unauthorized user to gain administrative access to a router or a firewall. Another protocol used for network diagnostics is Internet Control Message Protocol (ICMP), which is used by utilities such as ping and traceroute. Enabling ICMP leaves the network device open to denial of service (DoS) attacks where an attacker can overload the device with repeated ping requests, causing it not to respond to legitimate network requests. A DoS attack can quickly disable a router, effectively cutting off the communications flow for your network. ICMP can also be used for identification of systems are that live and accepting connections, which can lead to them being attacked.

Nonessential Services and Protocols and Security Auditing

O ne of the most overlooked problems with securing network activity is that of unknown ports, services, and protocols running on a system. For example, you could have a simple file server setup for file sharing but, when examined, the server might also be running software such as a web server, FTP server, and SMTP server. Although these running services might not be used on your system, they could create security vulnerabilities because unauthorized users can still connect to the file server using these alternate protocols and ports. By compromising the vulnerabilities inherent in those services, they might be able to gain access to the files on that system, bypassing any authentication or access control.

The main cause of this problem is that many OSs install certain services by default. For example, someone setting up a Microsoft Windows 2000 server might only want to use it for file sharing but, by installing it using a standard default configuration, the system could also install web server or other Internet services by default. When installing server OS software, it's critical to ensure that you only install the services and protocols you need for the purposes of that system. Deselect or disable any other services it installs by default during the installation process.

Travel Advisory

When installing OS and application software, use a custom installation method that enables you to pick and choose which services you want to run. Running the default installation could install a number of programs and services you don't need.

Unauthorized users, trying to find open security holes in a system or network, can use special software called *port scanners,* which will analyze a system or every service and protocol it's currently using. This is accomplished by looking for open service ports listening for requests. A Transmission Control Protocol/Internet Protocol (TCP/IP) port is a special numerical port used by a particular service. For example, HTTP web servers use port 80 by default. Other services, such as DNS and POP3, use ports 53 and 110, respectively. These services are usually waiting for a request, such as a DHCP server waiting for a client request for a new IP address. By scanning these ports, a hacker can determine what types of software and services are running on the server. From there, the hacker can use that information to use other methods for compromising the security of those services because of software bugs or security vulnerabilities that haven't been fixed.

> ### Exam Tip
> A port scanner can be used to analyze a system for open TCP/IP ports. For example, a web server that also runs SMTP might show port 80 and port 25 as open and waiting for connections. The port scanner can run through an entire port range looking for common open services.

To protect your systems, the administrator should examine each server carefully and ensure each is only running services and protocols needed for its specific function. Any other services should be disabled or uninstalled. The current service you do need to run should be examined to ensure all systems are using the latest version of the software with the most recent security patches installed.

> ### Exam Tip
> Know the port numbers of some of the most common protocols and services.

The administrator can run their own port scanner on their system to discover if any security holes exist. Table 8.1 lists the most common, well-known protocols and services, and their corresponding TCP/IP ports.

TABLE 8.1	List of Common TCP/IP Ports
Service	**TCP/IP Port Number**
HTTP	80
FTP (Data)	20
FTP (Control)	21
DNS	53
DHCP	67
SMTP	25
SNMP	161
TELNET	23
FINGER	79
POP3	110
IMAP	143
NTP	123
NNTP	119
SSH	22
LDAP	389

Access Control Lists

Access control lists (ACL) are used by routers and other networking devices to control traffic that comes in and out of your network. These access lists can be general in nature or specific to certain types of communications. *Access lists* are typically used in firewalls to control communications between public and private networks, but they can also be used on internal routers to regulate traffic within the network. An access list entry (ALE), which is contained inside the ACL, usually includes where the network packet is coming from, where it's going, what the protocol is (whether TCP or UDP), the TCP/IP port it uses, and, finally, whether access is allowed or denied. The types of parameters that can be controlled using an access list include the following:

- **Source Address** This parameter specifies the originating source IP address of a packet. The source address can be an internal or external machine, or an internal address that it proxies to an external address.
- **Destination Address** The destination IP address specifies where the packet is going. This can be internal or external to the network.

- **Port Numbers**   This parameter specifies the TCP/IP port number the communication is using. Each type of TCP/IP service uses a standard port.

- **Protocol**   This parameter identifies the protocol being used in the transmission, such as File Transfer Protocol (FTP), Hypertext Transfer Protocol (HTTP), or Dynamic Host Configuration Protocol (DHCP). This is usually used in conjunction with a port number that's standard to that protocol or service. This parameter can also be used to define whether the protocol is using TCP or UDP.

- **Permit or Deny**   This parameter is used to permit or deny the communication specified in the access list entry.

The following is an example of an ACL entry for a router:

8-1
```
permit source 192.168.13.2 destination 10.1.5.25 tcp port 80
```

The syntax used by your router or network device will be similar to this entry, but it varies from vendor to vendor. In this example, the ACL entry permits TCP traffic on port 80 (the default port for HTTP) from a host 192.168.13.2 to a host on another network 10.1.5.25. The destination might be some type of secured web server that only needs to be accessed from a web browser client on the source host. This prevents any other system—internal or external—from connecting to that web server, as shown in Figure 8.1.

ACLs can be a valuable security tool for locking down access to certain networks or hosts. This type of access control is critical for preventing spoofing attacks, where an unauthorized user tries to masquerade their external host as an internal system by spoofing the IP address to look like it's coming from the internal network. An ACL can be set up to prevent external traffic coming in as an internal address.

Travel Advisory

Denying all access by default is most efficient because then you only add the access to certain systems and service ports that you need. This way, you start off with full security and slowly add rules to allow access as needed.

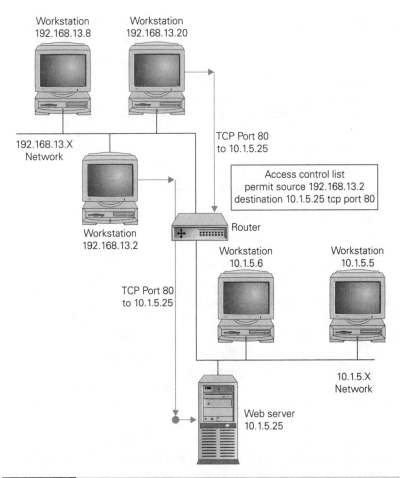

FIGURE 8.1 The ACL of the router only permits the specified host to connect to the web server.

Operating System Hardening

As the main software that controls how your system works and how it interoperates with your hardware, the OS is the most critical part of your computer system. Since its initial release, the OS you use has probably been examined for software bugs and security vulnerabilities. Newer versions of the software, or bug fixes and patches have been released to correct these security issues.

Beyond software updates, many other areas of your OS need to be examined for security vulnerabilities. These include auditing your user accounts, setting configuration options, available services, and file system security.

Operating System Updates

To ensure your OS software doesn't contain any known software bugs or security vulnerabilities, it should be operating at the latest version, with the most recent security patches applied.

OS vendors regularly release updates to their software. These are most often rolled into larger updates, called *service packs* or *updates*. Smaller bug fixes or patches that fix any critical security vulnerabilities are usually released quickly, so administrators can patch their systems before hackers can take advantage of the vulnerability. Vendors usually provide these patches and service packs as downloads from their web sites. Some OSs have updater functions that can automatically connect to the vendor's web site and download the latest versions of software components. Other vendors release CD-ROMs every few months, which contain all the latest patches and bug fixes since the last version.

Especially important is to perform this updating when a new system has just been installed. Usually the version of the OS is the original one that shipped with the hardware and, since that time, a number of service packs and patches have probably been released.

Travel Advisory

Even if you just installed a service pack for your OS, you need to install any security patches that have come out since that service pack to be fully protected and current.

Account Auditing

To log in to your system or network OS, users need to be authenticated before being allowed to access the system resources. Most OSs include some form of login and password authentication, and store a database of user and group accounts.

These accounts need to be regularly audited to ensure the current accounts reflect the current users of the system. Any accounts of users who aren't currently using the system need to be disabled or deleted. All other accounts should be examined to ensure the password and accounts procedures are being followed per your company's security policy. Passwords should be a certain minimum length and contain a variety of alphanumeric characters. Users should be forced to change their password at regular intervals to ensure password integrity. See Chapter 1 for more details on account and password management.

Account security should also be enabled to limit login attempts, in case someone tries to break into a user's account. Guest or anonymous accounts need to be disabled or deleted, to ensure that all users are properly authenticated. Time and host machine restrictions can also be set, so users can only log in during working hours or only from machines on your internal network.

Services and OS Configuration

After the installation of your OS, a number of administrative- and security-related configuration options can increase the security of your system. Other options might make your system more vulnerable to attack. Installing or enabling only the necessary options for that particular system is critical. By enabling unnecessary options, you only create potential vulnerabilities for unauthorized users to exploit.

This is especially important when you're enabling services to be run on your system. Examples of services that might not be needed, but could be running, are file- and print-sharing services, and Internet services such as HTTP, FTP, SMTP, DNS, and DHCP. If the system you're configuring doesn't need to share files, this service should be disabled, so no one on the network can connect to a network share on that system. Enabled Internet services can open a variety of security vulnerabilities because this could open network ports on your system to which unauthorized users can connect. For example, enabling web server services on your system enables hackers to connect to your system by issuing HTTP request to the server, where they can try a variety of attacks on your system to gain access or to disrupt communications.

As a general baseline, services that aren't needed by the system should be disabled or removed, while existing services should be configured to provide maximum security.

File Systems

For file servers that share files to other users and computer systems, it's critical to ensure the file system you use properly addresses any security concerns for locking down file sharing. Older types of disk file systems, such as file allocation table (FAT), don't provide the same security as NTFS on Microsoft systems or

EXT3 on Linux. Newer file system formats allow for greater access controls, such as specific security permissions on files and directories. Some file systems also provide encryption capabilities, so no one can read the contents of a file system without the proper encryption key.

Another aspect of file system security is how access permissions are configured for files on the server. Without proper access control, users can read or modify files that could be confidential in nature. This is critical for OS files, which contain administrative programs and sensitive configuration files. Access to system files should only be granted to system administrators. And user files should be stored on a separate disk or partition to ensure these system files aren't accidentally accessed or removed.

Users should each have their own separate home directory, to which only they have access. Group or department directories should be set up for files that must be shared among groups of people.

Application Hardening

The final step in securing your systems and services is analyzing your software applications for security vulnerabilities. A poorly designed application program can provide as many critical security flaws and unauthorized access as a network or OS vulnerability. If an unauthorized user can penetrate the security of an application, they can move on to other aspects of the system, such as the OS itself. Because of the variety of software applications that run on your network, especially those used by external Internet users, it's vital that you're aware of the security vulnerabilities that could occur because of running a certain type of service. For example, running a Simple Mail Transport Protocol (SMTP) server to allow the users to send e-mail without proper security precautions could allow users from outside the network to send mail through your server.

The following sections deal with hardening the security of your applications and services to prevent unauthorized users from exploiting vulnerabilities in those programs.

Application Updates

Your application software can contain a variety of bugs and security vulnerabilities that can be exploited by malicious users. Software bugs are unintentional errors made by programmers when they create a software package. For internal application software, such as word processing, spreadsheets, or custom-built applications, these bugs are usually annoying at most and might not provide real security threats. The usual effect of such bugs is simply interruption or corruption of services, affecting performance, productivity, and data integrity. Software applications specifically made for the Internet, however, can provide more than only annoyances because security vulnerabilities could allow an unauthorized user access to your internal network through the faulty application or service.

To protect yourself from any inherent bugs or security vulnerabilities, all application software should be upgraded to the latest versions, and the latest service and security patches installed. By having the most recent version of the software, you ensure that any previous problems have been corrected. This doesn't, however, protect you from any problems that might have arisen since the latest version was distributed. Product research and testing, and the proliferation of compromised security incidents might require the software vendor to release an interim update or patch (typically called a *security patch* or *security fix*) for the affected program.

Vendor web sites should be regularly checked for software updates for any applications running on your systems. Many vendors can automatically notify you through e-mail updates if you registered the software for technical support. Or, the software itself could contain a procedure that checks for the latest versions of its components. Other companies might send out CD-ROMs containing all the latest updates since the last major release of the product.

Server Types

Servers on the Internet can provide a variety of services, such as file transfer, e-mail, and database transactions. The nature of the Internet means these servers are wide open to abuse from external users. Each type of server has its own way of providing information and services, and could contain a number of security vulnerabilities that might allow them to be compromised by unauthorized users. The following sections outline some of the more popular Internet servers and what security vulnerabilities they could contain. See Chapter 2 for more details on attacks against Internet servers.

Exam Tip

Ensure you're aware of the different types of security vulnerabilities inherent with each type of Internet server and how to prevent them from being exploited.

Web Servers   Internet web servers accept HTTP requests from client web browsers and they send back the requested information to the client. Web servers are the most common forms of servers on the Internet and, as a result, they're the most often attacked. The attack can be for a variety of reasons. Many attacks seek merely to disrupt users from accessing the information on a web site for political, religious, or corporate reasons. Other types of attacks are used to spread worms and viruses quickly over the Internet. Some web sites have been vandalized and the information on their pages has been defaced or replaced with false information.

Most of these attacks take advantage of security vulnerabilities in the web server. These exploits include malformed requests, buffer overflow attacks, worms, and DoS.

- **Malformed Request**   A request that contains some type or sequence of information that causes the web server to malfunction. This type of attack is caused by bugs in the web server software that cause certain input coming from a web browser to have adverse effects on the system.

- **Buffer Overflow**   This type of attack is caused by sending a parameter that's outside the bounds of the system's programs. Its data buffer can overflow with information, causing it to crash or even provide administrative access to the system.

- **Worms**   These are malicious code transmitted through normal HTTP communications. The web site can be infected by the worm from an infected client. The worm then tries to replicate itself to other servers and clients, by scanning the Internet for servers using the HTTP service port 80. Clients can be infected by simply connecting to the affected web server.

- **Denial of Service**   This type of attack is used to prevent other users from accessing the web site. This is accomplished by flooding the web server with requests, so it can't process legitimate ones. These attacks can be from one system or a coordinated attack from a number of systems over the Internet.

These attacks can be easily prevented by ensuring the web server and browser software is current and the most recent security patches are applied. This ensures software is free of bugs and vulnerabilities that might have affected earlier versions of the software.

E-mail Servers   An *e-mail server* can be a server that stores messages and enables users to send and retrieve e-mail. Other types of e-mail servers are used only as a message transfer agent (MTA), whose purpose is to relay mail from site-to-site. Security for e-mail systems is a great concern because e-mail is one of the most common targets for viruses and worms that can infect user's computers through their e-mail. Unsecured e-mail servers can also be used for sending out spam e-mail to thousands of other users, while protecting the identity of the original sender. As with another application, e-mail software should be current with the latest revisions and service patches.

Protocols for checking e-mail on a server include Post Office Protocol 3 (POP3) and Internet Message Access Protocol (IMAP). Both these protocols use authentication before allowing users access to an e-mail mailbox. To enhance security, these communications should be used in encrypted form, to prevent unauthorized users from intercepting clear text messages containing login and password information.

For sending mail, the standard protocol is SMTP. An SMTP server forwards e-mail sent from clients to its proper destination. Unfortunately, insecure SMTP servers have been used by unauthorized users to forward spam e-mail to thousands of users in a single operation. The spammer usually spoofs the originating address, so it appears the e-mail came from your network. This occurs because the SMTP relay agent is configured to accept any requests, including those from outside the network. The SMTP server relays the e-mail, just as if it originated from inside the network. To prevent unauthorized relay, any user sending e-mail should be authenticated with a login and password, just like the authentication used for retrieving e-mail. SMTP servers can also be configured to allow only outgoing mail from trusted sources within the network.

FTP Servers   *FTP servers* are used to transfer files from one system to another across the Internet. A server hosting files will be running an FTP server service, which awaits file transfer requests originating from clients using FTP client software. Many FTP server sites on the Internet are public in nature and allow anonymous users to log in and download or upload files to the system. Other companies use authenticated FTP servers to enable clients to download engineering or technical support files. To access the server, the client needs to authenticate using a login and password. Basic types of FTP communications aren't encrypted, so any login and password information is sent over the network in cleartext and can be easily intercepted by a hacker. Secure FTP software uses encrypted communications to prevent interception by unauthorized users.

Exam Tip
FTP communications, including login and password authentication, are transmitted in cleartext.

FTP servers are a widely used resource on the Internet, so they are one of the most popular servers for hacking attempts and abuse. FTP server software can be vulnerable to certain types of attacks because of inherent bugs in its programming. Any FTP server software you use should be the latest version, with the most recent security patches installed. Software bugs in FTP programs allow unauthorized individuals to gain administrative access to the machine on which it resides. The hacker can then use that machine as a starting point for other activities, such as performing DoS attacks or hacking attempts on other machines.

Another problem with FTP servers is they're usually installed by default with some kind of anonymous account. This account enables users to access the FTP server without having to authenticate. If this is a private server containing confidential data that should only be accessed by authorized users, this anonymous account should be disabled.

DNS Servers   Domain name service (DNS) servers provide a way to translate Internet domain names into IP addresses. For example, the web site *www.server.net* can be translated to an IP address of 192.168.1.12. This allows network applications and services to refer to Internet domains by their fully qualified domain name (FQDN), rather than their IP address, which can be difficult to remember and can often change. If a company changes its system's IP address, it can simply update the DNS tables to reflect this. External users won't see a difference because they'll still be connecting to it by name.

DNS servers perform an extremely valuable function on the Internet and wide-scale communication interruptions can occur if a network DNS server is disabled. Most client machines use DNS each time they try to connect to a network host. The client's DNS server is configured using its network settings, which can be set manually or automatically through services such as DHCP. Each time a client tries to access a host, such as a web site, the local DNS server is queried for the IP address of the domain name. The DNS server translates the name into an IP address, which the client uses to initiate its connection.

DNS servers can suffer from DoS and malformed request attacks. In a DoS attack, the DNS server is inundated with DNS or ping requests. The load becomes so much, it can't respond to legitimate DNS queries. DNS queries to servers can also be manipulated to include a malformed input that could crash the server. Ensure your DNS software is the latest version, with the most recent security patches installed, to prevent these types of attacks.

NNTP Servers   Network News Transfer Protocol (NNTP) servers are used to retrieve and send Usenet newsgroups and news articles. Thousands of public Usenet newsgroups allow users to read and post articles about a particular subject. Because of the administrative- and bandwidth-related overhead of hosting an Internet news server, most companies don't run these types of public servers. Some companies create their own internal news server for company announcements and message boards. Some groups can be made public, such as a company that wants to maintain a news group specific to the technical support for one of their products.

To protect your system and network against abuse of the news server, authentication mechanisms should be set up so users who need to read or send news using the server must authenticate with a login and password. Many news servers can also create ACLs that can scan the IP addresses of incoming requests and reject those that originate from outside the network.

NNTP servers suffer from the same security vulnerabilities as other Internet servers, such as Web or FTP, insecure or buggy code, or unauthorized use without authentication. NNTP server software should be current with the latest service packs and security patches. Authentication of users is important because it prevents unauthorized individuals from sending unsolicited spam news articles to news servers all over the world.

File and Print Servers   File and print servers form the base for the majority of your users' daily operations. *File servers* are used to store the user's data, including personal work files, and departmental or company-wide information. *Print servers* are used to administer print services and print queues, where user's print jobs are organized and sent to the appropriate printer.

Security concerns with file and print servers center around authentication and access permissions. File servers should be configured, so no one can access the server through the network without first being authenticated using a user name and a password. Beyond that, various directories and files, depending on their ownership and confidentiality, need to be secured with access permissions.

Most files servers have their directories set up as a hierarchy, typically split into user and departmental or group directories. For example, each user should have their own personal data directory, where only they have access to create, delete, and modify the files and directories within. This prevents other users from accessing their files. For example, the head of the company wouldn't want other people in the company to have access to his files. Typically, a company will have other directories set up as departmental or group directories. This allows a separate area for an entire department to store files to which everyone in that department needs access. For example, a directory could be set up for the finance department, so each person in the finance group can access the confidential accounting files in that directory. The access permissions would be set so no other user or department could access that directory except those in the finance group.

Other directories can be set up only to allow read-only permissions, such as a directory of company policy and benefit files, which all employees need to access for reference, but shouldn't be allowed to modify or delete.

This same methodology should be used for printing services. Most printers are set up so anyone can send print jobs to them. For more confidential printers, such as a human resources department where employment or termination notices might be created, the printer should have its access permissions set so only the human resources department can print to that printer. More granular security-access permissions can be set, so users can't modify or delete jobs after they've been sent to the printer. Most of these controls, however, are usually for the administrator's purposes, so they can control the flow of print queues.

DHCP Servers   A DHCP server is used to allocate IP addresses and other network information automatically, such as DNS and Windows Internet Naming Service (WINS) information to network clients as they access the network. DHCP servers take the place of having to configure each client on the network manually with specific information. This greatly reduces administrative overhead because the use of static manual addressing means if something changes on the network, such as the address of a DNS server, you'll have to change the information manually on every client.

The main vulnerability with DHCP servers is no authentication mechanism exists to allow or disallow clients. Any client system that accesses the network and is configured for DHCP will be allocated network information, so it can communicate with the network. This means any unauthorized user can plug their system into a network and be automatically configured for access. A malicious user can also attack a DHCP server using DoS methods to overload it or by trying to use up all the available IP addresses in the DHCP pool. Then, no new clients can be assigned an address to communicate with the network. Some DHCP servers can be configured only to communicate to clients with specific MAC addresses. This list of MAC addresses should only contain computers and devices on your internal network. This way, when a DHCP server sees a configuration request from an unknown host, it can deny or ignore it.

Another security concern is the capability for an unauthorized user to set up their own DHCP server on the network. If the server manages to answer a client's request for configuration information before the real DHCP server, the client might be configured with bogus information that could cause their communications to be redirected to other servers under the control of the hacker. The only way to prevent this type of scenario is to scan your network regularly for rogue servers running these services and to control physical access to the facility.

Directory Services   *Directory services* are a repository of information regarding the users and resources of a network. Directory service software applications and protocols are often left open and unprotected because the information they contain sometimes isn't considered important, compared to file server or database server information. Directory services, however, depending on the level of information they provide, can be an excellent resource for unauthorized users and hackers to gain knowledge of the workings of the network and the resources and user account they contain.

A simple Lightweight Directory Access Protocol (LDAP) database that contains user names, e-mail addresses, phone numbers, and locations of users can be a resource for unauthorized users looking for the type of user account they're attempting to hack, such as an accounting user or an engineering user, if the hacker is performing corporate espionage.

Other types of directory services, such as Novell Directory Services or Microsoft Active Directory, can contain more critical network and user information, such as network addresses, user account logins and passwords, and access information for servers.

At the bare minimum, users who query directory services should be authenticated through a login and password. This will at least prevent casual unauthorized users from accessing the data on the network's directory services through queries. This is especially important when protecting more critical network-wide directory services, such as Novell NDS and Microsoft Active Directory. Only the administrators of the network should have access to read and change the highest levels of the directory hierarchy, while common users should only be able to look up information for basic information, such as the e-mail address of another user. To increase security, directory services should be used in conjunction with secured, encrypted communications protocols, such as Secure Sockets Layer (SSL) or Transport Layer Security (TLS).

Database Servers *Database servers* typically contain transactional types of data used as a back-end repository of information for front-end applications and web services. The most popular forms of database software are Oracle, Microsoft SQL, and MySQL.

The front-end applications that access the database usually send their commands as a set of procedures for the database to run on the data and to return the required result. A malicious user can insert their own code into these procedures to run some query on the database that can reveal or damage confidential data. This is similar to buffer overflow and invalid data types of attacks that can be performed from a web browser by passing certain parameters of input that transcend the boundaries of the software's thresholds. If the database software or query function isn't configured or programmed correctly, the parameters could bypass built-in security to reveal confidential data or destroy thousands of data records. By keeping your database and application software current, these security vulnerabilities can be avoided.

To protect data privacy and integrity, the use of authentication and access permissions should be configured for a database server. This creates a layered security model that first must authenticate the user before using the database, and then restrict the user's access through the use of permissions and access control lists. For example, for certain types of data, you might want most users to have read-only access. Other users who need more access can be granted permission to add, delete, and modify records.

When creating user accounts and logins, the same type of care used for general network authentication should be employed, such as requiring minimum lengths and types of secure passwords. Ensure the default database accounts, such as the supervisor or administrator account, or any other type of database service account, have had their default passwords changed to something more secure.

✔**Objective 8.01: Security Baselines** Security baselines should be set up to maintain a minimum standard of security. The initial baseline can be created with the use of industry standards, and also specific information related to your environment and activities. The three main areas to be examined are networking, OS, and software applications. All software and firmware should be upgraded to the latest versions and all recent security patches should be applied. Disable any unused services and ports that might create security vulnerabilities. Control access to protocols and services through the use of network ACLs.

✔**Objective 8.02: Nonessential Services and Protocols and Security Auditing** Audit all server processes to ensure any nonessential services are turned off. Examine each server carefully and ensure each is only running services and protocols needed for its specific function. Any other services should be disabled or uninstalled.

REVIEW QUESTIONS

1. What feature of a network device, such as a router or switch, can control access permissions for network data?

   A. DNS protocol

   B. Firmware update

   C. Firewall

   D. Access Control Lists

2. Which part of a network hardware device can be upgraded to provide better security and reliability?

   A. Firmware

   B. Port scanner

   C. Flash memory

   D. Configuration file

3. Which of the following protocols should be disabled on a critical network device such as a router?

A. TCP/IP

B. ICMP

C. IPX/SPX

D. RIP

4. Which of the following protocols would be disabled on an e-mail server to prevent an unauthorized user from exploiting security vulnerabilities in network monitoring software?

A. IMAP

B. POP3

C. TCP/IP

D. SNMP

5. What should be done to user accounts for users who no longer belong to the organization?

A. Reset the password to a default value

B. Turn on logging to audit access of those accounts

C. Disable the accounts

D. Change the password to something more difficult

6. What should be disabled on a server that won't be storing or providing access to any files or print services?

A. POP3

B. File sharing

C. Ping

D. DNS

7. A security patch for your OS was released about a week after you applied the latest service pack. What should you do?

A. Wait until the release of the next full service pack

B. Only download the patch if you experience problems with the OS.

C. Nothing—the security patch was probably included with the service pack

D. Download and install the security patch

8. Some kind of HTTP worm is trying to infect a file server, which seems to be also running an HTTP web server on port 80. The server doesn't need any type of web services. What should be done?

   A. Install antivirus software

   B. Change the web server to use a different port

   C. Disable the web server

   D. Update your firewall software to the latest version

9. What should be done to an e-mail server to prevent external users from sending e-mail through it?

   A. Install antivirus and antispam software

   B. Restrict SMTP relay

   C. Disable POP3 and IMAP access

   D. Enable encrypted logins

10. What can be enabled on a DHCP server to prevent unauthorized clients from obtaining an IP address from the server?

    A. Port scanning

    B. MAC address access list

    C. Intrusion detection

    D. DNS

REVIEW ANSWERS

1. **D**   A list of rules can be entered on a network device to control access between networks. For example, all FTP access can be denied from one network to another, except for a certain host.

2. **A**   The firmware of a network device is similar to an OS that controls how the network hardware should function. Like any other software, firmware should be updated to the latest release to ensure any previous software bugs or security vulnerabilities are fixed.

3. **B**   Internet Control Message Protocol is a reporting protocol used by utilities such as ping and traceroute to acknowledge network activity from a device. Unfortunately, this protocol can also be used as a basis for DoS attacks, such as a ping flood, to prevent the device from acknowledging legitimate requests. Such utilities are also used by an intruder to discover which hosts exist on the network.

4. **D**   Simple Network Management Protocol is used by many network monitoring programs to collect information about a device or system. Unfortunately, SNMP is known to have a number of security vulnerabilities and should be disabled if not needed.

5. **C**   Any account for a user who doesn't belong to the organization any longer should be immediately disabled or deleted to prevent anyone from accessing that account.

6. **B**   Many OSs install file-sharing services by default. If the server isn't sharing any files, this service should be removed to prevent unauthorized users from accessing files on that server.

7. **D**   Even though you just installed the latest service pack, a security vulnerability might have just been discovered, necessitating the need for an immediate security patch. You won't be protected from the vulnerability if you don't install the security patch and it might be too dangerous to wait for it to be included in the next service pack.

8. **C**   Any application or service that isn't needed by the server should be disabled or deleted. Leaving services, such as a web server, on could make the server vulnerable to web server attacks, such as viruses and worms.

9. **B**   Restricting the ability for external users to send e-mail through the server will prevent them from sending unsolicited spam e-mail from your server.

10. **B**   To prevent unknown clients from obtaining TCP/IP information from a DHCP server, an access list can be set up to only allow clients whose MAC addresses match the predefined list.

Basics of Cryptography

Understanding Algorithms

	NEWBIE	SOME EXPERIENCE	EXPERT
ETA	4 hours	2 hours	1 hour

Cryptography is concerned with keeping communications private. The protection of sensitive communications has been the basis of cryptography throughout history. Modern cryptography performs essentially the same function, but with some added functionality, such as authentication and data integrity, for today's computerized world.

The central function of cryptography is *encryption,* which is the transformation of data into some unreadable form. This ensures privacy by keeping the information hidden from those for whom the information was not intended. Even though a user might be able to read the encrypted data, it won't make any sense until it's properly decrypted. *Decryption,* the reverse of encryption, is concerned with the transformation of encrypted data back into some intelligible form.

The encryption and decryption process involves taking data in plaintext (sometimes called *cleartext*) and manipulating its form to create what's called a *ciphertext. Plaintext* is data that is readable and understandable. Once it's been transformed into ciphertext, plaintext becomes inaccessible unless it's decrypted. The entire process is illustrated in Figure 9.1.

This process enables the transmission of confidential information over insecure communications paths, greatly lowering the possibility of the data being compromised. In a file storage system, data is protected by authentication and access controls that prevent unauthorized users from accessing the files. When this data is transmitted over a network, these controls no longer exist and the data becomes vulnerable to interception. If the information or the communications channel itself is encrypted, the chance of someone intercepting and deciphering the data is extremely slim.

This chapter details the subjects of cryptography and encryption, including mathematical algorithms, public key infrastructure systems, and encryption standards and protocols.

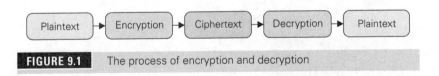

FIGURE 9.1   The process of encryption and decryption

Concepts of Using Cryptography

Objective 9.01

Today's cryptography is more than hiding secrets with encryption systems. With the world using more technological means to perform business and legal functions, such as purchasing items from a web-based store, online banking, and the digital signing of documents, the need for strong and secure encryptions systems to protect these transactions has become vital.

Information Assurance

The concept of *information assurance* is defined as protecting information and information systems by ensuring their confidentiality, integrity, authentication, and nonrepudiation.

- **Confidentiality**   *Confidentiality* is the concept of ensuring that data is not made available or disclosed to unauthorized people. Processes such as encryption must be used on the data, network infrastructure, and communication channels to protect against data interception and disclosure.

- **Integrity**   Data *integrity* is the protection of information from damage or deliberate manipulation. Integrity is extremely critical for any kind of business or electronic commerce. Data integrity ensures that when information has been stored or communicated, it hasn't been changed or manipulated in transit.

- **Authentication**   *Authentication* is the concept of uniquely identifying individuals to provide assurance of a user's identity. It is simply the act of ensuring that a person is who they claim to be. Typical physical and logical authentication methods include the use of ID cards, door locks and keys, and network logins and passwords. For modern e-commerce and legal applications, this type of authentication needs to be tightly controlled. Encrypted digital certificates are used to identify users electronically on a network. Encrypted forms of authentication can also be used in smart cards, which are a more secure medium than a typical ID badge.

- **Nonrepudiation**   *Nonrepudiation* is the term used to describe the inability of a person to deny or repudiate the origin of a signature or document, or the receipt of a message or document. For example, a user could legally prove that an electronic document or transaction didn't originate from them. The user could have digitally signed a contract that was transmitted through e-mail, but if the data or transmission wasn't considered secure because of lack of encryption, the user might legally claim it was tampered with and call its integrity into question. By implementing nonrepudiation processes, a cryptographic system can be considered secure for business and legal transactions.

Exam Tip

A specific type of encryption scheme, algorithm, or protocol could only cover certain parts of the information assurance objectives. For example, certain encryption protocols only concern themselves with authentication, while others might cover all the objectives of confidentiality, integrity, authentication, and nonrepudiation.

Access Control

Access control refers to the process of enabling or denying access to a resource. Access control is used to protect things of physical value, such as server hardware, or a confidential database of information. The act of authentication is also a critical piece of access control processes. Users must be able to identify themselves before the verifier can ascertain what access control they have. Older methods of authentication and access control weren't secure. For example, an employee might have lost their magnetic access card in the parking lot of their facility. A stranger could pick up the card, and then use it to open any doors to which the card has access. This access control method has no form of authentication because no process or mechanism identifies which person can use that particular card.

New technologies have emerged, such as smart cards, which are like credit cards, but they contain data about the owner of the card. To use the card for access control, it's inserted into a card reader, which then requires the user to enter a password, personal identification number (PIN), or secret key to continue. This key matches the information on the card, verifying the identity of the user. To protect the information on smart cards from being compromised, the data is encrypted.

This technology is also used in telecommunications, such as Pay TV or satellite TV services. To view an encoded channel or service, the user needs to install a smart card that contains the information to decrypt the transmissions. Because of their weak encryption algorithms and other vulnerabilities, hackers have been able to defeat the security mechanism on these cards to use the information to receive these services without paying for them. Telecommunications and smart card vendors have had to keep up with the hackers by constantly changing and strengthening the security of their systems.

Objective 9.02 Algorithms

A system that provides encryption and decryption services is called a crypto-system. The *cryptosystem* uses a mathematical encryption algorithm to turn data into ciphertext. An *algorithm* is a complex mathematical formula that dictates how the encryption and decryption process takes place. Because these mathematical algorithms usually are publicly known, the cryptosystem is strengthened with the addition of a secret key, as shown in Figure 9.2. A *key* is like a password that's combined with the algorithm to create the ciphertext. The encryption can't be deciphered unless the same key is used to decrypt it. This ensures that someone can't simply unravel the algorithm to decode the message because they also need the key. Depending on the encryption mechanism used, the same key might be used for both encryption and decryption, while for other systems, the keys used for encryption and decryption might be different.

The strength of the key is dependent on the algorithm's *keyspace*, which is a specific range of values—usually measured in bits—that's created by the algorithm to contain keys. A key is made up of random values within the keyspace range.

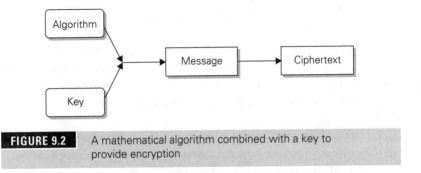

FIGURE 9.2 A mathematical algorithm combined with a key to provide encryption

A larger keyspace containing more bits means more available values exist to use for different keys, effectively increasing the difficulty for a hacker to compromise the system. The smaller the keyspace, the greater the chance someone can decipher the key value.

The strength of the cryptosystem lies in the strength and effectiveness of its algorithm and the size of the keyspace. Most hackers use some method of brute force attack to figure out the cryptosystem by processing large numbers of values to subvert the algorithm. No matter how strong the algorithm is, it will be rendered useless if a hacker obtains the key, so the key must be protected by encryption.

Travel Advisory

Most attacks on encryption usually center around the intercepting of keys rather than trying to subvert the algorithm, which requires large processing resources.

There are two main types of cipher encryption: substitution and transposition:

- **Substitution**   In its most simplified form, a *substitution* cipher takes plaintext and substitutes the characters in the data with other characters. For example, the letters "ABC" can be substituted by reversing the alphabet, so the cipher form will read "ZYX". Modern substitution encryption ciphers are much more complex, performing many types of substitutions with more than one alphabet.

- **Transposition**   In a *transposition* cipher, the characters are scrambled through mathematical permutations. When used with difficult mathematical formulas, these ciphers can be extremely complex.

Most modern ciphers use a combination of long sequences of substitution and transposition schemes. The data is put through an algorithm that performs these complex substitution and transposition operations to arrive at the ciphertext.

Two main types of encryption use key values and complex algorithms: symmetric and asymmetric.

Exam Tip

In a symmetric encryption scheme, both parties use the same key for encryption and decryption purposes. In an asymmetric encryption scheme, everyone uses a different but mathematically-related key for encryption and decryption.

Symmetric

In a *symmetric encryption scheme*, both parties use the same key for encryption and decryption purposes. Each user must possess the same key to send encrypted messages to each other, as shown in Figure 9.3. The sender uses the key to encrypt

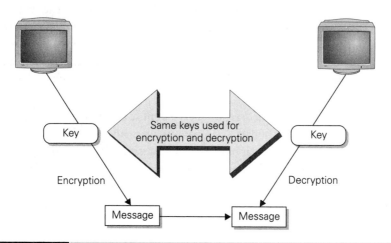

FIGURE 9.3   Users use the same keys in a symmetric encryption scheme.

their message, and then transmits it to the receiver. The receiver, who is in possession of the same key, uses it to decrypt the message.

The security of this encryption model relies on the end users to protect the secret key properly. If an unauthorized user were able to intercept the key, they would be able to read any encrypted messages sent by other users. It's extremely important that the users protect both the keys themselves, as well as any communications in which they transmit the key to another person.

One of the main disadvantages of symmetric encryption schemes is it doesn't scale well with large numbers of users. A user needs different keys for each person they are communicating with so, with more users, the amount of keys that need to be distributed and tracked can become enormous. Another disadvantage is the system needs a secure mechanism to deliver keys to the end users. Symmetric systems can only offer confidentiality; they offer little in the way of authentication and nonrepudiation.

Symmetric systems, however, can be hard to crack if a large key size is used. A symmetric system is also much faster than asymmetric encryption because the underlying algorithms are more simple and efficient.

There are two main types of symmetric systems: a stream cipher and a block cipher.

- **Stream Cipher** A *stream cipher* encrypts data one bit at a time, as opposed to a block cipher, which works on blocks of text. Stream ciphers, by design, are fast compared to block ciphers. The encryption of any plaintext data with a block cipher results in the same ciphertext when the same key is used. With stream ciphers, each bit of the plaintext stream is transformed into a different ciphertext bit. A stream cipher generates a keystream that's combined with the plaintext data to provide encryption.

- **Block Cipher** A *block cipher* encrypts entire blocks of data, rather than smaller bits of data like stream cipher methods. A block cipher transforms a particular block of plaintext data into a block of ciphertext data of the same length. For many block ciphers, the block size is 64 bits.

Types of Symmetric Encryption Systems

The following are different types of symmetric encryption systems that use the same key for encryption and decryption. Each system, however, uses different methods to achieve this functionality.

Exam Tip
For the exam, know which specific encryption systems are symmetric.

DES   The Data Encryption Standard (DES) is a block cipher defined by the United States government in 1977 as an official standard. The actual encryption system used was originally created by IBM. DES has become the most well-known and widely used cryptosystem in the world.

DES is a symmetric cryptosystem using a 64-bit block size and a 56-bit key. It requires both the sender and receiver to possess the same secret key, which is used both to encrypt and decrypt the message. DES can also be used by a single user for encrypting data for storage on a hard disk or other medium.

After so many years in use, the government ceased to authorize DES as a standard; it moved on to more secure methods of encryption, such as Triple DES (3DES) and the AES standard. The reasoning was this: having the same standard for so long increased the chance for the encryption scheme to be broken.

Travel Advisory
Despite its criticisms and published weaknesses, DES is still in wide use today.

Triple DES (3DES)   Over time, and after tests with multi-CPU systems proved the standard could be broken though brute force, DES encryption was considered insecure. A Double-DES encryption scheme was created that contained a key length of 112 bits, but its work factor wasn't considered much different than the original DES.

3DES is a 168-bit encryption standard that's resistant to cryptanalysis because it uses 48 rounds of cryptographic computations. 3DES is considered 2^{56} times stronger than DES. The main disadvantage of 3DES is that encryption and decryption is much slower than DES by almost three times, but it's considered powerful enough to be implemented in many banking and financial applications.

AES   Advanced encryption standard (AES) is the government-defined encryption standard created to replace DES, which was considered vulnerable. The new standard uses a symmetric block cipher supporting variable block and key lengths, such as 128, 192, and 256 bits.

Blowfish   *Blowfish* is a block cipher that uses 64-bit blocks of data. Its key length is 448 bits and it uses 16 rounds of cryptographic computations. Blowfish was designed specifically for 32-bit machines and is significantly faster than DES.

IDEA   International Data Encryption Algorithm (IDEA) is a block cipher that uses 64-bit blocks of data, with a key length of 128 bits. The data blocks are divided into 16 smaller sections, which are subjected to eight rounds of cryptographic computation. The speed of IDEA in software is similar to that of DES. IDEA is the cipher used in the popular encryption program Pretty Good Privacy (PGP).

RC5   *RC5* is a block cipher patented by RSA Data Security. It uses a variety of parameters to offer data block sizes such 32, 64, and 128 bit. The number of computational rounds can range from 0 to 255. The key can be anywhere from 0 bits to 2,048 bits in size. Such built-in variability provides flexibility in levels of security and efficiency.

Skipjack   *Skipjack* is the encryption algorithm that was used in the infamous *Clipper chip*, which was designed by the government to be built into all computers. Skipjack uses an 80-bit key to encrypt 64-bit blocks of data. Skipjack can be more secure than DES because it uses 80-bit keys and computes the data for 32 rounds. By contrast, DES uses 56-bit keys and scrambles the data for only 16 rounds.

As the details of Skipjack were classified and, therefore, unable to be fully tested, the public didn't trust its effectiveness or the government's motives. Many people were suspicious that Skipjack wasn't secure, either because of system design or by the deliberate introduction of a secret backdoor, so the government could decrypt any messages encrypted with the algorithm. Because of public outcry, the Clipper chip ceased to be supported by the government.

Asymmetric

In an *asymmetric encryption scheme*, everyone uses different, but mathematically-related, keys for encryption and decryption purposes, as shown in Figure 9.4. Even though the keys are mathematically similar, they can't be derived from each other. An asymmetric scheme is the basis for the public key system. Two keys are created for encryption and decryption purposes. One key is the public key, which is known to all users, while the private key remains secret. To use this system, a user will encrypt a message or file with the receiver's public key. To decrypt this message, the receiver will use their private key. These public keys can be passed directly among users or found in directories of public keys.

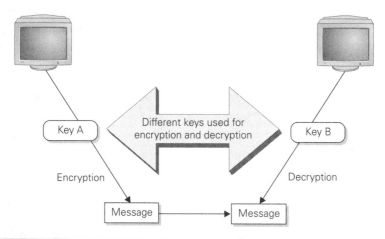

FIGURE 9.4   Users use different keys in an asymmetric encryption scheme.

The advantage of this system over symmetric schemes is it offers a level of authentication. By decrypting a message with a user's public key, the receiver knows this message came from the sender. The sender is authenticated because, to be decrypted with a public key, the private key had to be used to perform the initial encryption. This format of encryption is called *open message format.*

On the other hand, to have maximum confidentiality, a sender would encrypt the message with the receiver's public key, so only the receiver's private key could unlock the message. This format is called *secure message format.*

To provide a *secure and signed format* that both authenticates and provides confidentiality, the sender would encrypt the message with their private key, and then encrypt it again with the receiver's public key. To decrypt the message, the receiver would need to use their private key, as well as the sender's public key.

Exam Tip	
Recognize how the different combinations of key-pair encryption methods can provide different kinds of functionality like authentication, confidentiality, or integrity.	

The main disadvantage of asymmetric encryption is it can be much slower than symmetric schemes. Unlike symmetric systems, however, asymmetric schemes offer confidentiality, authentication, and also nonrepudiation, which prevents a user from repudiating a signed communication. Asymmetric schemes also provide more manageable and efficient ways for dealing with key distribution.

The following algorithms are all based on asymmetric encryption, which uses different keys for encryption and decryption.

RSA

RSA is one of the most popular asymmetric public key algorithms, and it's the main standard for encryption and digital signatures. The acronym RSA stands for Rivest, Shamir, and Adelman, the inventors of this technique. RSA is also used in many web browsers that use Secure Sockets Layer (SSL), and its algorithm is based on the factoring of prime numbers to obtain private and public key pairs. RSA is used primarily for encryption and digital signatures.

Elliptic Curve Cryptosystems (ECC)

Elliptic Curve Cryptosystems (ECC) provides the same functionality, such as encryption and digital signatures, as RSA. The ECC cryptosystem uses complex mathematical structures to create secure algorithms and keys. ECC was created for devices with smaller processing capabilities, such as cell phones, PDAs, and other wireless devices. ECC offers the same functionality as RSA, but with smaller size keys. Larger keys need more processing power to compute.

El Gamal

El Gamal is public key algorithm based on complex logarithmic operations. It can be used for encryption, key generation and exchange, and digital signatures.

DSA/DSS

The Digital Signature Algorithm (DSA) was published by the National Institute of Standards and Technology (NIST) in the Digital Signature Standard (DSS), which is a part of a United States government project. DSS was selected by NIST, in cooperation with the NSA, as the digital authentication standard of the United States government.

DSA is based on discrete logarithms and is used for authentication only. The algorithm is considered secure when the key size is large enough. DSS was originally proposed with a 512-bit key size and was eventually revised to support key sizes up to 1,024 bits.

Because of its lack of key exchange capabilities, relative slowness, and public distrust of the process and government involvement that created it, many people prefer RSA for digital signatures and encryption, but both standards are used widely.

Diffie-Hellman

Diffie-Hellman isn't an actual encryption algorithm; it's a key agreement protocol that enables users to exchange a private key over an insecure medium. The Diffie-Hellman protocol depends on the discrete logarithmic formulas for its security.

The main vulnerability with the protocol is the key exchange doesn't authenticate the participants. Further enhancements on the Diffie-Hellman protocol allow the two parties to authenticate each other through the addition of digital signatures and public-key certificates. This system is used in the Public Key Infrastructure (PKI).

Hashing

A *hashing* value is used in encryption systems to create a "fingerprint" for a message. This prevents the message from being tampered with en route to its destination. In the overall information assurance model, hashing is used to protect the integrity of a message and is most often used with digital signatures.

The most commonly used hashing function is the one-way hash. A *one-way hash* is a mathematical function that takes a variable-sized message and transforms it into a fixed-length value, referred to as either a *hash value* or a *message digest*. This function is referred to as "one-way" because it's difficult to invert the procedure and the procedure is never decrypted. The hash value represents the longer message from which it was created. This hash value is then appended to the message that's sent to another user. The receiver then performs the same hashing function on the message and compares the resulting hash value with the one sent with the message. If they're identical, the message wasn't tampered with.

> **Exam Tip**
>
> The main security provided by one-way hashing is it can't be performed in reverse.

Attacks against one-way hash functions can be prevented by longer hash values that are less susceptible to brute force attacks. A good minimum starting point for the size of a hash value is 128 bits. The most common problem with weak hashing algorithms is the possibility of hash value collisions. This occurs when two hashed messages result in the same hashing value. When these collisions are discovered, they can be used to try and reveal the underlying algorithm. Birthday attacks, explained in the following section, are often used to find collisions of hash functions.

> **Local Lingo**
>
> **Birthday Attack** The name used to refer to a class of brute-force attacks. *Birthday attack* gets its name from this surprising result: the probability that two or more people in a group of 23 share the same birthday is greater than one half. Such a result is called a *birthday paradox*. In encryption terms, if an attacker finds two hashed values that are the same, they have a greater chance of cracking the algorithm with this information.

The following sections describe some of the most common hashing algorithms in use today.

Message Digest

Message digest hashing algorithms are used for digital signature applications where a large message has to be hashed in a secure manner. A digital signature is obtained when the digest of the message is encrypted using the sender's private key. These algorithms take a message of variable length and produce a 128-bit message digest. The following are three versions of the message digest algorithm.

Exam Tip
A digital signature is obtained when the digest of the message is encrypted using the sender's private key.

MD2   Message Digest 2 (MD2) is a one-way hashing algorithm that can produce a 128-bit hash. Developed in 1989, *MD2* is optimized for 8-bit machines. In the MD2 algorithm, the message is first padded so its length in bytes is divisible by 16. A 16-byte checksum is then appended to the message and the hash value is computed on this resulting message.

MD4   Message Digest 4 (MD4) is a one-way hash function that produces a 128-bit hash message digest value. Developed in 1990, *MD4* is much faster than MD2 and is optimized for 32-bit machines. In MD4, the message is padded to ensure its length in bits plus 448 is divisible by 512. Next, a 64-bit binary representation of the original length of the message is added to the message. The message is then processed in 512-bit blocks, and then each block is processed in three rounds. Over time, MD4 has been shown to be easily broken.

MD5   Message Digest 5 (MD5), developed in 1991, is a slower, but more complex version of MD4. *MD5* produces a 128-bit hash value, but its complex algorithms make it much harder to crack. The algorithm consists of four distinct rounds, which have a slightly different design from that of MD4.

SHA

Secure Hash Algorithm (SHA) was developed by the NSA and NIST for use with digital signature standards. Similar to MD4, SHA produces a 160-bit hash value, which is then put through the Digital Signature Algorithm (DSA). This results in the signature for the message. The sender encrypts the 160-bit hash value with their private key, which is attached to the message before it's sent. The receiver decrypts the message with the sender's public key and runs the hashing function to compare the two values. If the values are identical, the message hasn't been tampered with.

Hash of Variable Length (HAVAL)

Hash of Variable Length (HAVAL) is a modification of MD5 that results in a variable length, one-way hash function. The data blocks are 1,024 bits, making them twice the size of those used in MD5. While MD4 and MD5 have been fully or partially broken, no successful attack on HAVAL has been reported so far.

Exam Tip
Know the different types of hashing algorithms available.

Digital Signatures

A *digital signature* is an encrypted hash value used to ensure the identity and integrity of a message. The signature can be attached to a message to uniquely identify the sender. Like a written signature, the purpose of a digital signature is to guarantee the individual sending the message is who they claim to be. The sender runs a hash function on their message, takes the resulting hash value, encrypts it with their private key, and sends it along with the message. When the receiver gets the signed message, they perform their own hashing function on the message, and, if the resulting value is the same as the original hash value, the message hasn't been altered in transmission.

Public Key Infrastructure (PKI)

Objective 9.03

Traditional cryptography methods based on symmetric key cryptography describe the use of the same secret key between the sender and the receiver of a transmission. The key the sender uses to encrypt the message is the same as the one used to decrypt the message. The disadvantage of this type of scheme is it can be difficult transmitting this secret securely from one user to another. If an unauthorized user intercepts this key, they can decrypt, read, forge, and modify all messages encrypted or authenticated using that key. Key management issues in these systems are difficult, especially ones that serve large numbers of users.

Public key cryptography was introduced in 1976 by Diffie and Hellman, whose public key protocol was created to solve this key management problem. In public key cryptography, each user received two keys: the public key and the private key. The private key is kept secret, while the public key can be published for any user to see or use. The problem faced using symmetric keys is solved because no need exists to share a secret key. All transmissions involve only the public keys; no private key is ever transmitted or shared. With public key cryptography, asymmetric cryptography is used to exchange symmetric keys. The sender encrypts the message with the receiver's public key. The receiver then decrypts the message with their own private key, as shown in Figure 9.5. The security mechanism is safe as long as the private keys aren't compromised.

PKI is a standard infrastructure consisting of a framework of procedures, standards, and protocols, based on public key cryptography. PKI is a hybrid of asymmetric and symmetric key algorithms, and provides the full range of the information assurance objectives for confidentiality, integrity, authentication, and nonrepudiation. The asymmetric keys are used for authentication and, after

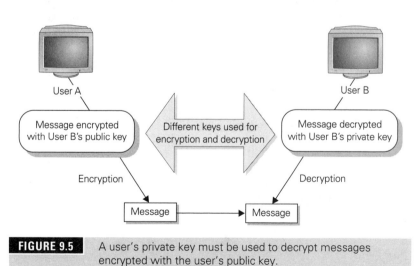

FIGURE 9.5   A user's private key must be used to decrypt messages encrypted with the user's public key.

this is successfully done, one or more symmetric keys are generated and exchanged using the asymmetric encryption. A message is encrypted using a symmetric algorithm and that key is then encrypted asymmetrically using the recipient's public key. The entire message (symmetrically encrypted body and asymmetrically encrypted key) is sent together to the recipient. The message might also be digitally signed. This is achieved through the use of digital certificates.

Exam Tip

Public key cryptography uses a hybrid of symmetric and asymmetric encryption systems. A message is encrypted using a symmetric algorithm, and that key is then encrypted asymmetrically using the recipient's public key. The entire message (symmetrically encrypted body and asymmetrically encrypted key) is sent together to the recipient.

Digital Certificates

A *digital certificate* is a credential required by PKI systems that can securely identify an individual, as well as create an association between their authenticated identity and their public keys. A trusted third party, called a certificate authority (CA), is used to sign and issue certificates. The CA is responsible for verifying the identity of a key owner and binding them to a public key. This enables users who have never met to exchange encrypted communications because the authentication is performed by the third-party CA.

Each certificate contains a unique serial number, identity and public key information of the user, and the validity dates for the life of the certificate.

Certificate Authorities

A CA is an organization or entity that issues and manages digital certificates. The CA is responsible for authenticating and identifying users who participate in the Public Key Infrastructure (PKI). This service doesn't necessarily involve a third party; it can be internal to an organization. A CA server can be set up to act as the manager of certificates and the user's public keys.

Third-party CAs are special organizations dedicated to certificate management. Some of the larger companies that offer this service, such as Verisign and Entrust, have their functionality built-in to popular web browsers to perform certificate services automatically.

Exam Tip

A certificate authority is an organization or entity that issues and manages digital certificates. The CA is responsible for authenticating and identifying users who participate in the Public Key Infrastructure (PKI).

Some of the actual authentication and identification services for certificates are taken care of by other organizations called Registration Authorities (RAs). These organizations offload some of work from CAs by confirming the identities of users, issuing key pairs, and initiating the certificate process with a CA on behalf of the user. The RA acts as a middleman between the user and the CA and doesn't issue certificates on its own.

To verify a user's identity, the Certificate and Registration Authority usually requires some form of identification, such as a driver's license, Social Security number, address, and phone number. Once the identification is established, the CA generates a public and private key for the user. A certificate is then generated with the identification and key information embedded within it. Once the user is registered and receives their certificate, they can begin using their certificate to send encrypted messages. When the receiver gets the message, their software can verify the certificate to ensure the message is from the stated sender.

Exam Tip

A certificate contains the authenticated identification of a user and their public key information.

Certificate Policies and Practice Statements

Certificate policies are rules indicating the applicability of a certificate to a type of application implementation with certain security requirements. A Certification Practice Statement (CPS) is a statement of the practices that a CA employs in managing the certificates it issues. The CPS should describe how the Certificate Policy is interpreted in the context of the system architecture and operating procedures of the organization. The Certificate Policy generally states *what* is to be adhered to, while the CPS states *how* it's adhered to.

The following list is a framework of components that should be included in a Certificate Policy and a CPS:

- **Identification**   This identifies the user community conforming to the stated policies, the identification of the Certificate and Registration Authorities, and the naming conventions for certificates.

- **Identification and Authentication**   The practice statement should describe the mechanisms used to authenticate the identity and the role of all important persons dealing with the CA, such as the network administrator and company security officials.

- **Key Management**   The key management component should describe how the key life-cycles through each of the system components, such as the Certificate and Registration Authorities, as well as how end users are managed. This should also include the algorithms used for certificates and their validity periods.

- **Security Practices**   Security practices are those relating to the PKI environment, such as physical security and access control, and network and system security.

- **Operational Practices**   This refers to the operating procedures regarding certificate revocation and renewal, and disaster and recovery.

Certificate Policies and Practice Statements are key components in establishing the degree of assurance or trust that can be placed in certificates issued by CAs.

Certificate Revocation

Certificate revocation is the act of rendering a certificate invalid and preventing its further use. The most common reason a certificate is revoked is because the user who is using that certificate is no longer authorized to use it, as in the case of a company employee who has quit or been fired. Or, the certificate subscriber's data might have changed, such as the name of the company, or it could have been incorrect when the certificate was applied for.

Other reasons include the possibility of a key pair or certificate being compromised. If the private key is lost or comprised, the details in the corresponding certificate will no longer be valid. By immediately revoking the certificate, it can't be used for any authentication, encryption, or digital signature purposes. When a certificate is revoked, it's placed on a certificate authorities Certificate Revocation List (CRL), which is distributed publicly to allow for current, efficient status checking.

Trust Models

Trust models define how users trust other users, companies, and Certificate and Registration Authorities, within the PKI. These models provide a chain of trust from a user's public key through to the root key of a CA. The validated chain then implies authenticity of all the certificates. The following are the most common trust models used in PKI.

Web of Trust

The *web of trust* is the simplistic trust model that relies on each user creating and signing their own certificate for individual users, as shown in Figure 9.6. This is the basis for encryption applications, such as PGP, where no central authority exists.

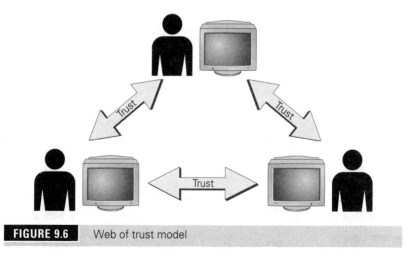

FIGURE 9.6   Web of trust model

With this model, each user is responsible for authentication and trust, and anyone can sign someone's public key. When a user signs another's key, that user is introducing that person's key to anyone who trusts them. Each user is considered a trusted introducer in the model.

Third-Party (Single Authority) Trust
A third-party central certifying agency signs a given key and authenticates the owner of the key. Trusting that authority means, by association, you trust all keys issued by that authority, as shown in Figure 9.7. Each user authenticates the other through the exchange of certificates. The users know the CA has performed all the necessary identification of the owner of the certificate and therefore, can trust the owner of the message.

Hierarchical Model
The hierarchical model is an extension of the third-party model, where root CAs issue certificates to other lower-level Certificate and Registration Authorities, as shown in Figure 9.8. Each user's most trusted key is the root CA's public key. The trust chain can be followed from the certificate back to the root CA. This model allows enforcement of policies and standards throughout the infrastructure, producing a higher level of overall assurance than other trust models.

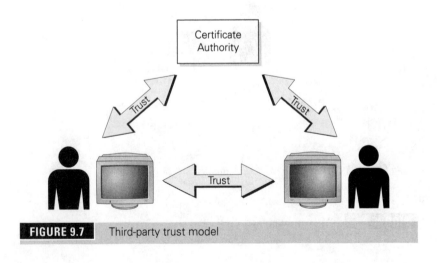

FIGURE 9.7 Third-party trust model

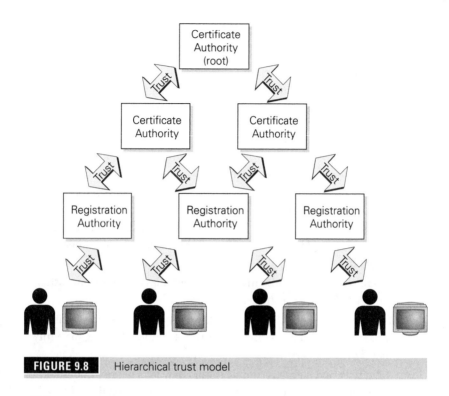

Hierarchical trust model

Objective 9.04   Standards and Protocols

The following sections detail official, unofficial, and industry standards for PKI infrastructure implementations. As in any area of technology, a variety of complementary and competing standards have arisen from international standards' organizations and individual industry leaders, such as RSA.

X.509

The X.509 International Telecommunication Union (ITU) recommendation is the most widely used standard for defining digital certificates. Because the ITU is a recommendation and not an official standard, different vendors have implemented the standard in different ways. Both Netscape and Microsoft use X.509 certificates to implement SSL in their web servers and browsers, but an X.509 certificate generated by Netscape might not be readable by Microsoft products.

The X.509 standard defines what information can go into a certificate and describes its data format. All X.509 certificates have the following data, in addition to the signature:

- **Version** This identifies which version of the X.509 standard applies to this certificate, which affects what information can be specified in it.

- **Serial Number** The entity that created the certificate is responsible for assigning this certificate a serial number to distinguish it from other certificates the entity issues. This information is used in numerous ways: for example, when a certificate is revoked, its serial number is placed in a CRL.

- **Signature Algorithm Identifier** This identifies the algorithm used by the CA to sign the certificate.

- **Issuer Name** The X.500 name of the entity that signed the certificate. This is normally a CA. Using this certificate implies trusting the entity that signed this certificate.

- **Validity Period** Each certificate is valid only for a limited amount of time. This is the expected period that entities can rely on the public value of the certificate, if the associated private key hasn't been compromised.

- **Subject Name** The name of the entity whose public key the certificate identifies, using the X.500 standard, Common Name, Organizational Unit, Organization, and Country.

- **Subject Public Key Information** This is the public key of the entity being named, together with an algorithm identifier that specifies which public key cryptosystem this key belongs to and any associated key parameters.

PKCS (RSA)

The Public-Key Cryptography Standards (PKCS) are unofficial standards produced by security company RSA Laboratories in cooperation with other secure systems developers. These standards, first published in 1991, were the result of meetings among developers, organizations, and companies who were early adopters of public key cryptography. The purpose of PKCS is to accelerate the deployment of public key cryptography. The documents that form the PKCS standard have become widely referenced and implemented. They include such topics as encryption algorithms, Diffie-Hellman and elliptic curve, password-based cryptography, certificates, and private key standards.

PKIX

The Internet Engineering Task Force (IETF) PKIX Working Group was established in 1995, with the intent of developing Internet standards needed to support an X.509-based PKI. The areas of standardization include the following:

- Profiles of X.509 Public Key Certificates and CRLs
- Management protocols
- Operational protocols using LDAP, FTP, and HTTP for PKI purposes
- Certificate policies and CPSs
- Time stamping and data certification/validation services

IEEE 1363

The Institute of Electrical and Electronics Engineers (IEEE) 1363 standard defines specifications for public key cryptography and brings together all the public key cryptography algorithms in one volume of standard.

The IEEE 1363 standard defines a full range of common public-key techniques, such as key agreement, public-key encryption, and digital signatures for the principal cryptographic families, including discrete logarithms, integer factorization, and elliptic curves. The standard supports a wide range of application and security requirements. It offers detailed descriptions of the main algorithms employed in today's most popular public-key cryptographic technologies, including the RSA public-key cryptosystem, Diffie-Hellman key agreement, and elliptic curve cryptography.

IEEE 1363 brings the algorithms into one place for the first time, and is intended to increase interoperability across protocols by providing a common reference for information about security and its implementation.

CHECKPOINT

✔ **Objective 9.01: Concepts of Using Cryptography** Information assurance is defined as protecting information and information systems by ensuring their confidentiality, integrity, authentication, and nonrepudiation.

✔ **Objective 9.02: Algorithms** In a symmetric encryption scheme, both parties use the same key for encryption and decryption purposes. Examples include DES, 3DES, AES, Blowfish, and RC5. In an asymmetric encryption scheme, everyone uses a different, but mathematically related, key for encryption and decryption purposes. Examples include RSA, RCC, El Gamal, and Diffie-Hellman. Hashing is used to protect the integrity of the message and is most often used with digital signatures. Examples include MD5, SHA, and HAVAL.

✔ **Objective 9.03: PKI** Public Key Infrastructure (PKI) is a standard infrastructure consisting of a framework of procedures, standards, and protocols, based on public key cryptography. A digital certificate is a credential required by PKI systems that can securely identify an individual, and create an association between their authenticated identity and their public keys. A trusted third party, called a Certificate Authority (CA), is used to sign and issue certificates. The Certificate Practice Statement (CPS) should describe how the Certificate Policy is interpreted in the context of the system architecture and operating procedures of the organization. Certificate revocation is the act of rendering a certificate invalid and preventing its further use. The trust models for PKI include web of trust, single authority, and hierarchical.

✔ **Objective 9.04: Standards and Protocols** Official, unofficial, and industry standards for PKI infrastructure implementations include X.509 for digital certificates, PKCS by RSA, PKIX by IETF, and IEEE 1363.

REVIEW QUESTIONS

1. When plaintext data is encrypted, what does it become?

   A. Certificate

   B. Symmetric

   C. Public Key

   D. Ciphertext

2. Which of the following isn't a function of information assurance within encryption systems?

   A. Efficiency

   B. Confidentiality

   C. Integrity

   D. Nonrepudiation

3. Which encryption scheme relies on the sender and receiver of a message to use the same secret key for encryption and decryption?

   A. Asymmetric

   B. Symmetric

   C. RSA

   D. Diffie-Hellman

4. Which of the following standards replaced DES as the government's encryption scheme?

   A. DSA

   B. ECC

   C. 3DES

   D. AES

5. Which encryption scheme relies on the sender and the receiver of a message to use different keys for encryption and decryption?

   A. Skipjack

   B. Blowfish

   C. Asymmetric

   D. Symmetric

6. Which of the following algorithms and encryption protocols is used as the basis for the Public Key Infrastructure system?

   A. MD4

   B. SHA

   C. Diffie-Hellman

   D. Skipjack

7. If the hash values of two different messages result in the same value, what is this called?

   A. Birthday attack

   B. Collision

   C. Digital signature

   D. Public key

8. Which entity issues, manages, and distributes digital certificates?

   A. Certificate authority

   B. Registration authority

   C. Government (NSA)

   D. PKI

9. The validity of a certificate refers to what?

   A. Validity of the Certificate Authority

   B. Validity of the owner

   C. Validity of the public key

   D. Time period for which the certificate can be used

10. In a hierarchical model of trust between certificate organizations and end users, which of the following is the common aspect of the certificates issued?

    A. Revocation policies

    B. Validity dates

    C. Private key

    D. Root certificate

REVIEW ANSWERS

1. **D**   Plaintext is transformed into ciphertext after being put through some type of cipher or encryption algorithm system. The ciphertext is unreadable unless it is decrypted back into plaintext form.

2. **A**   The four basic functions pertaining to information assurance are confidentiality, integrity, authentication, and nonrepudiation.

3. **B**   In a symmetric encryption scheme, both parties use the same key for encryption and decryption purposes. Both users must possess the same key to send encrypted messages to each other.

4. **D**   Advanced encryption standard (AES) is the government-defined encryption standard created as a replacement for DES, which was considered vulnerable to cryptographic attack because of weaknesses in its algorithm.

5. **C**   An asymmetric encryption scheme relies on the sender and receiver of a message to use different keys for encryption and decryption. The keys are mathematically related, but can't be derived from each other.

6. **C**   Diffie-Hellman isn't actually an encryption algorithm, but it's a key agreement protocol that enables users to exchange a private key over an insecure medium, which is the basis for PKI.

7. **B**   A collision occurs within a hashing algorithm when the hashed values of two different messages result in the same value. Collisions can be used to aid in cracking a hacking algorithm.

8. **A**   The Certificate Authority is responsible for identifying and authenticating a user, and then issuing a certificate with that user's credentials and public key. A Registration Authority is simply a middleman between the user and the Certificate Authority, and forwards a request on behalf of the end user.

9. **D**   Each certificate is valid only for a limited amount of time. This is the expected period that entities can rely on the public value of the certificate, if the associated private key hasn't been compromised.

10. **D**   In a hierarchical trust model, a central Certificate Authority issues a root certificate that validates all certificates released by lower-level authorities.

Key Management/
Certificate Lifecycle

	NEWBIE	SOME EXPERIENCE	EXPERT
ETA	4 hours	2 hours	1 hour

Key Management / Certificate Lifecycle

Objective 10.01

Encryption key management deals with the generation, distribution, storage, and backup of keys. Securing encryption keys is an extremely important aspect of encryption and cryptography. Once a key is generated, it must be secured to avoid the discovery of the key. Attacks on public-key systems are typically focused on the key management system, rather than trying to break the encryption algorithm itself. No matter how secure or difficult a cryptographical algorithm is, the entire process can be compromised by poor key management.

As part of key management, keys need to be generated and securely sent to the correct user. The user must then store that key in a secure place so it can't be compromised by another user. The key can be encrypted and stored on a hard drive, floppy disk, CD-ROM, or even a portable USB device and PDAs. The keys should also be recoverable if they're lost, damaged, or passwords for them are forgotten. Key storage is an important aspect of secure key management, which can be centralized either to a particular server or third-party service. Key storage can involve both hardware and software storage methods.

In the overall encryption trust model, all aspects, including the users, the administrators, the key management server, or third-party key management company, must be able to trust one another so the keys and identities of those using the keys are secured. As part of identifying users of keys, certificates were created, so users' identities and their public keys can be fully authenticated. Certificates go through a lifecycle that identify how long they're valid, how the certificate is renewed, when they can be suspended and revoked if compromised, and when they can be destroyed when no longer needed. This protects and secures the certificate mechanism itself because the entire key infrastructure could be undermined if it's compromised.

The following sections detail the aspects of secure key management and the lifecycle of certificates.

Centralized vs. Decentralized Storage

As part of the Public Key Infrastructure (PKI), the client key pair generated for a user needs to be securely stored somewhere. In the early days of encryption key management, cryptographic keys were stored in secure boxes and delivered by hand. The cryptographic keys could be given to the systems administrator who distributes them from a main server or by visiting each workstation. This type of administrative overhead for key management could almost be a job in itself and, obviously, doesn't scale well with larger enterprise networks. In today's networks, key distribution and storage are typically performed automatically through a special key management system, such as a key management server, or through a third-party service like Verisign or Entrust.

Centralized Storage

Key management can be an extremely time-consuming process for network administrators in a large enterprise network. Most modern encryption infrastructures use the concept of centralized storage for key management. A *centralized storage system* is a single place where all key management takes place. It typically involves a centralized server on your own network that takes care of key management for you. The server can issue key pairs, store and back them up, and take care of certificates. The following points outline the advantages of a centralized key management system:

- **Administration** Managing the accounts and keys of users at one centralized location is much more secure and convenient, relieving the administrator and the users of the administrative overhead. Signature verification is automatic because the validity information is colocated with the actual key and other account information.

- **Scalability** Key management servers are built to scale to any size enterprise network.

- **Integrity** Keys stored at a server can easily be backed up, eliminating the potential for the loss of a vital verification or an encryption key.

- **Security** Decentralized user management of keys can be insecure because of lack of education or operating system (OS) vulnerabilities. A key storage server is a secure environment where audited controls are required for access to the physical hardware and the keys are protected with specialized cryptographic devices.

Exam Tip

Centralized key-storage solutions provide greater security and integrity of keys. They're much more manageable and scalable than decentralized solutions.

Decentralized Storage

A *decentralized storage system* is typically used by individual users or a small network. Once the user has created their keys, their private key is stored locally on their system or some other secure device. They then send their public key with a certificate request to a certification authority (CA) who, after authenticating the user, sends back a certificate, which is again stored locally.

The advantage for the end user is they're always in control of their private keys and certificates. The users trust themselves with the security because they feel a server or a third-party service might not properly protect their information or could give their private key out to third parties, such as government authorities.

A decentralized storage method has many more disadvantages. For example, if the user encrypts data on their hard drive and they misplace their private key, they won't be able to recover any information encrypted with their private key. Another concern in a corporate network is this: after a disgruntled employee leaves an organization, they might not reveal the key needed to decrypt information that was protected on the corporate network.

Keys can also be damaged or lost and, if the user didn't properly back them up, those keys will be permanently lost. This means the data they encrypted will also be lost permanently because there will be no existing key to decrypt the information.

> **Travel Advisory**
>
> Decentralized methods are typically used by individual users. Centralized types of key storage are used for larger networks of users, where individual key management would be insecure and time-consuming.

Key Storage and Protection

Once a key pair has been generated, the private key must be safely stored to protect it from being compromised, lost, or damaged. The type of security used to encrypt and protect the private key should be as strong as those that encrypt and protect the actual message or files. A number of ways exist to protect the private key, including both hardware and software methods.

Hardware and Software Key Protection

The most important aspect of hardware key protection is being able to protect the hardware itself. Many users store their private key on the hard disk of their computers. Their computers might be hooked up to a network, potentially allowing access to anyone on that network. To prevent this sort of attack, private keys are usually stored on removable media, which can be more easily protected and can be physically carried with the person. This hardware can be typical media, such as a floppy disk, a CD, or a PDA. More recently, more convenient ways of storing encryption keys have been created, such as special smart cards, memory sticks, and USB devices. These small devices can fit into a wallet or pocket and they can contain flash memory that holds small files, such as encryption keys. The main disadvantage to these small devices is they can easily be lost or stolen, which is why the stored key should be encrypted.

When storing your private key, it should never be stored anywhere in its plaintext form. If an unauthorized user manages to find the file or steals the device in which the file is located, that user could uncover the private key. The simplest method of protection is to secure the private key with a password and store it locally on a disk. Most web browsers will let you set a password on the file, and then automatically encrypt the key on the hard drive in a hidden location. When you need to use the key, the browser will ask for the password before continuing. The password should be as carefully crafted as your network password, so it can't be guessed easily or discovered through brute-force attack methods.

Exam Tip	
The private key should never be stored in plaintext form. It needs to be encrypted and protected with a password.	

For enterprise-level networks, the installation of a key management system takes the burden of key storage and protection away from the user and lets the OS or application take care of storing keys on a centralized server.

An additional method of protection includes the generation of another key pair to be used to encrypt the private key. This key is usually kept with a third party using a key escrow type service.

Key Escrow

The concept of key escrow has been heavily overshadowed over the years by debates between privacy groups and the government because it concerns the issues of data privacy versus national security.

Key escrow means some form of third party, whether a government agency or an authorized organization, holds a special third key, on top of your private and public key pair. The third key is used to encrypt the private key, which is then stored in a secure location. This third key can be used to unlock the encrypted copy of the private key, in case of loss or the theft of the original key. Although the main concern of privacy activists is the possible abuse by the government regarding individual data privacy, the main security issue for most companies is the idea of a third-party entity controlling a crucial part of your security infrastructure. A common key escrow entity can be a certificate authority (CA), which is responsible for authorized and distributing certificates and encryption key pairs.

As part of your overall security plan, the capability for your CA to protect your information is crucial. CAs are a popular target of hacker attacks because of the valuable information they contain. These attacks are usually targeted at the CA's own private keys. The CA's key pairs are common targets of cryptanalytic attacks in an effort to break weak keys through brute force. CAs need to be both secure and practical because their public key might be written into software used by a large number of users. If the key needs to be changed, everyone's software will need to be updated to accept the new key.

> ## Travel Advisory
> When examining a key escrow service, pay careful attention to their methods of security, including the secure storage and transfer of keys and certificates.

Key Recovery

As the main key to unlocking the encryption on a file or other critical data, the private key must be carefully protected. If the private key is ever lost or destroyed, there will be no way of unlocking anything that's been encrypted with that key. The problem with the storage and backup of private keys is this:

a balance must be maintained between the security of the key and the capability to archive it in the event of the need for recovery.

Unfortunately, the concept of key recovery has been clouded with the issue of governmental control and the possibility that the government, in the interest of national security, would require a mandatory key recovery system. This mandatory key recovery system might enable the government to decrypt private data through the use of key escrow and key management companies. Whatever the outcome of that debate, secure methods of key recovery are available that keep the responsibility and capability of key recovery within the end user's hands.

One method gaining in popularity is for a company to maintain protection of the backup of its private keys, but to use a third-party company to store a unique key that can be used to unlock the backup of the private keys. This system prevents any of your private keys from leaving your premises and leaves little room for compromising the security of those keys. The private keys are stored on your site, while the key to unlock those private keys is offsite.

Another method uses what is known as *M of N control,* which refers to a method of storing a private key, protected and encrypted with a separate unique key. The key used for recovery is split into different parts and distributed to various individuals, called *key recovery operators,* and usually stored in a smart card or other memory device. To use the recovery key, a certain number of the operators must be present with their part of the key. M of N control refers to the number of operator keys that must be present to create the recovery key, such as 2 of 3 or 4 of 7. For example, in a 4 of 7 scheme, a recovery key is split into seven parts and only four of those parts are needed to create the recovery key that will decrypt the backup of the private key.

Exam Tip

M of N control refers to the number of keys that must be present to create the recovery key, such as 3 of 5.

Travel Advisory

M of N control can be somewhat difficult to maintain, especially with employee turnover where new replacements must be entered into the scheme.

Multiple Key Pairs

The issue of using multiple key pairs in a PKI implementation greatly increases both the security and the complexity of data encryption. Using multiple keys directly involves the problems associated with backing up certain types of key pairs for recovery.

In a typical PKI setup, a private and a public key are generated to be used for encryption and digital signatures. These keys can be used for three basic purposes:

- **Encryption** To encrypt data to protect its contents
- **Authentication** To identify users through their public keys and certificates
- **Nonrepudiation** To make it impossible for someone to deny having signed a transaction or file

The problem with a single key pair for these functions is the single key pair can often conflict with the backup and recovery requirements of the organization. A key pair used for encryption should be backed up in case the private key is lost or destroyed, so it can be recovered to decrypt the locked data. The backup of the same key pair used for nonrepudiation purposes, however, could be harmful. A digital signature intended to be legally binding can be repudiated if the signer proves it could be invalid because of the existence of another copy of the private key.

Exam Tip

Know the concept of nonrepudiation and how a dual key system can resolve the conflict with key backup.

To solve this conflict, a dual key-pair system can be used that can satisfy all security and backup requirements. One key pair can be used for encryption and decryption, while the second key pair can be used exclusively for digital signatures and nonrepudiation needs. The key pair used for encryption can be safely backed up for recovery purposes, while the second key needn't be backed up conforming to nonrepudiation procedures.

Another important concept is the problem of key history. When using multiple keys and discarding old ones in favor of new ones, you might have archived data protected with encryption keys that you don't use anymore. As part of your key backup strategy, you need to retain copies of keys for encryption that's still in use on your network.

Travel Advisory
Without some form of key history, you won't be able to recover data files that have been encrypted with older keys you no longer possess. 

Certificate Lifecycle

Certificates are issued as a form of identification of the user or corporate entity, and their corresponding public keys. This forms a basis of trust where encryption keys can be passed back and forth, knowing the certificates establish the proper identity of the owner and their keys.

Certificates go through a lifecycle that identifies how long they're valid, how they're renewed, when they can be suspended and revoked if compromised, and when they can be destroyed when no longer needed. This protects and secures the certificate process itself because, if compromised, this could undermine the entire key infrastructure.

If the public keys corresponding with a certain certificate have been compromised, then any messages or files that were encrypted might be vulnerable. The only way to ensure the validity of the key is to check the status of the certificate.

Exam Tip
Know the various aspects of the certificate cycle and what scenarios can cause certificates to be suspended or revoked.

The lifecycle of a certificate goes through the following stages, as detailed in Figure 10.1:

- Certificate Requested
- Certificate Issued
- Certificate Published
- Certificate Received
- Suspension/Revocation
- Expiration
- Key Destruction
- Renewal

This section deals specifically with the lifecycle of the certificate after it's been received by the owner, including suspension and revocation, expiry, renewal, and destruction.

Suspension and Revocation

A number of reasons exist why a particular certificate can be suspended and revoked before its expiration date. The most common reason is the user who's using that certificate isn't authorized to use it anymore, as in the case of a company

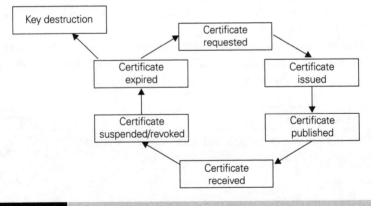

FIGURE 10.1   The certificate lifecycle

employee who quit or has been fired. The certificate subscriber's data, such as the name of the company, might have changed or it could have been incorrect when the certificate was applied for. Other reasons include the problem of a key pair or certificate being compromised. If the private key is lost or comprised, the details in the corresponding certificate will no longer be valid. By immediately revoking the certificate, it can't be used for any authentication, encryption, or digital signature purposes. Suspension is a temporary revocation of the certificate until the problem concerning the certificate or the certificate owner's identity can be corrected. A suspension of a certificate can be undone, but a revocation is permanent.

The owner of the certificate must initiate communication with the CA to begin the revocation process. This needs to be performed in a secure way, through a signed message, in person, or any other authenticated channel. The private key corresponding to a certificate being revoked can be used to authenticate a revocation request, but if this is because the key has been compromised, it can't be used to support authentication for a new certificate.

When a certificate is revoked, it's placed on a certificate authority's Certificate Revocation List (CRL).

Certificate Revocation Lists (CRLs)

A Certificate Revocation List (CRL) is a list of certificates that have been revoked before their expiration date. A CRL is used as a way for other users and organizations to identify certificates that are no longer valid.

CRLs can be distributed in two main ways:

* **Pull Model**   The CRL is downloaded from the CA by those who want to see it to verify a certificate. In this model, the end user or organization is responsible for regularly downloading the latest CRL for the most recent list.
* **Push Model**   In the push model, the CA automatically sends the CRL out to verifiers at regular intervals.

These models can also be hierarchical in nature, where a specific CRL of a CA is pushed to other sites, from where other users and organizations can download it. CRLs are maintained in a distributed manner, but various central repositories contain the latest CRLs from a number of CAs.

Web sites and companies that deal with large numbers of secure transactions might need their own local version of a CRL that can quickly be compared to the large number of certificates accepted.

To check the status of a certificate, the CRL of that CA is needed. This CRL can be obtained from that specific CA or from a centralized database of CRLs released by a collection of authorities. To help automate this process, certificate status checks have been built into software applications, such as e-mail programs and web browsers that automatically check the status of a received certificate. Status checks can also be made manually by checking the web site of a CA and entering the serial number of a certificate.

Exam Tip

Know the purpose of a CRL and how it can be used to verify certificates.

Expiration

Within each certificate is a specific date for the beginning and ending of that certificate's lifecycle. Most certificates are valid for approximately one to three years. The length of time the certificate is valid depends on the type of certificate issued and its purpose. A high-security defense contractor might switch their key pairs on a regular basis, meaning the certificates they use could only be valid for a short time.

The purpose of certificate expiry is to protect certificates from brute force attacks. The longer certificates are in use, the more likely they will be cracked. This is similar to a password expiry and retention scheme for a network where users must regularly change their passwords to prevent them from being compromised.

If you want to use a certificate after its time of validity is complete, you'll need to renew the certificate.

Exam Tip

Once a certificate has expired, it can't be renewed. A new certificate and key pair need to be generated.

Renewal

To continue to use a certificate, it must be renewed before its expiry date. Typically, the CA will contact the owner of the certificate when the certificate's expiration date is impending. The certificate owner has the responsibility to renew the certificate before the expiration date. If this renewal isn't performed before the expiry date, that certificate will become invalid, and anyone trusting the source of that certificate will be unable to transact or communicate with the certificate owner. For companies that rely on certificates for digital transactions, this could be fatal. In addition, a request for a new certificate will need to be issued, which might take time to process before you receive the new certificate and keys. The policies and procedures of the CA must be examined carefully to ensure certificates are renewed on time, especially because the certificate authorities usually need extra time before the expiry date to register the renewal properly. The recommendation is that you renew certificates at least 30 days before they expire to ensure enough time to have them renewed.

One important aspect of renewal is whether or not to generate a new key pair to go along with the new certificate. Many certificate authorities, in the process of renewal, merely repackage the certificate with the same public key. Because cryptographical keys can be compromised over time through sustained computational brute-force methods, the longer you keep the same key pair, the more insecure it will become over time. Therefore, it's extremely important for cryptographical security to generate a new key when renewing a certificate. This might not be so important for an individual who only uses encryption sparingly for personal purposes but, for companies with high-security needs, this is vital.

Destruction

If a certificate and key pair have been compromised or are no longer in use, the key pair should be destroyed to prevent further use. The *key pair* consists of a private and a public key. Because the public key has been distributed many times during its lifetime, it can obviously be difficult to destroy completely. Therefore, the destruction of the private key is essential to ensure certificates or digital signatures can no longer be created with those keys.

Some private keys, however, need to be retained, for example, if they're used for key management or data privacy, such as an encrypted file on a corporate network file server. The private key might need to be maintained as part of a key history, so items being stored with an older encryption key can be unlocked if necessary. A balance must be struck between the security need for key destruction and the need to access archived information.

Another aspect of key destruction is that of the certificate that validates those keys. If the certificate is still valid, according to its creation and expiry date, then it needs to be revoked by contacting the CA, who will include the certificate's serial number in its CRL.

Destroying the private key can be a fairly simple process, but it must be thorough to ensure the private key can't be recovered in any way. If the key is simply stored on a local hard disk, it can be deleted. The drawback to this, however, is that many OSs don't delete the file; they only delete the file name from the disk directory. The actual file is still stored on disk, so it can be retrieved through a data recovery program, such as Microsoft Windows recycle bin. In some cases, if the computer were stolen, the hacker could take the hard drive and analyze it or send it to a special recovery lab that can restore the data still on the disk. Many utilities can be used to delete files permanently from magnetic media. Other options include the actual physical destruction of the media itself, whether it be a hard drive, floppy disk, CD, smart card, or flash memory device.

CHECKPOINT

✔ **Objective 10.01: Key Management/Certificate Lifecycle**   Decentralized storage is used by individual users and centralized storage is used for enterprise networks. Private keys need to be stored securely and, preferably, encrypted with a password. Key escrow companies can store the encryption key that can unlock the encryption on your private key, which is stored at your location. Backups need to be made of keys to prevent loss of data because of lost, stolen, or damaged keys. Keys for digital signing shouldn't be backed up because of nonrepudiation requirements. A dual-pair key system can generate separate keys for encryption and digital signing. M of N control stores different parts of a key distributed among several people. Only a certain number of key parts are needed to provide the key. Certificates need to be renewed before expiry or else a new certificate must be generated. A certificate should be suspended or revoked if the keys related to that certificate are compromised. Check the CRL for certificates that have been revoked.

REVIEW QUESTIONS

1. When you save a private key on a local hard drive, how do you ensure its security?

    A. Needs to be password protected

    B. Save the backup to a floppy

    C. Store a written copy in an envelope

    D. Store it in the same directory as the public key

2. A key management server is considered a type of what?

    A. Local storage

    B. Centralized storage

    C. Decentralized storage

    D. Distributed storage

3. What should be stored to prevent a loss of data that was encrypted with older encryption keys?

    A. Public key

    B. Key history

    C. Expired certificates

    D. Escrow key

4. Which of the following would be the most secure way to store a private key?

    A. Save it on a hard drive in plaintext

    B. Seal it in an envelope and store it in a desk

    C. Encrypt it on a smart card

    D. Store it on a portable USB device in plaintext

5. In a key escrow model, what is stored offsite with a third party?

   A. Encryption key to decrypt a private key file

   B. Encryption key to decrypt a public key file

   C. Copy of a public key

   D. Copy of a certificate

6. An encryption key split into separate parts and distributed to a number of certain users is an example of what type of key recovery scheme?

   A. Key backup

   B. Key management server

   C. Key escrow

   D. M of N control

7. Which of the following describes the inability for someone to deny having signed a transaction or file with their encryption key?

   A. Nonrepudiation

   B. Authentication

   C. Encryption signing

   D. Digital signature

8. A network administrator has recently been fired from a company. What should be done with their current certificate?

   A. Renewed for the new administrator

   B. Revoked

   C. Suspended

   D. Expired

9. When a certificate is revoked, where are its serial number and information published?

   A. Certificate destruction list

   B. Certificate suspension list

   C. Certificate revocation list

   D. Certificate expiry list

10. When should a certificate be renewed?

   A. On its expiry date

   B. After it expires

   C. After it's revoked

   D. Thirty days before expiry

REVIEW ANSWERS

1. **A**   To ensure the security of a private key, especially when it's stored locally on some kind of device, the private key should be protected with a password. If the key or device that it's stored on is stolen, the unauthorized user won't be able to unlock the key.

2. **B**   A key management server takes care of the process of distributing, storing, and backing up keys for users of an enterprise network. The administrative overhead associated with manually managing keys for so many users would be overwhelming.

3. **B**   By saving a history of keys that have been used in the past, you'll be able to decrypt archived files saved with those keys. If those keys are lost, the data can't be unlocked.

4. **C**   Private keys should never be stored in plaintext. If they're stolen, the unauthorized user will be able to use them to decrypt messages and files.

5. **A**   In a key escrow storage scheme, an encryption key used to encrypt the private key file is stored offsite with a third party. If access is needed to the backup copy of the private key, the encryption key needs to be obtained from the third-party company after you've been properly authenticated.

6. **D**   In this key recovery scheme, a certain number of the key owners must be present with their part of the key. M of N control refers to the number of operator keys that must be present to create the recovery key, such as 2 of 3, or 4 of 7. For example, if a recovery key is split into seven parts, only four of those are needed to create the recovery key that will decrypt the backup of the private key.

7. **A**   A person can deny having signed a transaction or file with their encryption by proving another copy of the private key exists. This is a drawback of some key backup and recovery models. The use of dual key pairs facilitates having a separate key for digital signing that shouldn't be backed up.

8. **B**   The certificate should be revoked because the user assigned to that certificate is no longer with the company. This prevents the user from continuing to use that certificate for encryption and authentication.

9. **C**   A CRL is published by a CA to show what certificates have been revoked. A verifier can examine the list to check the validity of another user's certificate.

10. **D**   Most certificate authorities require a certificate to be renewed a certain amount of time before the actual expiry date. This gives enough time for the renewal process to renew the certificate and deliver it back to the client for distribution.

Operational/ Organizational Security

Physical Security Issues

	NEWBIE	SOME EXPERIENCE	EXPERT
ETA	3 hours	1 hours	0.5 hour

Objective 11.01 Physical Security

Physical security is different from computer security. When securing a computer system or network, you're attempting to prevent unauthorized users from accessing the resources of your system. Physical security, however, is used to prevent unauthorized users from accessing an environment. The environment can be anything from the entire facility itself to a small network closet that contains networking equipment and wiring.

Much time and expense is spent on securing a computer network from unauthorized external access but, typically, not enough resources are used on physical security to prevent unauthorized internal access. The possible result of lax physical security includes equipment theft, physical damage and vandalism, service interruptions, and the unauthorized release of confidential data.

Physical security is needed to protect employees, company data, equipment, and the facility itself. Physical security concepts include planning, facilities security, access control, and physical and environmental protections.

Access Control

To secure access to your facility, you need to install access systems that can identify employees and control what areas of your facility they can access. *Access control security* also includes surveillance and monitoring of your property, and the installation of physical barriers to prevent unauthorized intruders from trespassing on your company's property.

Building Security

Your first line of defense is the security of the perimeter of the facility or the boundaries of its property. It's critical that unauthorized people are prevented from accessing the property or its buildings. This could involve unique security mechanisms for use during daily working hours and for use when the facility is closed. Building security includes the use of physical barriers, surveillance, and access control.

Physical Barriers To deter unauthorized access to a facility, physical barriers can often be the most effective form of security. *Fencing* is a simple way to close off your perimeter from people who are simply passing by and could be inclined to trespass on your property. Depending on the level of protection you require, fencing can be as simple as a low, four-foot fence that can provide protection against casual trespassers or neighborhood animals. Higher fences of at least eight feet should be constructed to make it difficult for the average person to climb over them. For the most protection, barbed wire can be installed on the top of the fence.

Lighting   In the interest of security and safety, all areas of the property should have proper lighting installed to discourage intruders and provide a safe environment for employees. This not only includes all of the company's building, but also the parking lot. The most effective type of lights are flood lights, which can illuminate a large area. The entire lighting system should also be set on a timer or you can use photoelectric technology to detect when it's getting too dark outside.

Surveillance and Monitoring   To maintain the physical security of your property, surveillance and monitoring devices should be employed. The simplest form of *surveillance* is the use of common security procedures, such as using security guards. Another option is through the use of cameras set up throughout the facility, which can be constantly monitored by the security guards. Although effective, these options can be costly because of the high price of surveillance equipment and the ongoing wages that must be paid to have security guards on duty monitoring this equipment.

Another type of surveillance includes cameras coupled with recording equipment that can monitor and record all activity. If a burglary or vandalism occurs, the culprits could be captured on video, which can then be analyzed to identify the unauthorized intruders.

The use of intruder detection equipment can ensure that your surveillance and monitoring system is proactive by alerting you to suspicious behavior without the need and expense of constant monitoring by security guards. Several intrusion detection technologies options are available.

- **Proximity Detector**   A *proximity detector* is used to sense changes in an electromagnetic field that surrounds a small area or object. When a change is detected, an alarm will sound.
- **Motion Detector**   A *motion detector* can detect motion in a certain area. This is most often used in conjunction with flood lights that turn

on when motion is detected in the area. The light serves as a warning that an intruder has been detected.

- **Photoelectric Detector** A *photoelectric detector* can sense changes in light patterns that indicate someone is in the area. The photoelectric device emits a beam of light, which, when disrupted, sounds an alarm.

- **Infrared Detector** An *infrared detector* can sense changes in the heat patterns of an area that indicate the presence of an intruder.

- **Sound Detector** A *sound detector* is sensitive to sounds and vibrations. It can detect changes in the noise levels in an area.

Travel Advisory

The main drawback of most intrusion-detection systems is the large number of false alarms that can occur because of abnormal weather conditions, animals, and improper calibration.

Physical Access Control The most basic and least expensive of *physical-access control* methods is the use of a lock and key system. Unfortunately, in large environments, this can quickly become an administrative nightmare because the amount of keys that must be distributed for each lock can grow quickly. Also, you have the problem of employees losing keys, duplicating them, or letting other users borrow them. When employees are terminated, they might not always return their keys, and then every lock would have to be changed.

Depending on the environment, different types of locks can be used. For perimeter security, often only a simple padlock on a chained fence will suffice. For more high-security areas, electronic or mechanical locks with programmable keys can be installed. These require a combination or keycode to open, instead of a physical key.

Travel Advisory

Electronic locks should be linked with the alarm system. In case of a fire or other emergency, the locks should automatically disengage to allow people to leave the building.

More advanced personnel-access control techniques include the use of security badge access cards. A *security badge* should be some sort of photo identification that can immediately identify the wearer as an authorized user. Security badges should be worn at all times where they can be seen by other employees. The card should identify who the person is and what their job function is. By listing their job function, it can be quickly ascertained if that person is allowed into a certain part of the facility. Simple security badges, however, require the use of security guards and security-conscious employees. The most common method of personnel access control used today is the access card. Typically, each employee receives a card with a magnetic strip that contains their access information. These cards can be swiped in magnetic card readers, which are stationed outside important access points, such as doors or elevators. The information on the card is then compared with the security access of the area they're about to enter. If they don't have access to that particular area, then the door won't open.

Travel Advisory

Magnetic access cards should have no type of company identification on them. If one of these cards is lost or stolen, the unauthorized user will have no idea from which company or facility the card came.

Another type of access card system is the proximity reader, which doesn't require the physical insertion of a card. The *proximity reader* can sense the card if it's within a certain minimum distance. The information is read through an electromagnetic field.

Travel Advisory

For higher security areas, the cards should be complemented with access codes or personal identification numbers (PIN). In case the card is lost or stolen, it can't be used for access, except with the corresponding PIN number.

Network Infrastructure Security   Physical access to your special network and computer equipment rooms should be secured as carefully as access to your facilities. These rooms are the brains of your operations, concentrating a variety of critical functions, such as network communications, database servers, and backup systems. If an unauthorized user gains access to the central network room, the damage that person can cause could be considerable.

The main door to the network or server room should be secured with some type of lock, preferably with some sort of card access system, as described earlier. Only those employees who need to be in the room to perform their job functions should be allowed access. Inside, servers and other sensitive equipment should be housed inside a lockable cage or rack and not left running in an open area where they could be tampered with or accidentally damaged. Many types of networking equipment servers come with their own locks that require keys to open them for access. Cabling should be carefully laid out so it can't be easily disturbed by people walking through the room. Cables should either be run under the floor or around the perimeter of the room in special cable trays.

Personal Computers and Laptops   It's easy for an unauthorized user to walk by an unattended desk or system rack and quickly remove expensive equipment. Not only does the stolen equipment need to be replaced but, often, the sensitive data saved on that equipment must be recovered. If the item was stolen for the purpose of corporate espionage, the results of the lost information can be devastating.

Any expensive or sensitive equipment—especially portable items such as laptops, PDAs, networking equipment, and small computer devices—should be kept out of sight or locked up when unattended. Device locks are available for both desktop computers and portable laptops. A desktop computer can be housed in a lockable cage that would require a great deal of effort to open. Also, alarm cards, which will sound a loud alarm whenever the computer is moved, can be installed in computers. Peripheral devices attached to a computer can be protected with cable traps that prevent their removal. Laptop computers should be fitted with a special cable and lock that can securely attach it to its current work area. If you'll be away from the laptop for an extended period of time, it should be locked inside a desk or cabinet.

Biometrics

Although typically only available to extremely high-security installations because of the great cost, biometric access controls offer the most complete and technologically advanced method for securing access to a facility. *Biometrics* offers the capability to identify someone through a unique physical attribute, such as a finger print, voice scan, or retinal scan.

Initially, the user requesting access must have the respective attribute scanned, so a perfect copy is on file for comparison when the user tries to gain access in the future. These types of biometric systems are complex and sensitive, and they can often result in many false permissions and denials for access. They must be constantly calibrated and repeated measurements of a user's biometric data are required.

The following are the most common types of biometric access systems:

- **Palm/Fingerprint Scan**   No two fingerprints are alike, as most law enforcement officials are aware. A user must place their hand on the biometric scanner, which will compare them to the palm scan and fingerprints on file for that user. This is the most effective of all biometric methods.

- **Hand Geometry Scan**   The size and shape of a person's hand varies significantly among different people. Similar to a fingerprint scan, the user places their hand on a biometric scanner, which measures the length and width of the hand, including the sizes of the fingers.

- **Retinal/Iris Scan**   A person's retina contains a varied pattern of blood vessels and can be a unique attribute, similar to a fingerprint. The user must place their eye up to a device that projects a light beam into the eye to capture the retina pattern. The *iris,* the colored part of an eye that surrounds the pupil, can also be used for scanning because it contains many unique characteristics.

- **Voice Scan**   The voice is a unique characteristic between people. By recording the user speaking a set of access words, the captured voice print can be compared to the same spoken words the next time the user tries to gain access.

- **Face Scan**   A facial scan records the unique characteristics of each person's face, such as bone structure, and the shape of the eyes and nose. These characteristics can be captured in the scan and compared to the facial scan on file.

- **Signature Scan**   Considered one of the weakest types of biometric security, a signature scan records the written signature of a user, and then compares it to subsequent signatures when the user attempts to gain access. Two types of signature scans exist: static and dynamic. A *static scan* merely compares the two signatures for accuracy and can't be considered accurate. A *dynamic scan* can record the motions of the signature using electrical signals. These unique characters make a dynamic signature scan much more reliable.

Exam Tip
Be aware of which biometric access control systems are more reliable than others in identifying authorized users.

Social Engineering

Social engineering is defined as the use of subterfuge or trickery to reveal personal or confidential information. Most often this comes in the form of an unauthorized user posing as an authority who requires access to that information. In the context of physical security, social engineering could involve deception in allowing an unauthorized user to gain access to a facility. For example, an unauthorized individual might arrive at the front gates of a secured facility claiming to have forgotten their access card at home. Distracted by the user's friendly manner and banter, an unsuspecting security guard or receptionist might let the person through without checking credentials.

Fake or stolen identification could also be used to gain access to a facility that uses photo ID or a magnetic swipe access card. If the security guard only gets a passing glance at the photo, they might not realize the person wielding the card is someone who only vaguely resembles the photo. You must emphasize to all employees never to let strangers access any secured areas of the facility without proper identification or security access. Employees should never let another user borrow their identification or access card, or give out passwords without the consent of management and security.

Facilities Environmental Protection

Security is often thought of only as protection against theft, vandalism, or unauthorized access to a company's computer systems. Typically, not enough thought and planning are performed for the security of your actual facility, which is the first line of defense for your employees and your company's assets. Threats from unauthorized access are a great concern, but protecting your building from environmental concerns, such as fires and floods, is equally important.

At the minimum, the facility itself must adhere to any local and national safety standards as they pertain to building construction, fire ratings, and electrical code. Many of these issues need to be taken care of before and during the time the facility is being constructed.

To protect your employees and sensitive equipment that resides inside the building, care must be taken in providing a regulated environment that controls the temperature, humidity, electrical systems, ventilation, and fire-suppression systems.

Facility Construction Issues

Before the foundation of a new company facility is laid, an incredible amount of planning goes into the construction process. Part of that process should involve the physical security and safety of the new facility. Several issues must be dealt with, often even before the new location is chosen.

These main issues include location planning, building construction, and computer room construction.

Location Planning When planning the location for a proposed company facility, several factors must be taken into consideration. Unless secrecy of the facility is desired, the building should be in a visible area and situated comfortably within the surrounding terrain. The building should be easily accessible from major roads, highways, or even railway or coastal ports, depending on the type of business. Most important, the site should be analyzed in respect to its susceptibility to natural disasters. If the building is located in a valley, could flooding occur? Is the building situated in an area prone to tornadoes, hurricanes, or earthquakes? All these factors should be incorporated into your overall site plan.

Facility Construction After the site has been chosen, the actual construction of the facility must be carefully planned and executed. The construction materials need to be studied for their compliance with local and national safety standards, including fire and structural-strength ratings. Building security must also be a high priority during construction. The following outlines some of the key components of building construction, including some recommendations to enhance security:

- **Walls** Must be examined for fire and strength ratings. For high security areas, walls might need to be reinforced with stronger materials.

- **Doors** Should be resistant to forced entry and fitted with security mechanisms, such as basic or electronic locks. Emergency doors must be carefully placed for access during an emergency.

- **Ceilings**   Should be examined for their fire rating and materials should be made of noncombustible materials. The decision to use a drop ceiling is a balance between security and convenience. Although a *drop ceiling* is good for cable management, it also inadvertently provides access to other areas and rooms.

- **Windows**   Should be resistant to shattering and placed accordingly to prevent access to sensitive areas of the building. For added security, the windows can be made opaque or reflective, so no one can see into them from the outside.

- **Flooring**   Should be carefully chosen for its fire rating and susceptibility to combustion. The flooring surfaces should be conducive to a nonconductive, nonstatic environment.

Computer Room Construction   To preserve the integrity and security of a sensitive company computer and networking equipment, these components should be housed in a separate, environmentally and security controlled room. This room should not be accessible by other doors, rooms, corridors, or stairs. Only one secured doorway should exist, in which employees can enter and exit from the room.

Inside, servers and networking equipment are usually stacked in a rack or cabinet that can be secured by a lock. Cabling is typically run up to the ceiling, down through the floor, or high up on the walls, using special cable management trays. This prevents people from tripping over equipment or wiring that might be strewn haphazardly over the floor.

The room should also be designed for maximum air ventilation, and installed with environmental controls to regulate both temperature and humidity.

Exam Tip

Ensure that you know the special considerations that must be made for computer network room security compared to other parts of the building.

Environment Issues

Computers and electronic equipment are sensitive to environmental factors such as temperature and humidity, and air and power quality. Imbalances in any of these utilities can result in severe damage to computer equipment, and they can potentially cause even greater perils to both the people and the facilities.

Environmental controls must be installed and continuously supervised for proper operation.

Temperature and Humidity   Sensitive computer and electronic equipment needs to operate in a climate-controlled environment. To provide a proper operating environment, the temperature and humidity of a computer facility must be carefully controlled and maintained. Overheating of computer equipment can cause operating disruption or even total equipment failure. When devices overheat, they cause their components to expand and retract, which can eventually damage them permanently. In a computer system itself, several fans circulate the air and cool the components inside. In addition to this, computer facilities should be equipped with an industrial air conditioner to keep the entire room at a steady, cool temperature.

Humidity levels are also important to the overall operating health of computer equipment because high humidity can cause corrosion of the internal parts of a system. Low humidity levels create a dry environment, where the buildup of static electricity can cause great harm to electronic equipment, so humidity levels should be set between 40 to 50 percent. Static electricity can also be minimized in the environment through the use of special antistatic mats and antistatic bands, which can be worn by technicians who regularly touch the equipment.

Ventilation   The quality of the air circulating through the computer facility must be maintained through the proper use of ventilation techniques. Without proper ventilation, a risk of airborne contaminants occurs. These contaminants could be dust or other microscopic particles that can get inside and clog such critical equipment as the fans, which need to be running to keep the system cool.

Electrical Power   Another important environmental concern is the electrical power system that runs your equipment. *Electrical power* must be provided with consistent voltage levels and a minimum of interference. Even small fluctuations in power can cause irreparable damage to sensitive electronic equipment. Power protection has two aspects: ensuring the consistency and quality of your primary power source, and maintaining the availability of alternate power in a power outage.

Several types of fluctuations can occur:

- **Blackout**   A *blackout* is a prolonged period without any power.
- **Brownout**   A *brownout* defines a prolonged period of lower than normal power.
- **Spike**   A voltage *spike* is a momentary jump to a high voltage.

- **Sag** A *sag* is a moment of low voltage.
- **Surge** A power *surge* is defined as a prolonged period of high voltage.

To protect your equipment against these different types of perils, several devices can be used. Simple power-surge protectors generally aren't rated for expensive types of computer equipment. Usually, these types of power bars only contain some type of fuse or circuit breaker that cuts off the power in a spike or a surge. By the time the breaker cuts in, the moment of high voltage has already been reached and, possibly, damaged the equipment that's plugged into the power bar. The recommendation is for most computer systems, servers, and network infrastructures to use an uninterruptible power supply (UPS). A *UPS* works on a variety of levels as both a high-end surge protector and during a power failure. The battery normally contains enough power to run the system for a short time, so it can be brought down properly and shut off before the battery runs out. Most modern UPSs come with software that shuts down during a power outage. A more expensive option for backup power is the use of a backup power generator that runs on a battery or fuel.

Travel Advisory

Don't plug power bars or high-load peripherals, such as laser printers, into UPS power outlets because they can quickly overload the UPS.

To provide clean and consistent power to computer equipment, a device called a line or power conditioner can be used. This *line* or *power conditioner* plugs directly into the power supply outlet, and ensures the power that reaches the computer equipment is free of voltage fluctuations and interference.

Cable Shielding

Network cabling can be extremely sensitive to environmental electrical interference. This type of disruption can cause loss of information, network latency, and the complete disabling of the network. These types of problems are most pronounced in manufacturing environments where computers and networking cabling run side-by-side with large machines. The following are the most common type of problems that affect network cabling.

- **EMI**   *Electromagnetic interference* is caused by the electrical "noise" created by motors, lighting, and any type of electronic or mechanical equipment. This interference can potentially disrupt communications on network cabling because of the noise in the line that distorts the network signals.

- **Crosstalk**   *Crosstalk* is caused by the electrical signals of one wire disrupting the signals of another wire. Without proper shielding, network cabling is susceptible to crosstalk, especially twisted-pair type of wiring.

- **Attenuation**   As an electronic signal travels, it slowly degrades over a certain distance. The longer a network cable is, the more susceptible it is to this type of signal degradation. The rate of *attenuation* increases when the type of network signaling is using higher frequencies for faster data transfer. Attenuation can also be caused by damaged or faulty network cabling.

To prevent these problems from affecting your network communications, the cabling you use should be properly shielded. Different types of cabling use different kinds of shielding methods.

Exam Tip
Be aware of the different types of interference that can affect network cabling.

Coaxial   *Coaxial cabling* consists of a special copper core wire that's surrounded by several layers of protection. The copper wire is insulated by PVC or Teflon-based material, as shown in Figure 11.1. This, in turn, is wrapped with a braided shielding material, and then the cable is covered with a protective outer sheath. This cabling is resistant to EMI and, most often, is installed in manufacturing

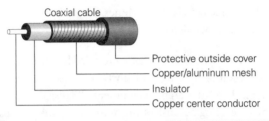

FIGURE 11.1 Cross-section of coaxial network cabling

environments because of the large amounts of interference that can result from nearby electrical and mechanical equipment.

Twisted Pair *Twisted-pair cabling* consists of several insulated copper wires, surrounded by a protective sheath. The copper wires are twisted together to protect them from EMI and to balance the crosstalk between the individual wires. Two types of twisted-pair cabling exist: shielded and unshielded. Shielded twisted-pair (STP) cabling contains an extra layer of foil shielding for added protection, as shown in Figure 11.2. Unshielded twisted-pair (UTP) cabling, which doesn't have this protection, is shown in Figure 11.3. UTP is the most common form of cabling because the extra shielding of STP makes it much more expensive.

Fiber-Optic Because fiber-optic technology uses light as the medium for communication, it isn't susceptible to electromagnetic interference, crosstalk, or

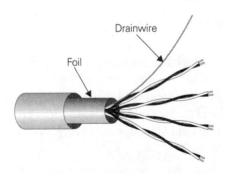

FIGURE 11.2 Cross-section of shielded twisted-pair wiring (STP)

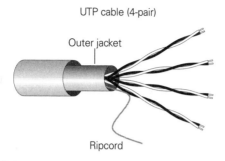

UTP cable (4-pair)

Outer jacket

Ripcord

FIGURE 11.3 Cross section of unshielded twisted-pair wiring (UTP)

attenuation. Fiber-optic cabling is expensive and is typically used in large local area networks (LANs) as the backbone among smaller networks using coaxial or twisted-pair cabling. Figure 11.4 shows a cross section of a fiber-optic cable.

Wireless Cells

Although no physical wires are involved with wireless communications, wireless networks can still be disrupted in many ways. Because wireless networks use a common frequency band—typically in the 2.4 GHz range—they can suffer from interference from other devices that use those frequencies, such as cordless phones and microwave ovens.

Another problem is that the overlapping of wireless cells can cause disruptions in communications, especially when a user is tied to a specific access point. An *access point* is a wireless base station that connects the wireless clients to a wired network. A *cell* is a specific area of influence of that access point or other cellular system base station. Users suffer signal degradation as they travel farther

Outer covering

Optical fiber

Glass cladding

FIGURE 11.4 Cross section of a fiber-optic cable

from the access point. The ranges for wireless access points are typically 500 feet indoors and 1,000 feet outdoors.

Local Lingo

Wireless Cell   A division of wireless networks containing a certain amount of frequencies that can be used.

Fire Suppression

Although this, typically, is already part of your facility plans, fire suppression for a computer environment can be different from techniques used to protect building structures and their contents. The most obvious difference is this: when suppressing a fire in a computer facility that's filled with a large number of electronic servers, personal computers, laptops, printers, and network devices, the use of water can be as damaging as the fire itself. Other effects of a fire, such as smoke and high temperatures, can also be damaging to computer equipment. The key elements of fire protection are early detection and suppression.

Early detection is a must in preventing fires from escalating from a small, minor fire to a raging inferno. Timing is of the essence and you can detect a fire in several ways.

Smoke Detection   *Smoke detectors* are the most common form of warning device. Through the use of optical or photoelectric technology, a beam of light is emitted and the smoke detector sets off an alarm if it detects a change in the light's intensity. As smoke filters into the unit, it senses the changes in the light pattern.

Flame Detection   A *flame detection unit* can sense the movements of a flame or detect the energy that's a result of combustion. Flame detection units tend to be more expensive than other options and they're typically used in high-security environments that require advanced fire-detection techniques.

Heat Detection   *Heat detector units* can detect fires by sensing when a predetermined temperature threshold has been reached. Once the temperature from the fire grows to a certain level, the alarm is triggered. Heat detector units can also detect rapid changes of temperature that indicate the presence of a fire.

Once a fire is detected, a mechanism must be initiated to suppress the fire. A fire can be suppressed in several ways, each with its own positive and negative aspects, depending on the type of fire and the environment of the location.

Water *Water* is the most common type of fire suppressant but, for computer facilities that contain a large amount of electrical equipment, water can also be damaging. The use of water during an electrical fire can make the fire worse, causing even more damage. Water sprinkler systems usually consist of sprinkler heads that are distributed evenly throughout the area to provide maximum coverage. The detection system should be configured to shut down the electrical supply before the water sprinklers turn on. Four main types of water sprinkler systems exist.

- **Dry Pipe** In a *dry pipe* system, water isn't released into the pipe until the alarm sounds. A delayed release valve turns the sprinklers on when filled and ready. This type of system is helpful in a false alarm because the system can be turned off before water is released.

- **Wet Pipe** In a *wet pipe* system, the system already contains water in the pipes that's released when a predetermined temperature is reached. This is the most common method and is considered the most reliable. The disadvantage of a wet pipe system is the possibility of the pipes freezing during cold weather and the water damage that can be caused by a broken or a faulty nozzle.

- **Preaction** The *preaction* system is a more expensive method, which combines the characteristics of the wet and dry pipe systems. Water is released into the pipes only when a predefined temperature is reached. The sprinkler system is initiated when a contact link on the nozzle has melted because of the fire and heat. This prevents water damage from false alarms or allows time to suppress smaller fires with conventional methods, such as a fire extinguisher.

- **Deluge** A *deluge* system is simply a dry-pipe architecture with nozzles that are left fully open to allow a maximum amount of water to be released. This is rarely used in computing environments because of the large amount of water damage that can occur.

Halon *Halon* is a special fire-suppressing gas that can neutralize the chemical combustion of a fire. Halon acts quickly, and it causes no damage to computers and electrical equipment. This is a good alternative to using water, which can quickly damage computer systems as much as the fire itself. Unfortunately, because of its environmental drawbacks, including depletion of ozone and the possibility of danger to humans when used in large amounts, Halon is no longer manufactured. Halon still currently exists in some building installations, though, if they were installed before restrictions on Halon were put in place. Several safe replacements exist for Halon, such as FM-200, and Argon.

✓**Objective 11.01: Physical Security** Physical security of your building includes both access control to your facilities and environmental controls, which maintain the safety and operating conditions of your workplace. *Access control methods* include the use of physical barriers, locks, access cards, biometrics, and surveillance and monitoring equipment. Environmental protection involves temperature and humidity management, proper ventilation, electrical protection, and fire suppression.

REVIEW QUESTIONS

1. Which of the following biometric methods is considered the most secure?

   A. Signature analysis

   B. Voice scan

   C. Palm/Fingerprint

   D. None of the above

2. You finished working on your laptop and you're going out for a one-hour lunch. What should you do before leaving?

   A. Tell a coworker to keep an eye on your laptop

   B. Log out of the laptop

   C. Shut it down and close the lid

   D. Ensure your laptop is secured to your desk or locked away in a cabinet

3. A user, claiming to be a manager, calls you on the phone, claims to have lost their password, and needs access immediately. What should you do?

A. Provide access immediately, and then check their credentials

B. Create a temporary login and password for them to use

C. Verify their identity before providing access

D. Give them your own password temporarily

4. For a new facility, you're asked to plan out special security considerations for a computer and networking room. Which of the following characteristics is the most important?

A. Creating proximity to the network administrator's desk

B. Providing adequate heating control

C. Installing only one secured access door to the room

D. Adding special nonstatic carpeting

5. In a power brownout, which of the following devices would be the most useful in maintaining proper power levels?

A. Backup power generator

B. UPS

C. Line conditioner

D. Power bar

6. Interference caused by the electrical signals of one wire disrupting the signals of another wire in a cable is called what?

A. Crosstalk

B. Attenuation

C. Spike

D. Surge

7. What is the primary purpose of an uninterruptible power supply (UPS)?

A. To provide power supply redundancy within a network server

B. To provide continuous power until the main power is restored

C. To provide temporary power to allow the safe shutdown of a system

D. To regulate and control power levels to prevent fluctuation

8. Which of the following types of network cabling is most resistant to EMI?

   A. Fiber-optic

   B. STP

   C. UTP

   D. Coaxial cable

9. A water-based fire suppression system, where the water to be released is already present in the piping system, is called what?

   A. Wet Pipe system

   B. Dry Pipe system

   C. Deluge system

   D. Preaction system

10. Which of the following fire-suppressing agents is the safest for both electronic equipment and personnel?

    A. Halon

    B. FM-200

    C. Water

    D. Sand

REVIEW ANSWERS

1. **C**   The uniqueness of each person's palm and fingerprints makes this method the most accurate and secure of biometric systems. Signatures and voices are much easier to duplicate and forge.

2. **D**   A passerby can remove a laptop unnoticed from an area in the blink of an eye. To prevent theft, the laptop should be always locked in place or stored away out of sight if you're going to be away for any length of time.

3. **C**   The user could be unauthorized. They might be using social engineering to try tricking you into giving them access to the system. Always verify the user's identity through other types of identification before allowing access.

4. **C**   To prevent unauthorized access, the room should have only one door, secured by a special lock or access system. This can only be planned during the prebuilding phase.

5. **C** This device is situated between the power source and the equipment. The line conditioner ensures the power coming from the source is at constant levels. Options, such as UPSs and power bars, typically don't offer this protection.

6. **A** Crosstalk is caused by the electrical signals of a wire in a cable interfering with the signals of another nearby wire. This is most pronounced in the twisted-pair type of cabling.

7. **C** A UPS battery typically contains only enough power to run a system for about ten to twenty minutes. This allows enough time for the systems to be safely shut down before the power runs out. Some UPSs have software that controls this shutdown automatically.

8. **A** Because this type of cabling media uses light to transfer information over the cable, fiber-optic cables aren't susceptible to electromagnetic interference.

9. **A** The piping on a wet pipe system is already filled with water in case of a fire. The disadvantages of this system are false alarms, and broken sprinkler heads that activate the system and cause water damage. Other types of systems fill the pipes with water only after the alarm is sounded and they release the water when the temperature reaches a certain point.

10. **B** Although Halon is much safer than water when extinguishing a fire near electrical equipment, it's considered dangerous to humans in high levels. Halon isn't manufactured any more and FM-200 is now one of the preferred replacements for Halon in a nonwater-based dire-suppressant system.

Disaster Recovery and Business Continuity

	NEWBIE	SOME EXPERIENCE	EXPERT
ETA	4 hours	2 hours	1 hour

Disaster recovery and business continuity are subjects often avoided by management personnel because of the added costs and time to put together a disaster recovery plan that adds little value to the company's bottom line. Unfortunately, when a disaster strikes and a company is unprepared for such natural disasters as fires, floods, earthquakes, and tornadoes, as well as unnatural disasters, such as vandalism, theft, hacking, and virus attacks, the final cost of implementing no disaster protection could prove fatal.

The most difficult task is analyzing your company's weaknesses to such risks and identifying the impact it will have on the operations of your business. When it becomes obvious that even a small-scale disaster can send your operations into a tailspin, then you must begin planning an overall disaster recovery plan to prevent such disasters from fully impacting your capability to function as a business. Contingency plans must be created, so representatives from each department know exactly what to do if an emergency occurs. Representatives must be trained thoroughly and the procedures documented carefully. The plan must be tested at least once a year or when company changes require alterations to the original procedures.

Travel Advisory

A disaster recovery plan is essential to protecting your employees, the company's capability to operate, its facilities and equipment, and its vital data.

Objective 12.01 Disaster Recovery

A disaster, although rare, can be fatal to any business that doesn't prepare for such an emergency. Even interruptions on a small scale, such as system or network outages, can quickly incur huge financial costs and a damaged reputation to customers. Many studies have shown that a majority of businesses who suffer a service interruption lasting more than one week are never able to recover and, consequently, go out of business.

Critical to a company's preparedness is having a proper backup and disaster recovery plan. Without any sort of data backup, a company risks having its entire data store wiped out forever. In most cases, this would cause the company to go under immediately or face a long rebuilding stage until it can be operational again.

A well-defined disaster recovery plan is coupled with a backup strategy. Although the expense and planning for such a large disaster can be costly and time-consuming because of the dedication of resources and equipment costs, it must be compared to the costs involved with losing the capability to do business for many days or even for weeks and months.

Backups

The most critical disaster recovery procedure that should be performed every day is data backup. The financial and productivity loss resulting from a large corruption or destruction of important data can be enormous. The relatively inexpensive nature of a good backup infrastructure far outweighs the result of the unrecoverable loss of vital company data. A good backup strategy must be clearly planned, defined, executed, documented, and tested.

Travel Advisory

One of the most important aspects of a backup strategy is regularly testing backups by performing test restores. Remember, your backups are no good unless you know the information can be restored.

Planning

The first step in establishing your backup strategy is to draft a plan that covers the following points.

Type of Data   Your company's data must be separated into what's considered as mission-critical data and more constant data that doesn't change much over time. Obviously, the most important data is the information the company requires during its daily business activities, especially if this information is something frequently accessed by customers. For example, a database company will ensure it fully protects its customer's data. If the company loses that data without any procedure for disaster recovery, its business is essentially lost.

Frequency   Depending on your type of data, a wide range of backup frequency schedules can be implemented. For example, a transactional database used every day by customers would be considered critical data that must be backed up every day. Other files such as operating system (OS) and application program files that don't change often can be backed up on a lighter schedule, say, once a week. Your frequency should depend on the critical nature of the data, as well as the costs involved with losing and re-creating data from the same point in time. Some high-end transactional databases need to be backed up many times a day because of the high rate of transactions.

Size of Data   The amount of data to be backed up will have a large bearing on the type of backup strategy you choose. Depending on how much information you need to save on a daily basis, you might be unable to perform a completely full backup of all your data every night because of the time it takes to perform the operation. To create a backup plan that can meet your objectives, a balance must be created between the type of data and the frequency with which it needs to be backed up. Instead of using full backups, other alternatives such as performing incremental or differential backups on information that has only recently changed can be used instead.

Retention   A decision must be made on how long you need to keep your backed-up data. Depending on the type of business and the type of data, you might need to archive your backup for long periods of time, so it will be available if you need to perform a restore. Other data might only be needed in the short term and this can be deleted after a certain period of time.

Travel Advisory

The legal policy of some companies is to retain information for a certain period of time before the information must be destroyed. Check with your legal department to create a policy for backup tape retention.

Backup Hardware

Several types of backup hardware and devices are available to suit the needs of the backup strategies of most companies. The most common type of backup system uses magnetic tape. These can be simple devices that only contain one tape drive to large jukebox tape libraries with robotic autoloaders. Magnetic tape drives and media are flexible, and offer relatively inexpensive storage, combined with speed and ease of use.

Other devices include the use of optical devices, such as CD and DVD-ROMs. These, however, are typically used for more permanent archival purposes, rather than everyday backup.

Backup hardware should be routinely inspected for faults. Because of their mechanical nature, backup hardware is more prone to failure than typical electrical devices. Magnetic tape drives should be cleaned periodically with a special cleaning tape to clean the magnetic heads that become dirty over time.

Backup Types

An important part of your backup strategy is deciding what type of backup you'll perform. Depending on the size of all the data you need to back up on a daily basis, it might be impossible to do a full backup of everything every night. The amount of backup media required and the time needed to perform the backup can render this option unfeasible. The goal is to achieve the most efficient backup plan possible, depending on your environment and the type of data to be backed up.

Each file on a computer system contains a special bit of information, called the *archive bit*. When a file is modified or a new file is created, the archive bit is set to indicate the file needs to be backed up. When a backup is performed, the archive bit is either cleared or left as is, depending on the type of backup method chosen.

Full Backup   A *full backup* will back up all files selected on a system. A full backup will clear the archive bit of each file after every session. The advantages of a full backup include the fact that all data you selected is saved during every session, so all your system's data is backed up in full. If you need to restore all the information back on to the server, the recovery time is much shorter because it's saved in a specific backup session. For example, if you perform a full backup on Wednesday night and the server crashes the next morning, your data loss will be minimal. The disadvantage of using a full backup is this: depending on the amount of data you have, the backup could take up a large amount of media and the time it takes to perform the backup could intrude on normal working hours, causing network delays and system latency.

Incremental Backup   With an *incremental backup*, only those files that have been modified since the previous backup are saved. The archive bit is cleared on those files that are backed up. Incremental backups are much quicker to perform than full backups and they use up much less backup media because you're only saving files that have been changed. The disadvantage of incremental backups is that to restore an entire system, you need to restore the last full backup and every incremental backup since then.

Differential Backup   A *differential backup* saves only files that have been changed since the last full backup. In this method, the archive bit isn't cleared so, with each differential backup, the list of files to save grows larger each day until the next full backup. The advantage of differential backups is that to restore an entire system, you only need the last full backup and the most recent differential backup. The disadvantage is the backups will take more time and use more media with each differential backup that takes place.

> **Exam Tip**
>
> Be aware of the advantages and disadvantages of each type of backup method, depending on the environment.

Media Rotation and Retention

Another important factor in your backup plan is determining the length of time that backup media and its data should be retained. Theoretically, you could save every backup tape you create forever, but this increases costs because of the large amount of backup media you'll need to purchase on a routine basis. Magnetic tape media usually deteriorates over time and, if you constantly use the same tapes over and over, they'll quickly wear out. The integrity of your backups might be compromised if you continue to use these tapes.

Media rotation and retention policies must be defined to form the most efficient and safe use of your backup media. Several methods can be used for rotation and retention, from simple to the most complex.

Son Backup Method   The *son backup method* is the simplest to use because it involves performing a full backup every day, using the same backup media each time. This method is only used for small backup requirements. The media can quickly wear out and must consistently be replaced. This method doesn't allow for archiving and, if you need to perform a restore, you can only use your last backup as a source. If the file you're looking for was deleted months ago, it can't be recovered.

Father-Son Backup Method   The *father-son backup method* uses a combination of full and differential or incremental backups on a weekly basis. For example, daily tapes are used for a differential or incremental backup from Monday to Thursday, while a Friday or weekend tape is used to perform a full backup. This method enables you to retrieve files archived from the previous week, using the weekly full backup. More tapes can be added to the strategy if further archiving is needed.

Grandfather-Father-Son Backup Method   The most common backup strategy is the *grandfather-father-son method*. This method is easy to administer and offers flexible archiving. Similar to the father-son method, daily backup media are assigned for incremental or differential backups. At the end of the week, a full backup is made, which is kept for one month. At the end of the month, a special monthly backup can be made, which is then kept for one year. This method enables you to archive data for at least a year.

Documentation

Your backup plan should be carefully documented, so if the primary backup operator is unavailable, another person can perform the backup operator's functions, such as changing tapes, sending tapes offsite, performing restores, and examining backup log files. The document should outline what systems are backed up, how often they're backed up and by what method, and the location and directories of the data. The documentation should also describe any special media labeling used and contact information for any offsite storage facilities.

The documentation should be constantly reviewed and updated when new hardware and software are installed. New systems with new data must be added to your backup routine immediately.

Travel Advisory

When adding a new system or a directory/file to a network server, ensure it's added to your backup schedule.

Restoration

The ultimate goal of any backup system is the capability to restore lost or corrupted data from the backup media. Amazing to note is most companies don't test the backups they've made. The only true way of testing a backup system is to perform routine test restores. Although your backup application logs might show no problems exist and backups have completed successfully, a hardware problem could exist with the tape drive that causes the written data to be corrupted.

When performing regular file restoration, the best practice is not to overwrite any original files of the ones you're trying to restore. Create a separate directory and restore the file there. This way, the user can decide which version they need. If the original file and directory have been completely deleted, then there's no need for this extra step.

All your backup media should be properly labeled so, in case of an emergency—where time is of the essence—the correct tape containing the data can be quickly located and restored.

Travel Advisory

Some tape autoloader systems come with a bar-code reader, so tapes can be labeled with bar codes for easier cataloging and searching.

Offsite Storage

In case of a disaster at your primary site, such as fire or a flood, your backup tapes stored there could also be destroyed. All the data that's saved to backup tape will be lost and you won't have other backups to fall back on. Offsite storage is an important part of your overall disaster recovery plan. Using an offsite storage facility means after you successfully complete your backups, they're sent to a different location, which could be another office building or a special storage company facility.

> ### Travel Advisory
> In case you want to keep your most recent backup media onsite, you can make two copies of your full backup, and then send one of them to the offsite storage company and keep the other. Creating the extra backup requires extra time and backup media, however.

When choosing an offsite storage facility, you must ensure it follows the same basic rules of facility security measures as you'd follow at your own site. You should visit the location where your backup media will be stored to examine the environment. For example, the storage area should be regulated for temperature, humidity, fire prevention, and static electricity prevention. Access control should be strictly enforced, so only authorized employees of your company can retrieve tapes from the facility. Depending on the type of data you're sending offsite, you should identify how quickly you'll need access to the tapes, if and when necessary. The storage facility should allow access at all hours in case you need a backup in an emergency.

Secure Recovery

The capability to recover from a disaster is greatly dependent on the facilities and equipment available if your main facility is heavily damaged or destroyed. Backup equipment and facilities are vital elements in planning for recovery. They should be examined for both onsite and offsite strategies.

Onsite Alternatives

Most disasters and disruptions are localized in nature and, typically, only involve one room or even one particular piece of equipment. Failed hardware is the most common type of service interruption, such as blown power supplies, damaged network cabling, failed hard drives, and broken tape backup drives.

Having spare hardware onsite to fix these small problems is vital to handling these smaller disruptions quickly. Many companies have vendor maintenance contracts that require the vendor to replace failed hardware but, in case of an emergency, the spare parts might not be delivered for many hours or even days. It's vital for hardware components that are commonly prone to failure to be switched quickly with an onsite spare. The following spare components should be kept onsite at all times:

- Hard drives
- RAID controllers
- SCSI controllers
- Hard-drive ribbon cabling
- Memory
- CPU
- Network cards
- Keyboard/mouse
- Video cards
- Monitor
- Power supplies
- Network switches, hubs, and routers
- Phone sets

For servers and computers, having spare server machines and PCs available to replace failed units is critical. For example, failed file server hardware can be quickly replaced and the data restored from backup. For expensive server machines, this might not be feasible but, for lower-end servers and desktops, it offers a fairly inexpensive way of replacing failed equipment immediately.

Alternate Sites

In case of a physical disaster, such as a fire or a flood, at your main company site, you need alternate facilities to house backup equipment to get your company operational again. In some cases, your original server and networking equipment could be damaged or destroyed, and then a new infrastructure must be created at a new site. For a company with no alternate site in its disaster recovery plan, this could mean many weeks before a facility is secured, and then new equipment must be set up in the new building. The purpose of alternate sites is to have a facility already secured and, in some cases, already populated with a network and server infrastructure to minimize downtime. The choice of alternate sites will come down to how time-sensitive your company's product or services are and how fast you need to be operational again.

Hot Site   A *hot site* is a facility that's ready to be operational within a short period of time. All equipment and networking infrastructure the company requires are already in place and can be activated quickly. The equipment should duplicate the setup installed in the original building. The hot site facility is usually provided by another company, which hosts your equipment. Hot sites should be tested frequently to ensure the switchover runs smoothly and quickly. This is an expensive solution, but for companies that offer critical services, the costs of losing money and customers during an extended downtime would be quickly recovered.

Warm Site   A *warm site* is similar to a hot site, but without most of the duplicate servers and computers that would be needed to facilitate an immediate switchover. The warm site is there to provide an immediate facility with some minimal networking in place. In case of a disaster, a company will transport its own equipment to the new facility or if the original equipment is destroyed with the facility, new equipment must be purchased and moved there. A warm site could take several days to bring the business back to full operation, so this makes more sense for companies who don't offer time-critical services. This is the most widely used alternate site option because of its relatively lower price compared to hot sites and its flexibility. The disadvantage of a warm site is it's not immediately available after a disaster and it isn't easily tested.

Cold Site   A *cold site* merely offers an empty facility with some basic features, such as wiring, and some environmental protection, but no equipment. This is the least expensive option, but this also means in case a disaster strikes, it might take several weeks before the facility and equipment are ready for operation. This is because almost all the networking and server infrastructure needs to be built and configured.

Exam Tip	
Be aware of the advantages and disadvantages of the different types of alternate sites, depending on your environment.	

Disaster Recovery Plan

Although the chances of a large disaster, whatever the cause, interrupting or halting business operations are fairly slim, all companies should be prepared for such an event. Most management personnel pay little attention to the subject because the expense and amount of work involved in creating a disaster recovery plan does little for the financial bottom line of the company. The reality of the threat, however, can have dire financial consequences on a company that isn't prepared.

The purpose of a disaster recovery plan is to prepare your company for a potential disaster. A detailed document can provide an initial analysis of the risks involved to the business because of a disaster, the potential business impact, and a contingency plan for restoring full operation.

The process of creating a disaster recovery plan includes the following phases:

- Creation of a disaster recovery team
- Risk analysis
- Business impact analysis
- Contingency plan
- Documentation
- Testing

Exam Tip

Ensure you know the different parts that make up a full disaster recovery plan and how each one relates to your overall procedures.

Disaster Recovery Team

The purpose of forming a disaster recovery team is to establish a central team responsible for executing the disaster recovery plan in case of an emergency situation. The team is responsible for creating, maintaining, and executing the plan, which outlines the goals to restore company operations and functionality as quickly as possible following a disaster. The disaster recovery team is also there to provide for the safety and support of the rest of the company's personnel and the protection of company property.

The team should include members from all departments, including management. Including all areas of the company's operations is important because each department has its own objectives and goals, depending on its function. These disaster recovery duties should be included in the job description of each department, even though this goes over and above regular duties. Designated backup team members should also be designated in case the original person isn't available to perform their function.

In a disaster, each team member is responsible for certain priorities and goals, which could include coordination of other department personnel, contact with outside emergency agencies, and equipment and service vendors. The bulk of the work will be the responsibility of the IT staff who need to coordinate the creation of a communications and networking infrastructure, as well as restore all system functionality, including the restoration of lost data.

Risk Analysis

A *risk analysis* identifies the areas of your facility and computer network that are vulnerable to certain types of disasters. The entire business operation of the company must be broken down and analyzed, so the impact of a disaster on a critical business function can be ascertained.

A risk analysis evaluates the potential outcome of any type of disaster on your company's infrastructure. All possible scenarios must be analyzed in full. For example, in case a flood strikes the area where the main company building is located, your facility must be carefully examined for areas that would be affected by this particular disaster. Similar analysis must be made for other potential disasters, such as earthquakes, fire, and unnatural disasters, such as software and hardware failure, hacking, or virus attack.

Diagrams of the facility must be created or obtained, such as building blueprints, seating plans, network cabling maps, and hardware and software inventory. The effect of each disaster scenario should be more easily ascertained with the aid of these diagrams.

When you finish, you'll have a detailed document outlining the possible risks for each type of disaster that might occur. Using this information, you can formulate a business impact analysis that will show how those risks can affect your business functionality.

Business Impact Analysis

A *business impact analysis* will outline your most critical functions and how they'll be affected during a disaster. The analysis will examine the loss of revenue, legal obligations, and customer service interruption that can arise as the result of a disaster. Your most important business functions should be prioritized so, during the disaster recovery process, they'll receive the attention needed to get them operational before any noncritical aspects of the business.

Exam Tip
Business functions should be prioritized so, in case of a disaster, they'll be made operational before other less-critical functions.

The business impact analysis should also include timelines on how long it will take to get the company operational again if a disaster occurs. The resources, equipment, and personnel required should be carefully detailed, especially the capability to recover and restore vital company information from backups.

Most important will be examining the total financial loss incurred by certain types of disasters. If it isn't prepared, the company probably won't survive a disaster that completely halts its operations. This information can be provided to management, who might help fund and organize a disaster recovery plan, based on the statistics of the impact of a disaster. Many companies don't like spending the time or expense on disaster recovery, but when the cost of the impact is analyzed and calculated, the capability to be prepared for a disaster will quickly pay for itself, if and when the time comes.

Types of Disasters

Many types of disasters can befall a company. Many disasters are small and inconvenient, only affecting a certain part of the company or only one server. They might only affect communications or software applications. Larger disasters can be devastating, causing the destruction of most or all of the company's physical facility.

Natural   Natural disasters, although rare, can be the most devastating emergency to affect your business. A natural disaster, such as fire, flood, earthquake, tornado, or hurricanes, can destroy your building and its infrastructure within minutes. The only way the company can be truly protected is if its data is regularly backed up and sent to an offsite location. Your company furniture and computer equipment can be relatively quickly replaced, but sensitive company data collected over many years can't.

Human Error and Sabotage   Something as simple as a mistakenly deleted file can cause a company much grief if that data is critical to the business operation. A spilled cup of coffee can render a server unusable within seconds. Human errors and mistakes can be expected and are much more common than natural disasters. Vandalism and sabotage, however, can be quite unexpected, but cause great damage. Theft or malicious destruction of company equipment by a disgruntled employee can cause as much damage as any natural disaster. The need for access controls and physical security is emphasized with these types of disasters.

Hacking   Cybertheft and vandalism are an increasingly annoying and dangerous problem for companies, especially those whose business is Internet-related. When a company is connected to the Internet permanently, it opens the door for unauthorized users to attempt to gain access to company resources. Some hacking attempts are simply a chance to try gaining access to a system for fun. More malicious unauthorized users might cause widespread damage within the company's network if they gain access. Some attacks could even come from within the network. A security professional will need to analyze threats coming from both outside and inside the network.

Viruses   Computer viruses are special programs able to replicate themselves, and often perform malicious activities on networks, servers, and personal computers. Viruses can be extremely destructive, causing massive network outages, computer crashes, and corruption or loss of data. Once one computer is infected with the virus, it can quickly spread to other computers and servers on the network. E-mail-based viruses can be spread quickly in a short amount of time. Protection against viruses includes the use of special antivirus software at both the personal computer and server level. User education about the computer viruses is also key to virus prevention.

Travel Advisory

Hacking and viruses are probably the most common disasters that befall a business. An e-mail virus can spread so fast it can overload your e-mail servers within a matter of minutes after initial infection.

Contingency Plan

As part of your disaster recovery process, a contingency plan must be put in place, so specific goals are defined and prioritized. This will result in clear objectives that must be met during the recovery phase.

Responsibilities must be clearly defined for those important individuals participating in the recovery as part of the disaster recovery team. Tasks should be divided and assigned to the appropriate people and departments. Each individual must be trained on the specific procedures and have them properly documented. Team leaders must be established; central authorities can guide the recovery process through each of its critical steps.

Decisions must be made on which aspect of the business is the most critical and must be up-and-running first if a disaster occurs. Different departments in the company have different objectives and priorities, but certain functions can be delayed if they don't immediately impact the capability of the company to function. Typically, the most important part of the company to get operational is basic communications, such as phone, fax, networking connectivity, and e-mail. Until these communication lines are functional, the capability to coordinate the disaster recovery effort will be greatly reduced, causing much confusion and chaos. Business critical items should come next, such as file servers, database servers, and Internet servers that run the company's main applications or anything specifically needed by a customer.

The capability for the company to restore full operations as quickly as possible depends on the efficiency with which objectives and goals, outlined in the contingency plan, are met.

Documentation

Each phase of the disaster recovery plan should be carefully documented and the resulting document should be readily available to all members of the disaster recovery team. The document should also be safely stored in both hard copy and software copies to prevent damage to, or loss of, the document. In case of a real disaster, a lack of documentation will cause nothing but chaos because no one will know how to get all aspects of the company running again, especially during a stressful and frantic time.

The disaster recovery plan must be precise and detailed, so anyone can follow the instructions without further clarification. Each person in the disaster recovery team will have clear responsibilities and duties that must be performed in the most efficient manner possible.

The plan should include the following items:

- **Notification lists**   A list of people and businesses to notify in case of a disaster.
- **Contact information**   Phone numbers and contact information for employees, vendors, data recovery agencies, and offsite facilities.
- **Networking and facilities diagrams**   Diagrams and blueprints of all networking and facilities infrastructure, so it can be re-created on the new site.
- **System configurations**   Configuration information for all servers, applications, and networking equipment.
- **Backup restoration procedures**   Step-by-step information on how to restore data from the backup media.

Finally, copies of the disaster recovery plan should be stored onsite and in an offsite facility, especially any designated alternative company site. If a physical disaster strikes your main facility, the plan will be useless if it's destroyed along with the building.

Exam Tip

Be aware of the types of information that should be documented in your plans.

Testing

To complete your disaster recovery plan, it must be fully tested to ensure all parts of the plan work as they should. Re-creating a disaster without affecting the current operations of your company might be difficult, but some form of test should be performed at least once a year.

Most disaster recovery tests involve the choice of a scenario, such as a fire in a certain part of the building. Your disaster recovery team must consult the recovery plan documentation and execute it accordingly. Depending on the size of the company, it might be feasible to involve only certain departments, but this should always include the IT department, whose main responsibilities are the network infrastructure and data recovery. During the testing, every phase should be fully documented through the use of a checklist. Any exceptions or problems encountered during the procedure should be thoroughly documented.

Once the test has been completed, the original disaster recovery plan should be reviewed for any procedures that didn't work correctly or need to be modified as a result of the test. The plan should be updated with any new information as a result of the testing. Any changes to the existing facilities or infrastructure should initiate a review of the current disaster recovery procedures. Any changes should be made immediately to reflect the new environment.

Objective 12.02 Business Continuity

As part of your disaster recovery program, other considerations exist for the protection of your network data and services. Most important is the continuation of your business activities in case of equipment failure or destruction. As part of your overall disaster recovery planning, the use of high-availability and fault-tolerant systems should be implemented. This involves implementing disaster recovery techniques at the system level. *High availability* is a term used to define a set of services and systems that must be available at all times.

Many companies measure their capability to provide services as a *service level*. For example, a web-server hosting company might promise 99 percent service availability when the systems and services it hosts are available. The other 1 percent of the time, the systems might be unavailable because of maintenance, equipment failure, or network downtime.

> ## Local Lingo
>
> **Service Level**   Specifies in measurable terms the level of service to be received, such as the percentage of time when services are available. Many Internet service providers (ISPs) provide their customers with a service-level agreement to guarantee a minimum level of service. Some IT departments now provide a measured service level to the rest of the company.

Maintaining a high availability is the premier goal of most businesses that guarantee access to data, and host services and content that must be always available to the customer. Fault-tolerance defines how able your system is to recover from software or hardware errors and failure. For example, a server that only contains one hard drive and one power supply isn't fault-tolerant. If the power supply fails, the entire server will be rendered useless because there's no power to the system. Similarly, if your hard drive crashes and is unrecoverable, all your data on that hard drive will be lost. Fault-tolerant systems are another important way to maintain business continuity.

High-Availability Utilities

Many special business continuity utilities are available that can be used to enhance systems with high-availability and fault-tolerance capabilities. Some of the most popular software utilities are those used for clustering. *Clustering* enables you to use several servers to perform the services of one. Clustering greatly enhances load balancing, as the resources of all the servers can be used to perform the same task as one server. Clustering can be also used for fault tolerance, so if one system goes down, one of the other servers in the cluster can take over.

Other utilities can be used to take clustering to the next level, where failover systems are located in buildings of other company locations. For example, a company operating in Los Angeles might have another facility operating in New York. Special software can be used to allow the servers in New York to take over the services offered by the Los Angeles servers if they suffer an interruption or disaster.

High Availability and Fault Tolerance

High availability and *fault tolerance* are extremely important factors in maintaining business continuity in case of equipment or communications failure. Protecting your information from corruption or data loss is vital in maintaining your capability to provide vital services. High availability and fault tolerance are implemented at the system level to provide redundancy, data protection, and maintain system uptime.

High Availability

The capability to provide uninterrupted service consistently is the goal of maintaining a high-availability system. This initially requires identifying which of your systems need to provide services at all times. The following questions must be answered when planning for high availability systems:

- What is the monetary cost of an extended service downtime?
- What is the cost to a customer relationship that can happen as a result of an extended service downtime directly affecting that customer?
- Which services must be available at all times? Rank them in order of priority.

If you host a number of services needed by customers, they should be given higher priority than your own systems because the service level you promised the customer must be maintained at all times.

The most common examples of servers and services that require high availability include the following:

- **Internet servers**   These include Internet services, such as web and FTP servers. These types of servers usually require their information and data to be available at all times.
- **E-mail**   E-mail is the most commonly used Internet service because all users need and use e-mail. Therefore, e-mail servers and gateways must maintain high levels of service availability.
- **Networking**   As the backbone of all computer communications, the networking equipment that provides the infrastructure for private and public networks must be available at all times.
- **File servers**   File servers house all data and information needed by the users. Without access to this data, users can't perform their job functions.
- **Database servers**   Usually required as back-end servers to web servers and other applications that use database transactions. Database servers, like file servers, must have their data available at all times.

To protect your computer and network equipment, and to provide redundancy to maintain high-availability service, the use of fault-tolerant systems must be implemented.

Fault Tolerance

To make a system fault tolerant, the system should contain a number of redundant components that will allow it to continue functioning if an equipment failure occurs. For example, a file server can be configured with two network cards. In case one network card fails, network communications can continue uninterrupted through the second network card. To ensure data integrity, it isn't enough to implement redundant hardware components, such as power supplies and network cards. The use of fault-tolerant Redundant Array of Independent Disks (RAID) systems is required to allow multiple copies of the same data to be saved across multiple disk media, so data won't be corrupted if one of the hard drives fails.

Local Lingo

RAID   Redundant Array of Independent Disks. Defines the concept of using a number of separate hard drives to create one logical drive. If one of the drives fails, the system can rebuild the information using the remaining disks.

Some fault-tolerant concepts must be understood before implementation:

- **Hot Swap**   Refers to the capability to insert and remove hardware while the entire system is still running. Most types of hardware require that the system be shut down before removing or inserting components. Hard drives in RAID systems are the most common type of hot swap device.

- **Warm Swap**   Refers to the capability to insert and remove hardware while a system is in a suspended state. Although less flexible than a hot-swap device, the capability to warm swap means you needn't shut the entire server down to replace hardware components. When the swap is complete, the server resumes its normal operations. Although services are shut down during the suspend, time is saved by not having to reboot the entire system.

- **Hot Spare**   Refers to a device already installed in the system that can take over at any time when the primary device fails. There's no need to physically insert or remove a hot spare device.

The following sections outline the types of system components that can be made fault tolerant.

Hard Drives   *Hard drives* are partly mechanical in nature. This makes a hard drive one of the most common components prone to failure on a server. The hard drives contain all the data and information and, if the hard drive fails, that data can be irretrievably lost.

> **Travel Advisory**
>
> If a hard drive fails or its data is corrupted, the information it contains can sometimes be retrieved by special hard-drive recovery specialists. This recovery process can be both lengthy and expensive.

The most common method of hard-drive redundancy is to use a RAID system. RAID allows data to spread across two or more hard drives so, if one hard drive fails, the data can be retrieved from the existing hard drives. Mirroring the contents of one hard drive on another is called *RAID 1.* Several RAID levels can be implemented, depending on the number of disks you have and the importance of the information being stored. Other RAID techniques include *striping,* which spreads the contents of a logical hard drive across several physical drives and includes parity information to help rebuild the data. If one of the hard drives fails, parity information is used to reconstruct the data. Most RAID systems use hot swap drives, which can be inserted and removed while the system is still running. To increase the fault tolerance of a RAID system, redundant RAID controllers can be installed to remove the disk controller as a single point of failure. Table 12.1 describes the most common RAID levels and their characteristics.

Power Supplies   Because of their electrical nature, power supplies are another one of the most common computer components prone to failure. As the central source of power for any computer or network device, a blown power supply can instantly render a critical computer system useless. Most modern servers come with multiple power supplies, which are running as hot spares. In

TABLE 12.1	Most Common RAID Levels	
RAID Level	**Minimum Number of Hard Drives**	**Characteristics**
0	2	Striping only, no fault tolerance
1	2	Disk mirroring
3	3	Disk striping with a parity disk
5	3	Disk striping, distributed parity
0+1	4	Disk striping with mirroring

case one of the power supplies fails, the other will immediately take over without an interruption in service. Some high-end servers have as many as three extra power supplies. Many network devices, such as switches and routers, now come with dual power supplies. Replacing a single power supply on such a small, enclosed device would be difficult.

Network Interface Cards   One of the most overlooked fault-tolerant-capable devices in a server system is the *network card*. Typically, little thought is given to the scenario of a failed network card. In the real world, losing connectivity to a server is the same as having the server itself crash because the server's resources can't be accessed. Many modern servers now come preinstalled with redundant network cards. Extra network cards can also be used for load balancing, as well as being available to take over if another network card fails.

CPU   Although central processing unit (CPU) failure is unlikely, this is still a scenario that requires fault-tolerance capabilities, especially for high-availability systems. Many large-scale server systems have multiple CPUs for load-balancing purposes to spread the processing across all CPUs. Extra CPUs, however, can also be used for fault tolerance. If a CPU happens to fail, another one in the system can take over.

UPS   Although redundant power supplies can provide fault tolerance in a server if one of the power supplies fails, they can't protect against the total loss of power from the building's main-power circuits. When this happens, your entire server will immediately shut down, losing any data that wasn't saved or possibly corrupting existing data. In this case, a battery backup is needed. An uninterruptible power supply (UPS) contains a battery that can run a server for a period of time after a power failure, enabling you to shut down the system safely and save any data.

> **Travel Advisory**
>
> Most UPSs come with software that can configure your server to automatically shut down when it detects the UPS has taken over because of a power failure.

Backups

The use of backups as a disaster recovery tool was covered in the earlier section "Backups." The use of backups in a business continuity sense involves not only the backup of important information and data, but also backing up the system files and configuration settings of your server and network equipment.

When equipment failure causes the loss of your server, you not only lose the data and services housed on that server, you also lose all your system settings and configuration. Depending on the type of server, these configuration settings can be complex and can take many hours, or even days, to set everything back to its original configuration. For example, an e-mail server is usually configured with many options and settings that are unique to your location. If the server has failed, or is destroyed and needs to be rebuilt, you'll need to reinstall the OS, install your e-mail server applications, and configure it properly before you can restore your mail files that were backed up to tape. If you didn't back up your system files, you'll need to recall and enter your system settings manually, which can take up too much time when a high-availability server is down.

Most modern backup applications have disaster recovery options that save important elements of the OS and application configuration files that can be instantly restored in case of a disaster. If you're recovering a server, you only need to install the OS and the required media device drivers for your tape driver to retrieve the rest of your server files and system configuration from tape.

CHECKPOINT

✔**Objective 12.01: Disaster Recovery** Perform backups to save and archive critical company data. Full backups are recommended if time and space permit but, if not, use incremental or differential schemes. Periodically test your backups by performing a restore. Consider using alternate sites for disaster recovery purposes. Create a disaster recovery plan that documents your risks, the business impact of a disaster, a contingency plan, and network and facility documentation.

✔**Objective 12.02: Business Continuity** Maintain high availability of your services by implementing redundancy, data integrity protection, and fault tolerance. Use RAID for disk storage systems. Determine the level of RAID redundancy, depending on the importance of the data you're protecting. Keep spare parts of common hardware on hand, so it can be replaced immediately.

REVIEW QUESTIONS

1. Which of the following is a disadvantage of using an incremental backup strategy?

   A. Takes longer than other methods

   B. Uses too much backup media

   C. Restores require all incremental backups since the last full backup

   D. Resets the archive bit after backup

2. Why do backup media need to be rotated?

   A. They slowly wear out after repeated use

   B. Full backups require media rotation

   C. The tapes need to be relabeled after every backup

   D. Rotation is used to reset the archive bit

3. What is the primary purpose of storing backup media at an offsite storage facility?

   A. The facility can copy the data to CD-ROM

   B. If the primary site is down, the offsite storage can reload your systems from backup at their facility

   C. For proper archive labeling and storage

   D. To prevent a disaster from destroying the only copies of your backup media

4. A facility that contains networking and server equipment, and is ready to be operational within a short period of time is referred to as what?

   A. Warm site

   B. Hot site

   C. Cold site

   D. Offsite

5. What is the purpose of a disaster-recovery risk analysis?

   A. To discover which network servers are most likely to fail

   B. To gather information on natural disasters in your area of the country

   C. To know which employees are most likely to be injured in a disaster

   D. To discover what aspects of your company are at risk during a disaster

6. Which of the following would be considered an unnatural disaster?

   A. Flood

   B. Hurricane

   C. Earthquake

   D. Viruses

7. The capability to provide uninterrupted service is referred to as what?

   A. Fault tolerance

   B. High availability

   C. Contingency planning

   D. Business impact analysis

8. The capability to insert and remove hardware while a system is still running is called what?

   A. Cold swap

   B. Suspend swap

   C. Warm swap

   D. Hot swap

9. Which RAID level defines disk mirroring?

   A. RAID 5

   B. RAID 1

   C. RAID 0

   D. RAID 3

10. What device can be used to operate server and network equipment in case a power failure occurs?

    A. RAID

    B. Router

    C. UPS

    D. Cluster

REVIEW ANSWERS

1. **C** In an incremental backup scheme, only files that have changed since the last full or incremental backup are saved. To perform a restore, you need the last full backup and any incremental backups since then.

2. **A** Magnetic tape media degrade after each use. The more times they are used, the more inclined they are to failure.

3. **D** All backup plans should require backup media to be sent to an offsite storage facility. If a disaster destroys your physical location, the backup tapes will be safe.

4. **B** A hot site contains enough networking and server equipment to continue your business operations in case a disaster strikes your primary facility. Warm sites and cold sites contain little to no existing equipment or infrastructure.

5. **D** A risk analysis will examine what parts of your facility and infrastructure are at risk during different types of disaster scenarios. This can help you create a business impact analysis and a contingency plan to avert those risks.

6. **D** A computer virus attack can quickly render your company's computer system useless within minutes and can be as destructive as the effects of a natural disaster, such as a hurricane, flood, or earthquake.

7. **B** The capability to provide uninterrupted service is referred to as high availability. This is important for businesses that require the services or products they offer to be available at all times.

8. **D** A hot swap device, such as a hard drive, can be inserted or removed without the need to shut down the server. This enables you to retain the availability of the services on that server.

9. **B** Disk mirroring is the process in which one hard drive's contents are duplicated on an identical drive in the system. In case the primary drive fails, the mirrored drive will take over.

10. **C** If a power outage occurs, an uninterruptible power supply (UPS) can run the system on battery power for a short period of time, enabling you to bring the systems down normally until power is restored.

Policy Procedures and Privilege Management

	NEWBIE	SOME EXPERIENCE	EXPERT
ETA	3 hours	1.5 hours	0.5 hour

As part of an overall company strategy, security should be officially recognized as a critical business objective, just like any other important business objective. In previous years, the IT department had to define security and access controls for the company network and data. Now that companies are doing business in the Internet world, corporate management had to adapt the legalities of the business world to computer networks by ensuring that electronic transfer of information is secure to protect both the customer and the company.

To ensure security across the organization and to assure customers they can be trusted, companies had to implement several policies and procedures that govern how they use computer networks, how they protect and distribute data, and how they offer services to their customers. These policies and procedures include rules on company Internet use, customer data privacy, company structure, data retention and disposal, and HR hiring and termination practices.

Privilege management is another aspect of company security that includes access controls and how users can interact with data. By assigning access privileges through user, group, and role-based models, and centralizing user account management, access to data can be governed from the top down throughout the organization.

Objective 13.01 Policy and Procedures

For effective security, the creation of security policies and procedures must begin at the top with senior management. These policies and procedures must then follow all the way through the company to ensure that security is useful and functional at every level of the organization. The security of the company must begin with an understanding of the basic laws, regulations, and legal liability issues to which the company must adhere to protect the company and its assets, as well as the employees.

Security policies and procedures are official company guidelines to ensure a standard level of security guidelines exists across the entire organization. These policies define how the employees interact with the computer systems of the company to perform their job function and service the company's clients. The upcoming sections outline policies and procedures in the following areas:

- Network Security Policies
- Access Control Guidelines
- Human Resources Policies

Network Security Policies

There are several policies that provide standard guidelines for network security within a company, and they encompass areas such as the Internet and internal network use, data privacy, and security incident response.

Acceptable Use Policy

An *Acceptable Use Policy* is a set of established guidelines for the appropriate use of computer networks. The policy is a written agreement that outlines the terms, conditions, and rules of the Internet and internal network use for the company, and it's signed by all employees.

An Acceptable Use Policy helps educate your employees about the kinds of tools they will use on the network and what they can expect from those tools. The policy also helps to define boundaries of behavior and, more critically, specify the consequences of violating those boundaries. An Acceptable Use Policy also specifies the actions that management and the system administrators might take to maintain or patrol the network for unacceptable use. They might outline general worse case consequences or specific responses to specific policy violation situations.

Exam Tip
An Acceptable Use Policy is a set of established guidelines for the appropriate use of computer networks.

Developing an Acceptable Use Policy for your company's computer network is important. Acceptable Use Policies should cover the following issues:

- **Legality**   The company's legal department needs to approve the policy before it's distributed for signing. The policy will be used as a legal document. This is to ensure the company isn't legally liable for any type of Internet-related incident and any other transgressions, such as hacking, vandalism, and sabotage.

- **Uniqueness to your environment**   The policy should be written to cover your specific network and the data it contains.

- **Completeness**   Your policy shouldn't only contain the rules of behavior. It should also include a statement concerning the company's position on Internet use.

- **Adaptability**   Because the Internet is constantly evolving, your policy will need to be updated as new issues arise. You can't anticipate every situation, so the Acceptable Use Policy should address the possibility that something could happen that isn't outlined.

- **Protection for employees** If your employees follow the rules of the Acceptable Use Policy, their exposure to questionable materials should be minimized. In addition, it can protect them from dangerous Internet behavior, such as giving out their names and e-mail addresses to strangers.

The focus of an Acceptable Use Policy should be on the responsible use of computer networks. Such networks include the Internet, including web and e-mail access, and the company intranet. Most Acceptable Use Policies contain the following components:

- A description of the strategies and goals to be supported by Internet access in the company
- A statement explaining the availability of computer networks to employees
- A statement explaining the responsibilities of employees when they use the Internet
- A code of conduct governing behavior on the Internet
- A description of the consequences of violating the policy
- A description of what constitutes acceptable and unacceptable use of the Internet
- A description of the rights of individuals using the networks in your company, such as user privacy
- A disclaimer absolving the company under specific circumstances from responsibility
- A form for employees to sign indicating their agreement to abide by the policy

Travel Advisory

Many company web sites contain an Acceptable Use Policy or Terms of Use statement that protects the companies from any liability from users of the site.

Due Care and Due Diligence

Due care and due diligence are terms that apply to the implementation of company-wide security policies. The company practices *due care* by taking responsibility for all activities that take place in corporate facilities. The company practices *due diligence* by implementing and maintaining these security procedures at all times to protect the company's facilities, assets, and employees.

Although many companies outline plans for security policies and standards, they often never officially implement them or the information isn't properly shared with the employees. Without training, guides, and manuals, and without employee input and feedback, no guidance comes from management regarding the policies and their use.

By practicing due care, the company shows it has taken the necessary steps to protect itself and its employees. By practicing due diligence, the company ensures these security policies are properly maintained, communicated, and implemented. If the company doesn't follow proper due care and due diligence initiatives, it might be considered legally negligent if company security is compromised.

Exam Tip

Due care is taking the necessary responsibility and steps to protect the company and the employees. Due diligence ensures these security policies are properly implemented.

Privacy

Privacy policies are agreements for protecting individually identifiable information in an online or electronic commerce environment. A company engaged in online activities or electronic commerce has a responsibility to adopt and implement a policy for protecting the privacy of individually identifiable information. Organizations should also take steps to ensure online privacy when interacting with other companies, such as business partners.

The following are recommendations for implementing privacy policies:

- A company's privacy policy must be easy to find, read, and understand, and it must be available prior to or at the time that individually identifiable information is collected or requested.

- The policy needs to state clearly what information is being collected, the use of that information, possible third-party distribution of that information, the choices available to an individual regarding collection, use, and distribution of the collected information, a statement of the organization's commitment to data security, and what steps the organization takes to ensure data quality and access.

- The policy should disclose the consequences, if any, of an individual's refusal to provide information.

- The policy should also include a clear statement of what accountability mechanism the organization uses, such as procedures for dealing with privacy breaches, including how to contact the organization and register complaints.

- Individuals must be given the opportunity to exercise choice regarding how individually identifiable information collected from them online could be used when such use is unrelated to the purpose for which the information was collected. At a minimum, individuals should be given the opportunity to opt out of such use.

- Where third-party distribution of information is collected online from the individual, unrelated to the purpose for which it was collected, the individual should be given the opportunity to opt out.

- Organizations creating, maintaining, using, or disseminating individually identifiable information should take appropriate measures to assure its reliability and should take reasonable precautions to protect it from loss, misuse, or alteration.

Each company must evaluate its use of the Internet to determine the policy it needs to protect all involved parties. The privacy policy will protect the company from legal issues, raising customers' comfort levels regarding the protection of their information. A policy should include the following elements:

- **Information Collection**   Collect, use, and exchange only data pertinent for the exact purpose, in an open and ethical manner. The information collected for one purpose shouldn't be used for another. Notify consumers of information you have on them, as well as its proposed use, handling, and enforcement policies.

- **Direct Marketing**   Sell only nonpersonal information and certify the information won't be resold. Sell only information that meets the criteria for customers to distribute marketing materials.

- **Information Accuracy**   Ensure the data is accurate, timely, and complete, and has been collected in a legal and fair manner. Allow the customer the right to access, verify, and change information about themselves in a timely, noncumbersome fashion. Inform the customer of the data sources and allow them the option of removing their names from the marketing lists.

- **Information Security**   Apply security measures to safeguard the data on databases. Establish employee training programs and policies on the proper handling of customer data. Limit the access to a need-to-know basis on personal information and divide the information, so no one employee or unit has the whole picture. Follow all government regulations concerning data handling and privacy.

Exam Tip

Privacy policies must be easy to find and provide information on how to opt out of any use of personal information.

Service Level Agreement

A service level agreement (SLA) is an understanding among a supplier of services and the users of those services that the service in question will be available for a certain percentage of time. For example, a web-hosting company could have an SLA with its customers that states the web servers that host the customer's web pages will be available 99.8 percent of the time. If the service level drops below this percentage, the customer might be reimbursed for business lost during the downtime. In some larger companies, this SLA can also be between departments, such as the IT department promising its network systems will be operational 99.9 percent of the time.

The reasons for the downtime could be hardware or software failure, or even compromised security, such as a denial of service (DoS) attack or a virus. As part of the SLA, the company takes responsibility for the security measures and fault tolerance that will maintain a high-service level for those systems. Systems that are required to maintain a high-service level should be equipped with redundant hard drives and power supply systems, including an uninterruptible power supply (UPS) in case of power failure. Proper protection against viruses and other network security threats should be employed. Any hardware or software configuration changes need to be fully tested before implementation and clients warned ahead of time of any scheduled downtime. The window of downtime should be kept to a minimum and proper fall-back procedures must be in place to return quickly to the original configuration in case of an upgrade failure.

Exam Tip

A service level agreement (SLA) is an understanding among a supplier of services and the users of those services that the service in question will be available for a certain percentage of time.

Incident Response Policy

An *Incident Response Policy* is another important policy that should be part of a company's overall security procedures. In case of some form of security incident, be it physical intruder, network hacker, or equipment theft and vandalism, some form of procedure should be in place to deal with these events as they happen.

Without any clear directives, the aftermath of a security breach can cause even more damage if the employees don't know how to handle an incident properly. A clearly defined incident response policy can help contain a problem and provide quick recovery to normal operations.

The policy should cover each type of compromised security scenario and list the procedures to follow when they happen. For example, in case a server is hacked, procedures might be in place to deal with having to remove the server from the network, shutting down related network servers and services, and the preservation of evidence, such as audit trails and logs. The incident response policy should cover the following areas:

- Contact information for emergency services and other outside resources
- Methods of securing and preserving evidence of a security breach
- Scenario-based procedures of what to do with computer and network equipment depending on the security problem
- How to document the problem and the evidence properly

Access Control Guidelines

The following concepts concern access control to data, including how to increase security through proper organizational structures and data security principles.

Separation of Duties

To ensure all employees and management personnel know their roles in the company, the organization's structure should be clear, with positions properly defined with formal job titles and descriptions, definitions of responsibilities, and reporting structures that define the lines of authority.

To increase security and reduce risk from security compromises, part of this effort should be directed toward both a clear organizational structure and a specific separation of duties. A *separation of duties* can ensure one individual isn't tasked with high security and high-risk responsibilities, and that users aren't accessing restricted resources because of jobs that haven't been defined properly.

To separate duties that involve high-security situations, a certain amount of collusion must take place. *Collusion* means that to proceed with a certain task, more than one person is required to allow the procedure to take place. The more people involved, the less chance of a poor security decision that could compromise security being made by one individual. In a banking situation, opening the main safe might require the authorization of at least two people because each authorized person possesses a key and both keys needs to be used together to open the safe. This prevents a single individual from opening the safe without supervision.

Need-to-Know Principle

The *Need-to-Know* principle is used to ensure users only have the access rights they need to perform their job function. This requires giving users the least amount of privileges possible to prevent them from abusing more powerful access rights. For example, a user might need access to certain files to print them for their manager. The network administrator should only give the user enough access rights to read the file and print it, without including privileges to delete, modify, or add information to the file.

The function of management is to decide exactly what a person needs to know or for what areas they require access for their particular position. The network administrator must enact the decision. When in doubt, the network administrator should err on the side of caution and only allow minimal access until someone can authorize more privileges on behalf of the user. Increased privileges should never be handed out at the request of the user who needs them.

Exam Tip
Data access should be based on the Need-to-Know principle, which ensures users only have access to the data they need to perform their job function and nothing more.

Password Management

Password management, although typically created and enforced by the network administrators, is now becoming a special area of network security that should be covered through specific company policies. *Password management* ensures all users are aware of the rules and procedures in place for managing the user accounts and passwords that allow access to company resources. Password management should be part of the company's overall published security policies, such as the Acceptable Use Policy.

Typically, users most often use something easy to remember for their passwords. This includes the names of their family, pets, phone numbers, and birth dates, all of which can easily be discovered by someone who knows the user or even by a complete stranger who, through simple social engineering, only has to ask the user a few questions about their personal life. Other types of passwords that aren't secure are those based on any word found in the dictionary. Many password-cracking programs based on dictionary attacks are available that can find out any password in a short time if it's based on a common dictionary word.

The following are some basic, but important, password policies that can be set by the administrator to enforce strong passwords:

- **Minimum length**   The minimum length for a password can be enforced by the network administrator. This prevents users from using small, easy-to-guess passwords of only a few characters in length. The recommended minimum password length is approximately six to eight characters.

- **Password rotation**   Most login and password authentication systems can remember the last five to ten passwords a user has used and can prevent them from using the same one over and over again. If this option is available, it should be enabled, so a user's password will always be different.

- **Password aging**   The longer a password has been in existence, the easier it is to discover eventually, simply by narrowing the options over time. When you force users to change their passwords regularly, this prevents the discovery of a password through brute force attacks.

Data Retention and Destruction

Many companies have been affected legally by archived e-mail that offers evidence against them during court proceedings. To prevent legal liabilities, companies have implemented *data retention* policies to help reduce the possibility of legal problems.

Data retention policies should apply to electronic information, such as files and e-mails, and traditional paper documentation. Some clash might occur between data retention policies and backup policies, where certain files are required to be archived, while others should be disposed of after a certain period of time. Only management and the legal department can define which data is covered under either policy. The data retention policy needs to be specific about your information and take into account items that could be damaging legally, as well as information that can be damaging to business if it's lost. In the case of e-mail, the concept of data retention becomes complicated because e-mail can contain file attachments. Part of your policy might require e-mail to be retained for a certain amount of time before deletion, while the policy for actual electronic files could be different.

When data is to be disposed of, it must be done completely. When destroying paper documentation, most companies use a shredder to cut the document into pieces small enough so they can't easily be put back together. For electronic files, this process is more complicated. Merely deleting a file or e-mail from a hard drive doesn't necessarily delete the data. Many operations systems (OSs) use a special recovery method to enable you to recover deleted files easily. When a file is deleted, it usually still exists in its original location; only the locator for the file in the hard drive directory has been removed. To ensure complete destruction of data on magnetic media, it should be overwritten. Many "shredder" utilities are available that can overwrite the contents of a hard drive with random data to ensure any information on the drive was destroyed.

Human Resources Policies

A company's human resources (HR) department is an important link regarding company and employee security. The HR department is responsible for hiring employees, ensuring employees conform to company codes and policies during their term of employment, and maintaining company security in case of an employee termination. The following sections outline the responsibility of human resources during the three phases of the employment cycle.

Hiring

When hiring employees for a position within the company, the HR department is responsible for the initial screening of the employee. This usually takes place during the first interview, where an HR representative meets with the employee to discuss the company and to get a first impression of the employee's personality gauging whether this person would fit into the company's environment. This interview generally is nontechnical and personality-based. Further interviews are usually more skill-oriented and are conducted by the department advertising the position. The employee could possess excellent technical skills for the position, but their personality and communications skills might not be conducive to their work environment.

During the interview process, HR also does background checks of the applicant, and examines and confirms their educational and employment history. Reference checks are also performed, where HR can obtain information on the applicant from a third party to help confirm facts about the employee's past. Depending on the type of company or institution, such as the government or the military, the applicant might have to go through security clearance checks or even health and drug testing.

To protect the confidentiality of company information, the applicant is usually required to sign a nondisclosure agreement, which legally prevents the employee from disclosing sensitive company data to other companies in case of their termination. These agreements are particularly important with high-turnover positions, such as contract or temporary employment.

Once an employee is hired, the company also inherits any personality quirks or traits of that person. A solid hiring process can prevent future problems with these employees.

Codes of Conduct and Ethics

The HR department is also responsible for outlining a company's policy regarding codes of conduct and ethics. The codes are a general list of what the company expects from its employees in terms of every day conduct—dealing with fellow employees, managers, and subordinates, including people from outside the company, such as customers and clients.

This code of conduct could include restrictions and policies concerning drug and alcohol abuse, theft and vandalism, and violence in the workplace. If an employee transgresses any of these codes of conduct and ethics, they could be disciplined, suspended, or even terminated, depending on the severity of the infraction.

Termination

The dismissal of employees can be a stressful and chaotic time, especially because these terminations can happen quickly and without notice. An employee can be terminated for a variety of reasons, such as performance issues, personal and attitude problems, legal issues such as sabotage, espionage, theft, or the employee could be leaving to work for another company. The human resources department needs to have a specific set of procedures ready to follow in case an employee terminates. Without a step-by-step method of termination, some areas might have been ignored during the process that compromise company security.

A termination policy should exist for each type of situation. For example, you might follow slightly different procedures for terminating an employee who's going to work for an industry-unrelated position with another company than with an employee who's going to work for a direct competitor. In the latter case, the employee might be considered a security risk if they remain on the premises for their two-week notice period, where they could transmit company secrets to the competition.

A termination policy should include the following procedures for the immediate termination of an employee:

- **Securing Work Area**   When the termination time has been set, the employee in question should be escorted from their workstation area to the HR department. This prevents them from using their computer or other company resources once notice of termination is given. Their computer should be turned off and disconnected from the network. When the employee returns to their desk to collect personal items, someone should be with them to ensure no private company information is taken. Finally, the employee should be escorted out the building.

- **Return of Identification**   As part of the termination procedure, the employee's company identification should be returned. This includes identity badges, pass cards and keys for doors, and any other security device used for access control to company facilities. This prevents them from accessing the building once they've been escorted from the premises.

- **Return of Company Equipment**   All company-owned equipment must be returned immediately, such as desktops, laptops, cell phones, PDAs, organizers, or any other type of electronic equipment that could contain confidential company information.

- **Suspension of Computer Accounts**   An important part of the termination procedure is the notification to the network administrators of the situation. They should be notified shortly before the termination takes place to give them time to disable any network accounts and phone access for that employee. The network password of the account should be changed and any other network access the employee might have, such as remote access, should be disabled. The employee's file server data and e-mail should be preserved and archived to protect any work or important communications the company might need for operational or legal reasons.

Exam Tip
All user access, including physical and network access controls, needs to be disabled for an employee once they've been terminated. This prevents the employee from accessing the facility or network.

Objective 13.02   Privilege Management

P*rivilege management* involves the creation and use of policies defining the users and groups that access company resources, such as data files or printers. To control how users access data, the employees of the company need to be logically structured to define access privileges depending on the type of user, the groups they belong to, or their specific role in the company. The following sections outline some of the key topics concerned with privilege management.

MAC/DAC/RBAC

Access control models are policies that define how users access data. These policies form a framework based on the security and business goals of the organization. The rules of the framework are enforced through access control technologies. Three main access control types exist.

- **MAC** In a mandatory access control model (MAC), the OS of the network is in control of access to data. Data owners can assign permissions to their own files and share them however they see fit, but OS access controls override any data owner settings. This type of model is often used in high-security environments, such as the military or the government, where access control is tightly guarded through the OS.
- **DAC** Discretionary access control (DAC) enables the data owners to specify what users can access certain data. A data owner might own only one file or that owner could own several files and directories. For example, a department manager could own several directories of resources particular to that department.
- **RBAC** Role-based access control (RBAC) is also referred to as nondiscretionary access control. This centrally controlled model allows access to be based on the role the user holds within an organization. Instead of giving access to individual users, access control is granted to groups of users who perform a common function.

User/Group/Role Management

When designing a company's security infrastructure, you must visualize the relationships among your users and groups and the resources they need to perform their jobs. For a network administrator to assign access permissions individually to resources on a per-user basis would be inefficient and extremely time-consuming. While this might be viable for small networks, it would be an unwieldy strategy for mid-sized to large corporate networks. Grouping your users depending on similarities in their job functions is much more efficient. On top of this, you can also organize user security by their role in the company.

- **User** As a single user, an employee's access rights and privileges revolve around the data that they alone create, modify, and delete.
- **Group** In a group model, several users who need access to the same data are organized in a group. Privileges can be distributed to an entire group of users, rather than to each individual user. This is much more

efficient when applying permissions and provides greater overall control of access to resources.

- **Role** A user might have different security privileges according to their role in the company. For example, a user who's in the role of an auditor might have extra privileges accorded to that role, on top of or replacing those privileges acquired as a user or part of a group. Predetermined permissions for a role can be created, and then applied to users or groups who fit that role.

Centralized and Decentralized Management

The most common method of computer network authentication is through the use of a login and a password. In early computer systems, when networking wasn't as available as it is today, each computer contained a set of resources the user would access. If the user wanted to access the resources of a computer system, they had to use a specific login and password to gain access. Each specific computer and its resources needed a separate login and password. This was tedious for computer users and administrators alike because of the frequency that login accounts and passwords had to be reset for each computer if a user forgot them.

Nowadays, modern networks provide resources that are spread throughout a computer network that can be accessed by any user from any location. The user can be onsite on their own computer, or they can be logged in from home or on the road by using dial-up methods or through the Internet. With the vast amount of resources that can be contained on a large computer network, the concept of different login and password for each resource has been eliminated in favor of a single logon to the network. This way, the user only has to be authenticated once on the network to access the resources for that network. This type of centralized administration is a much more efficient way for a network administrator to control access to the network. User account policy templates can be created and used networkwide, to remove the need to configure each user's account settings individually, except for a unique login and password. The use of access control methods, such as directory and file permissions, is used to provide more granular security on the resource level.

Auditing

Although your company might have specific security policies in place, it's often difficult to monitor how well they're being used and enforced. For these security policies and procedures to be fully effective, they must be audited on a regular basis to test and assess their efficiency. Auditing ensures employees are conforming to company security procedures and policies. And, ultimately, auditing is a way of ensuring accountability. See Chapter 2 for specific information on auditing.

CHECKPOINT

✔ **Objective 13.01: Policy and Procedures**   An Acceptable Use Policy is a set of established guidelines for the appropriate use of computer networks. The company practices due care by taking responsibility for all activities that take place in corporate facilities. The company practices due diligence by implementing and maintaining these security procedures at all times to protect the company's facilities, assets, and employees. Privacy policies are agreements for protecting individually identifiable information in an online or electronic commerce environment. A service level agreement (SLA) is an understanding among a supplier of services and the users of those services that the service in question will be available for a certain percentage of time. A specific separation of duties ensures that one individual isn't tasked with high security and high-risk responsibilities. Users should only have the access rights they need to perform their job functions. The employee termination process includes securing the work area, returning identification and company equipment, and the suspension of computer accounts.

✔ **Objective 13.02: Privilege Management**   In a mandatory access control model (MAC), the OS of the network is in control of access to data. Discretionary access control (DAC) allows the data owners to specify what users can access certain data. Role-based access control (RBAC) allows access to be based on the role the user holds within an organization. Privileges can be assigned by user, group, or role in the company. Centralized management and single network sign-on increases network security across the organization and allows for easier user management.

REVIEW QUESTIONS

1. Which of the following policies concerns the use of protection and distribution of user's data?

   A. Privacy

   B. Due care

 C. Acceptable use

 D. SLA

2. Which of the following policies concerns the appropriate use of computer networks?

 A. SLA

 B. Due diligence

 C. Acceptable use

 D. Privacy

3. Which of the following policies is an agreement to provide service availability?

 A. Code of Ethics

 B. Privacy

 C. Due care

 D. SLA

4. Which of the following access control principles concerns giving a user minimum access rights to be able to perform their job function?

 A. SLA

 B. Separation of duties

 C. Need-to-know

 D. RBAC

5. What should be done to prevent someone from recovering deleted files from a hard drive?

 A. Password-protect the data

 B. Overwrite the data

 C. Format the hard drive

 D. Rub it with a magnet

6. Which of the following HR procedures should be performed to help confirm facts about an employee's skills and background?

 A. Drug test

 B. Skill test

 C. Reference check

 D. Security clearance check

7. When an employee is terminated, what should be done to prevent them from logging in to their computer?

   A. Remove the monitor

   B. Change the e-mail password

   C. Delete the user account

   D. Disable the user account

8. When an employee is terminated, which of the following items is the most important to retrieve from them?

   A. Facility access card

   B. Name tag

   C. Cell phone

   D. Office supplies

9. Which of the following privilege management access-control models concerns role-based access control?

   A. NDAC

   B. DAC

   C. RBAC

   D. MAC

10. Which of the following should be implemented to facilitate access control and user account management across several systems?

    A. Role-based access control

    B. Mandatory access control

    C. Remote access

    D. Single network logon

REVIEW ANSWERS

1. **A** The privacy policy concerns the protection and distribution of user's data. A company engaged in online activities or electronic commerce has a responsibility to adopt and implement a policy for protecting the privacy of individually identifiable information.

2. **C** The Acceptable Use Policy is concerned with the appropriate use of computer networks. The policy is a written agreement that outlines the terms, conditions, and rules of Internet and internal network use for the company, and is signed by all employees.

3. **D** A service level agreement (SLA) is an understanding among a supplier of services and the users of those services that the service in question will be available for a certain percentage of time.

4. **C** The Need-to-Know principle is used to ensure users only have the access rights they need to perform their job functions. This requires giving users the least amount of privileges possible, to prevent them from abusing more powerful access rights.

5. **B** Merely deleting a file or an e-mail from a hard drive doesn't necessarily delete the data. Many OSs use a special recovery method to enable you to recover deleted files easily. When a file is deleted, it usually still exists in its original location; only the locator for the file in the hard drive directory has been removed. To ensure complete destruction of data on magnetic media, it should be overwritten.

6. **C** As part of the background check of the applicant, the HR department should confirm the applicant's educational and employment history by performing a reference check.

7. **D** When an employee is terminated, their user account should be disabled to prevent them from logging in to their computer.

8. **A** The access card needs to be retrieved from the terminated employee, so they can't enter the facilities using the card.

9. **C** Role-based access control (RBAC) allows access to be based on the role the user holds within an organization. Instead of giving access to individual users, access control is granted to groups of users who perform a common function.

10. **D** With a single network logon, a user only has to be authenticated once on the network to access the resources for that network. This type of centralized administration is a much more efficient way for a network administrator to control access to the network.

Forensics, Risk Management, Education, and Documentation

CHAPTER 14

	NEWBIE	SOME EXPERIENCE	EXPERT
ETA	3 hours	2 hours	1 hour

Because the concept of computer crime and security is still fairly new, many companies have had to adapt quickly to this new environment of doing business on the Internet and to protect themselves, their employees, and the company's data in the process. Traditional crimes against companies—physical intrusion, theft, and vandalism—while still an important security issue, have been replaced by concerns with computer crimes and electronic security issues, such as viruses, hacking, and data integrity protection.

In adjusting to the legalities of prosecuting computer crimes, most companies have trained their employees in collecting and preserving forensic evidence of computer crimes. Because the evidence is usually electronic in nature, it can easily be tampered with, causing it to be legally invalid in a court of law. Therefore, the art of computer forensics is a critical part of preventing and prosecuting computer crimes.

To increase protection from the increased risks of the Internet world, companies have had to audit their security practices continually to identify the risks and threats to their assets, as well as how to protect them in the most possible cost-efficient manner. To help reduce the risk of security compromise and also any legal liabilities the company might incur, companies need to train and educate their users on proper security practices, as well as enforce documentation controls to prevent confidential documents from ending up in the wrong hands.

This chapter deals with security and legal issues, such as computer crime forensics, risk management, user education, and document controls.

Objective 14.01 Forensics

Forensics is the act of collecting and preserving evidence to use in a court of law for legal proceedings. Typical forensics of crimes, such as theft or murder, includes gathering evidence to help prosecute a suspect, such as fingerprints, weapons, and even DNA samples. In the computer world, evidence of a cybercrime can be difficult to obtain, preserve, and allow into a court of law. Because of its nature, most evidence of computer crimes is electronic, which can easily be erased, modified, and tampered with. After a computer crime—such as a hacked server—is committed, initial investigation by the network administrator can quickly ruin evidence the hacker left behind.

Travel Advisory

If a system is rebooted after a security compromise, certain evidence could be destroyed in the process, such as memory contents and system logs.

The following sections outline some of special procedures required when preserving and collecting evidence of a computer crime, which includes keeping audit trails and logs, preserving the environment, and retaining a chain of custody of the evidence.

Collection and Preservation of Evidence

If a computer crime occurs, an effort must be made to leave the original environment and evidence intact and unaltered until the authorities have been contacted. If people begin to pick apart the crime scene after a physical crime or if the network administrator begins poking around the file system after a cybercrime, the evidence could be disturbed and considered inadmissible in court.

A company must create an incident response policy that indicates what can and cannot be touched if a security compromise occurs. For example, a company suffering from a denial of service (DoS) attack might panic and pull the plug on its Internet connection. This, of course, stops the attacks, but now the entire network has been brought down and no communication exists with the outside world. This effectively stops all e-mail and Internet business communications. If the business runs its operations through a web page, this can be fatal. The incident handling and response procedures will provide information on what to do in a certain scenario. In the example of the DoS attack, to prevent the entire network from going down and to preserve any evidence of the attacks, the company might let the attack continue, so the network administrator can save logs and audit trails to help trace the source of the attack.

Collecting and preserving evidence from a computer crime usually centers around keeping and storing any logs or audit trails that detail, step-by-step, what the attacker was doing. In cases such as these, panic must not set in. If a network administrator suddenly reboots the server to ward off the attacker, they are not only disrupting access to that server for legitimate users, they could also destroy valuable evidence in the form of audit trails and timestamps on files that might have been changed by the intruder. When computer logs are to be used as evidence, they must be collected in the regular course of business. If the log was the result of a one-time monitoring in response to an incident, it might be considered hearsay evidence, meaning the evidence is secondhand. The company must also prove the logs themselves haven't been altered in any way from the time of the original data capture.

If the crime was physical in nature, such as the theft of equipment, the evidence needed would be some type of surveillance video. If the theft took place in a secured area, it might be possible to analyze the access logs of employees who were in the secured area at the time. If the company uses magnetic access cards for doors, a log can be created showing who went in and out at a certain time.

Chain of Custody

When collecting evidence of a computer crime, keeping a proper chain of custody is extremely important. Keeping a *chain of custody* requires that all evidence be properly labeled with information on who secured and validated it. This process must also happen for each individual who comes in contact with the evidence. Unfortunately, electronic evidence can be volatile and, in a court of law, it can be easily dismissed because of possible tampering. Computer media can be easily destroyed, erased, or modified, so handling this evidence requires strict procedures.

If a copy of data needs to be made, reliability and integrity must be assured, so the copies can be considered tamperproof. Any devices or media containing data need to be carefully catalogued and labeled, and then sealed away to prevent any further tampering. Magnetic media should be write-protected to prevent the data from being overwritten.

If all evidence has been properly secured, identified, labeled, and stored, then it can be considered solid and admissible in court. A clear chain of custody log ensures this process was completed without the possibility of data modification.

Exam Tip	
A chain of custody ensures that evidence has been handled with the utmost care and hasn't been tampered with.	

Objective 14.02 Risk Management

Risk management deals with identifying, assessing, and reducing the risk of security issues. By assessing the probability of a risk and estimating the amount of damage that can be caused as a result, steps can be taken to reduce the level of that risk.

As an example of risk management, you could have a file server that contains confidential company data. This asset is considered extremely valuable to the company, its clients, and its competitors. The amount of financial damage to the company from loss, damage, or theft of this file server is considerable. The risks and threats posed to the file server could be physical damage—such as from a natural disaster or a hardware malfunction—to nonphysical threats—such as viruses, network attacks from hackers, and data theft because the file server is easily accessible through a network. To help reduce these risks, you can take several actions: use multiple hard drives and power supplies for fault tolerance, implement a good backup scheme, protect the server through physical security such as access controls, install antivirus software, and configure software authentication and access control to prevent network attacks. The costs of reducing the risks are more than made up for by the potential cost of losing that data on the file server.

To identify the risks that pose a security threat to your company, you should perform a risk analysis on all parts of the company's resources and activities. By identifying risks and the amount of damage that could be caused by exploiting a vulnerability, you can ensure the most efficient method of securing that risk will be used. The risk analysis can identify where there's too little security or even where there's too much security, where the cost of security is more than the cost of the loss because of compromise. Ultimately, risk analysis is a cost/benefit analysis of your security infrastructure.

The three main phases of a risk analysis are the following:

- **Asset Identification**   Identify and quantify the company's assets
- **Risk and Threat Assessment**   Identify and assess the possible security vulnerabilities and threats
- **Identify Solutions and Countermeasures**   Identify a cost-effective solution to protect assets

Asset Identification

Asset identification involves defining what assets the company owns and how much they're worth. The assets can be anything from physical items such as computer and networking equipment to electronic items like a company's valuable data. To assign value to assets, an asset must be considered worth more than its purchase price. Other considerations include acquisition costs, maintenance, the value of the asset to the company, the value of the asset to a competitor, what clients would pay for the asset or service, the cost of replacement, and the cost if the asset is compromised. For example, a list of a company's clients can be easily re-created from backup if the original is lost or destroyed but, if the list finds its way into the hands of a competitor, the actual financial damage could be devastating. Ultimately, the value of the assets you're trying to protect is what drives the costs involved with securing that asset.

Exam Tip	
The cost of the solution shouldn't exceed the potential cost of the asset if it's lost.	

Risk and Threat Assessment

For each of your assets, you must perform a risk assessment to ascertain the risk to an asset in its current state. You must ensure to include all possibilities, both physical and nonphysical. Data can be stolen from a file server by someone physically stealing the system or by accessing the data through a network security vulnerability. You need to identify three items when you perform a risk and threat assessment:

- **Threat**   The origin of the problem, such as a fire, flood, virus, hacker, employee, or intruder.
- **Vulnerability**   The aspect of the asset that's vulnerable to a threat, such as lack of antivirus software, no fire-prevention mechanisms, weak physical security, or ineffective network access controls.
- **Risk**   The actual risk of a vulnerability being compromised by a threat. If a virus infects a server without any antivirus protection, the result could be lost or damaged data.

Threats

A *threat* is defined as something that creates the possibility of a vulnerability being compromised. A wide variety of threats can pose a security risk to a company. The following is a list of the most common threats a company can face.

- **Natural Disasters** A natural disaster typically is something like a fire or flood that causes physical damage to company assets—usually the facilities and the equipment within.
- **Equipment Malfunction** Electronic equipment is vulnerable to normal wear and tear that can result in failed components. This can be anything from a failed power supply fan to a failed hard drive.
- **Employees** Your assets face threats from employees, but this isn't always malicious in nature. The source of the threat could simply be human error, such as someone deleting a directory of files by mistake. Other threats include theft, vandalism, and corporate espionage.
- **Intruders** A threat by intruders refers to a physical intruder who compromises the access controls of a facility to gain access and perform theft, vandalism, or sabotage.
- **Hackers** A threat by hackers is a nonphysical threat that centers around a hacker's ability to compromise network security to access data assets on a company's network.

Travel Advisory
Although many companies take great efforts to secure their network and facility from external users, often little is done to protect attacks from the inside by employees.

Vulnerabilities

An *asset vulnerability* is a security weakness that can be potentially compromised by a particular threat. An operating system (OS) might be vulnerable to network attacks because it wasn't recently updated with security patches. A file server could be vulnerable to viruses because it doesn't have any antivirus software installed. Asset vulnerabilities are organized into physical and nonphysical categories.

Physical   *Physical* vulnerabilities are those that affect the physical protection of the asset. Physical assets, such as network servers, should be protected from natural disasters, such as fire and flood, by storing them in special rooms with protective mechanisms to prevent damage from these threats. Without this protection, the assets can be quickly damaged or destroyed if a natural disaster occurs.

Nonphysical   *Nonphysical* vulnerabilities are those that usually involve the software of computer equipment or network devices. Software security vulnerabilities are caused by a variety of reasons: improper software configuration, buggy software, lack of antivirus protection, weak access and authentication controls, and misconfigured or nonexistent firewalls.

Risk Assessment

Once the threats and vulnerabilities are identified, the next step is to understand the risk involved of having a threat compromise a vulnerability. This is the final result of what can happen in a security breach. For example, a combination of the lack of antivirus software protection and the introduction of a virus would result in a virus-infected server, which could damage or delete sensitive data.

The risk assessment reflects the worst possible scenario of a security compromise, and should be quantified with a direct financial value for losses and potential losses. A company should reflect on the amount of damage to reputation and financial loss if a hacker were to launch a successful DoS attack on the company's web servers. A loss of service—even for a few hours—can be severely damaging, as in the case of a company that offers stock-trading services. On top of immediate costs for equipment or data loss, the potential loss of prolonged downtime must be factored into the equation.

Once the potential loss is calculated for each type of risk, the result can be used to create solutions and countermeasures that are cost-efficient, depending on the risk situation.

Exam Tip

The risk assessment should reflect the worst possible scenario of a security compromise, and be quantified with a direct financial value for losses and potential losses.

Solutions and Countermeasures

As the result of the entire risk identification and management procedure, you'll have collected information on how valuable your assets are, the list of possible threats, the potential risk of each threat, and the potential loss if the threat manages to compromise a security vulnerability.

Each risk scenario should be ranked by probability, so the risks more likely to happen are ranked toward the top of the list because this is where the solution efforts should be most concentrated. For example, within a company that already practices strict physical security and access control methods, the priority of risk scenarios could be geared toward nonphysical threats, such as viruses and network hackers.

Once this process is complete, a list of solutions and countermeasures to protect against each threat should be reviewed. Examine your solutions with respect to what current security measures are in place and what needs to be done to make them more effective. Ensure that the functionality and effectiveness of the solution is enough to reduce the risk of compromise. Purchasing a fire extinguisher for the server room could seem like a fire-prevention solution, but only an automatic fire detection and suppression system can fully protect a room full of servers from a large, out-of-control fire in the middle of the night. Similarly, buying a firewall to protect your servers from outside Internet traffic is a great idea for network security but, if the network administrator hasn't been trained to configure it properly, the firewall might not be effective at all.

These solutions, however, must be cost-effective to ensure the benefits of the solution are in line with the actual cost of data loss. For example, there's no point in spending $100,000 on a security solution to protect data that's only worth $40,000 to the company if it's lost or damaged. Ongoing maintenance also needs to be factored into the final calculations. Although you have a large initial cost for a tape backup solution, you'll still be paying out for costs of new tapes when needed and offsite storage.

Security is always an ongoing primary concern and, to protect the network and infrastructure from new threats, the company must be diligent to ensure the current security mechanisms can effectively deal with these new risks. After implementation, the security solutions should be regularly tested and reevaluated to ensure their functionality and reliability, as well as that their costs are comparable to their benefits.

Objective 14.03 Education

For a company's security policies to be effective, they must be communicated properly to the employees to ensure knowledge and compliance. No one will follow any rules if they aren't aware of them. Many companies make use of consultants to create and draft security policies and procedures but, often, these policies aren't communicated to the user community, and then they aren't used at all. Employees need to be aware of any security issues and procedures to protect not only themselves, but also the company's services and data.

This effort must be directed from senior management and filtered throughout the company to every single employee. Different departments and divisions within a company need different security education depending on their job tasks and area of influence. The security procedures used by the financial department could be different from those used by sales or engineering. Finance might need special procedures to protect confidential company and employee financial data from being exposed to other employees or companies. Engineering's security efforts will revolve around the protection and integrity of the source code or research data. Front reception could be specially trained on security practices with incoming calls or the physical security of the main entrance. Each department must interpret the company's high-level goals into the functional procedures specific to their job function.

To propagate security policies and procedures effectively to the user community, the company must make a diligent effort to communicate these policies. If no one knows about the security policies, there's no point creating them. The best methods for overall user-security awareness are though proper documentation and training.

Documentation

The first step in user awareness is creating and maintaining proper documentation of all your security policies and procedures. Policies that apply to the company as a whole should be distributed to each employee. These policies might include such areas as acceptable Internet use, employee code of ethics and conduct, and safety and emergency contact information. More department-specific policies could only be distributed to employees in that department. The human resources (HR) department wouldn't publish policies for the protection of employee salary information to other departments of the company, so it wouldn't reveal or undermine any security procedures. The IT department would have different security policies because one of its main job functions is to be responsible for the security and protection of the company's network infrastructure and data.

As security policies tend to change over time, manual distribution isn't always the most efficient and timely way to communicate security information. Employees should have a way to access the most-current versions of these documents in a conspicuous place, such as in a binder located outside the HR area. Another more efficient method is to publish these documents on a company intranet, so employees can easily access the most-current versions of these documents. Printed versions should still be available but, because this documentation frequently changes, only a few central copies should be created to prevent excessive paper waste. The advantages of online versions of documents are they're instantly available through the employee's computer and they're always the most recent versions.

> **Exam Tip**
>
> The best place to store company documentation for easy access by employees is through the corporate intranet.

Education and Training

Providing access to documentation is only one part of user awareness. Although printed documentation might be handed out to all employees or electronic versions could be made available online, no guarantee exists that they'll read, understand, or implement the security procedures. To supplement the documentation and to ensure employee awareness, education and training sessions should be provided.

Training sessions should be mandatory for all employees and it's critical for all new employees to go through this security training. The purpose of the training courses is to ensure employees know the security policies and procedures the company has created and, most important, that they understand these policies and know how to enact them within their specific positions. Any policies or procedures an employee might not be sure of can be discussed within this environment.

Classes can be based on overall security procedures, such as virus awareness and dealing with outside clients and inquiries. These should be attended by all employees to ensure they know how to handle security problems properly with communications media used companywide, such as e-mail or the telephone.

Virus-awareness training can educate users on proper e-mail use and how to prevent viruses from infecting the company network. General security items, such as facility access control, can include training on identifying and authenticating users in the facility, so they can spot employees or strangers who are somewhere they shouldn't be. Network authentication standards, such as proper login and password management, are also applicable to all employees.

Specialized training can be presented to laptop and mobile device users who'll be traveling to ensure they protect company equipment and data when they're not on the premises. Other education initiatives can be more specific to an individual user or department, depending on their job function. The HR department can be given training on the security practices involved with hiring and terminating employees. The IT department should be given special training on specific networking security issues.

Education and training can ensure your employees are aware of and understand all company security policies and procedures, whether they apply to the company as a whole, or to specific departments and job functions.

Objective 14.04 Documentation

Your company produces a wide variety of documentation—from publications for internal use to confidential papers for senior management to publicly available documents. Without proper controls, that documentation could compromise company security. The company's document control standards and guidelines must ensure all documents produced by the company are classified, organized, and stored securely to prevent their loss, damage, or theft.

To ensure control over the protection and distribution of data, it needs to be classified with a certain designation. This data *classification* indicates what type of document it is, if the information it contains is confidential or can be made public, and to whom it can be distributed. The classification also defines what levels of data retention and storage are needed for that particular document. Finally, policies must exist on the legal status of documents concerning which can be destroyed and which need to be retained.

Standards and Guidelines

To ensure the continuity of documentation across the company as a whole, a set of documentation standards and guidelines should be introduced. These standards and guidelines can serve as templates for all documentation to ensure they have the same look and feel, and to ensure they'll all be distributed and stored securely, according to their scope or sensitivity.

The standards and guidelines should address the following topics:

- Data Classification
- Document Retention and Storage
- Destruction

Data Classification

A company's documentation can be voluminous, comprising a variety of documents with varying value and importance. Depending on the type of document, the amount of security and procedures used in storing and distributing that document can greatly vary. Some documents might be considered public, so they can be posted in a public form or distributed freely to anyone. Other documents can be extremely confidential and contain information that only certain individuals should be allowed to see.

To aid in this effort, documents need to be assigned security classifications to indicate the levels of confidentiality of the document. Each classification requires different standards and procedures of access, distribution, and storage. The classification also sets a minimum standard of privileges required by a user to access that data. If you don't have the necessary access privileges for that classification of data, you won't be able to access it.

Several levels of classification can be assigned, depending on the type of company or organization and its activities. A typical company could have only two classifications: private and public. *Private classified documents* are only for the internal user of the company and can't be distributed to anyone outside the company. *Public documents,* however, would be available to anyone. Government and military institutions might have several levels of confidentiality, such as sensitive, secret, top secret, and so on. Each document needs to be assigned a classification depending on the sensitivity of its data, its value to the company, its value to other companies such as business competition, the importance of its integrity, and the legal aspects of storing and distributing that data.

Exam Tip

The type of security protections, access controls, data retention, and storage and disposal policies to be used depends on a document's security classification.

Document Retention and Storage

Depending on the classification of a document, the procedures and policies for storing that document can be quite different. For example, a particular document might incur certain legal liabilities if it isn't properly stored, distributed, or destroyed. To ensure proper document management, depending on its classification, companies have implemented data-retention policies to help reduce the possibility of legal issues.

Certain documents are required to be archived, stored, and protected, while others should be disposed of after a certain period of time. These policies must be created by senior management and the legal department, which can define what retention policies apply to different classifications of documents. The data retention policy needs to be specific about your company's data. It also needs to take into account items that could be legally damaging and information that can be damaging to the business if it's lost or falls into the wrong hands.

To protect documentation properly, it should be stored offsite at a special document storage facility. In case of a disaster, such as a fire at the company facility, this will ensure all important documentation is secure and can be recovered.

Document Destruction

Document disposal can often be a tricky issue. In some cases, to prevent future legal or confidentiality ramifications from the existence of a certain document, it needs to be destroyed. In other cases, it's illegal to destroy certain documents that are required by law as evidence for court proceedings. Only your company's legal department can decide on retention and disposal for particular documents. Once decided, these policies need to be communicated to the employees to ensure that sensitive documents are either destroyed or retained as per their classification.

When data is to be disposed of, it must be done completely. When destroying paper documentation, most companies use a shredder to cut the document into pieces small enough so they can't easily be put back together. Simply putting documents in the trash or recycle bin isn't acceptable because anyone can sift through the garbage or recycle containers for these documents, a practice called *dumpster diving*. As part of corporate espionage, some companies hire private investigators to examine garbage dumpsters of a target company, and these investigators try to discover any proprietary and confidential information.

Travel Advisory

To combat the problems of dumpster diving for confidential company documents, the physical security of your facility should include your garbage disposal and recycling operations.

Types of Documentation

Beyond standard company documents, such as policies, procedures, guidelines, and training manuals, some specialized document sets require added attention regarding security and storage. Network architecture diagrams, change logs, and system logs and inventories are all documents created and managed specifically by the company's IT department. Because these documents can contain specific information on system and network devices such as logs, audit trails, network addresses, and configuration data, they are usually accessible only by authorized persons within the Information Technology (IT) department, and aren't accessible by other employees in the company.

Systems Architecture

The IT department should always have current diagrams of your overall company network architecture on-hand. When troubleshooting network problems or security issues, having network diagrams to identify devices and overall data flow within the company's network is helpful.

A variety of diagrams is needed to show different aspects of the architecture. Overall diagrams should be general and show the company network as a whole. These diagrams should possibly only indicate offices by name—with wide area network (WAN) links in between them—for companies that have geographically distant offices. More detailed diagrams can be made of the internal network structure, showing all the routers, switches, firewalls, hubs, printers, and servers, as in Figure 14.1.

Each device should be clearly labeled with identifying information, such as the system name and the network address. Including end-user workstations on

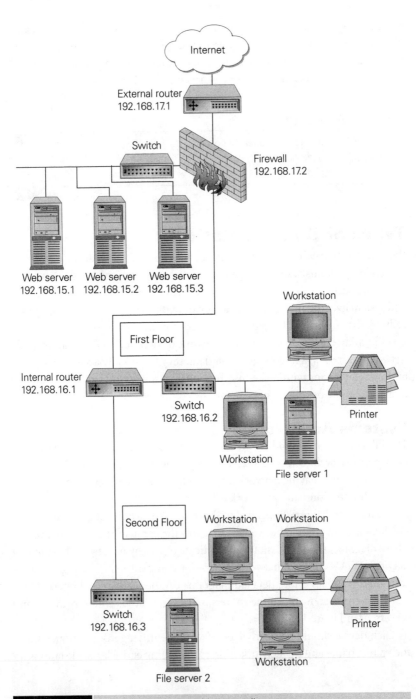

FIGURE 14.1   Typical network architecture diagram

systems architecture diagrams is rare because too many could exist to include on a single diagram. The general network used by the end users should be indicated, however.

As a security precaution, network diagrams shouldn't be generally published because the information can be used maliciously by a hacker to give them a roadmap of the company's network, including IP addresses of the most critical network devices and servers. Network architecture diagrams should only be accessed by authorized individuals from the IT department. Printouts of diagrams should never be posted in public places, such as on a notice board or even the office of the network administrator. The diagram can be easily stolen by someone walking by the area.

Exam Tip

System architecture diagrams should never be displayed or stored in a public area, especially if they contain system IP addresses and other information hackers can use to compromise a network.

Logs and Inventories

General application logs, audit logs, maintenance logs, and equipment inventory documentation are also important documents within an IT department. Most of this documentation is related with the maintenance and operation of the company's computer equipment, but certain logs, such as system activity logs, should be carefully archived and preserved as evidence in case of a security compromise.

System and audit logs provide snapshots of what's happening on a system at a specific point in time. These logs need to be retained for auditing in case of some security compromise. For example, the hacking of a certain server could have gone unnoticed for a long period of time. But if the logs of that system are retained and archived, they can be audited to reveal when the compromise began and how it happened. To ensure the company's backup procedures and policies are being followed, the IT department might have to retain and store copies of backup application logs, which indicate when certain data was backed up, and where it's now stored. Inventories of computer equipment enable the company to keep track of its assets and where they're located. Maintenance logs provide important evidence for service and warranty claims.

Change Control Documentation

Change control documents are used to identify current or forthcoming changes to some aspect of the company, such as the network or another critical operation.

For example, the IT department might issue a change control document to the employees to notify them of a network outage because of an upgrade. More detailed change control documents for IT internal use describe the specific technical changes to the company's systems or infrastructure.

Tracking and controlling the changes to your network is important, so any unplanned changes are quickly noticed and investigated. System changes without prior knowledge or approval of management and the IT department could indicate a hacker or an intruder has compromised a system.

CHECKPOINT

✔**Objective 14.01: Forensics**   To preserve evidence, leave the original system environment intact. Save audit and activity logs for evidence. Keep a chain of custody of evidence to preserve its integrity.

✔**Objective 14.02: Risk Management**   Perform asset identification to identify and quantify assets, including full potential loss. Identify and assess risks and threats to those assets. Identify a cost-effective solution and countermeasures to reduce the risk of a security compromise.

✔**Objective 14.03: Education**   To supplement the documentation and to ensure employee awareness, education and training sessions should be provided, especially to new employees. Maintain proper documentation of all security policies and procedures, and then publish them in a conspicuous place. Documentation should be stored online to facilitate quick retrieval of the most current versions of the documents.

✔**Objective 14.04: Documentation**   Classify data according to its confidentiality. Document retention, storage, and disposal procedures depend on the classification of the document. For disposal, documents must be fully destroyed, not simply thrown in the garbage or the recycle bin. Specific network documentation should be stored securely and accessible only by authorized individuals.

REVIEW QUESTIONS

1. A network administrator has discovered the company's FTP server has been hacked. Which of the following items would be the most important to collect and preserve as evidence?

    A. Server memory dump

    B. Activity log

    C. List of files on FTP server

    D. List of user accounts

2. Which of the following describes the procedures for preserving the ownership history of a piece of evidence?

    A. Screen capture

    B. Audit trail

    C. Wiretapping

    D. Chain of custody

3. To be beneficial to a company, which of the following is the most practical relationship between a security risk and its countermeasure?

    A. The cost of the countermeasure should be less than the potential cost of the risk

    B. The cost of the countermeasure should be greater than the potential cost of the risk

    C. The cost of the countermeasure should be less than the cost of the asset

    D. The cost of the countermeasure should be greater than the cost of the asset

4. Which of the following is the most dangerous threat to a fault-redundant file server located on the network administrator's desk and fully secured with an antivirus program, strict authentication, and access controls?

    A. Equipment failure

    B. Virus

    C. Hacking

    D. Theft

5. Which of the following vulnerabilities of a server room would be the most at risk from the threat of a natural disaster?

   A. Lack of antivirus software

   B. Network firewall not properly configured

   C. Lack of a fire detection and suppression system

   D. No lock on the server room door

6. Which of the following is the most efficient method for distributing and providing access to company documentation?

   A. Training course

   B. Company manual

   C. Centrally located notice board

   D. Intranet

7. Which of the following is the best way to assist a new employee in understanding and learning the company's security standards and policies?

   A. A training course

   B. Give them a large manual to read at home

   C. Learn-as-they-go on the job

   D. Send an e-mail with a link to online company materials

8. Which of the following is the best way to dispose of paper documentation?

   A. Ingestion

   B. Garbage

   C. Shredder

   D. Recycle bin

9. Which document classification would be considered the least secure?

   A. Sensitive

   B. Secret

   C. Top Secret

   D. Public

10. Which of the following IT documents should be secured in a safe place and not publicly distributed or displayed?

    A. Shift schedule

    B. System architecture

    C. Cell phone and pager numbers of IT staff

    D. Change control documents

REVIEW ANSWERS

1. **B**   The activity log will show what times the hacker was performing their activities and what those activities were. This evidence might be able to be used in court to help prosecute the hacker, if they're caught.

2. **D**   Keeping a chain of custody requires all evidence to be properly labeled with information on who secured and validated the evidence. This can ensure the evidence wasn't tampered with in any way since the time it was collected.

3. **A**   To provide an adequate cost/benefit comparison, the cost of the countermeasure of solution to the risk should be less than the potential cost of that risk happening. You don't want to spend more money on protecting an asset than its actual value if it's lost.

4. **D**   Because the file server isn't stored in a secure location, anyone walking by the area could steal it. All the other protections are for network-based threats.

5. **C**   Although the server could be protected from networking attacks or physical left, the lack of a fire detection and suppression system leaves the server vulnerable to a fire.

6. **D**   By publishing documentation on the company intranet, employees can easily access the most current versions of these documents.

7. **A**   Through mandatory security-training courses for new employees, you ensure they're aware of and understand all company security policies. If new employees only receive a manual, you have no assurance they'll read it.

8. **C**   By shredding a document, you ensure no one can piece the document together again. Documents thrown into the trash or recycle bins can be easily recovered.

9. **D**   A document classified as a public document can be accessed by, or distributed to, anyone within or outside the company or organization. The document contains information that isn't confidential or proprietary in nature.

10. **B**   As a security precaution, network diagrams shouldn't be generally published because the information can be used maliciously by a hacker, giving them a roadmap of the company's network, including IP addresses of the most critical network devices and servers.

About the CD-ROM

Mike Meyers' Certification Passport CD-ROM Instructions

To install the *Passport* Practice Exam software, perform these steps:

1. Insert the CD-ROM into your CD-ROM drive. An auto-run program will initiate, and a dialog box will appear indicating you're installing the Passport setup program. If the auto-run program doesn't launch on your system, select Run from the Start menu, and then type *d*:\setup.exe (where *d* is the "name" of your CD-ROM drive).

2. Follow the Installation Wizard's instructions to complete the installation of the software.

3. You can start the program by going to your desktop and double-clicking the Passport Exam Review icon or by going to Start | Program Files | Passport | Security+.

System Requirements

- **Operating systems supported**   Windows 98, Windows NT 4.0, Windows 2000, and Windows Me
- **CPU**   400 MHz or faster recommended
- **Memory**   64MB of RAM
- **CD-ROM**   4X or greater
- **Internet connection**   Required for optional exam upgrade

Technical Support

For basic *Passport* CD-ROM technical support, contact

Hudson Technical Support
Phone: 800-217-0059
E-mail: mcgraw-hill@hudsonsoft.com

For content/subject matter questions concerning the book or the CD-ROM, contact

MH Customer Service
Phone: 800-722-4726
E-mail: customer.service@mcgraw-hill.com

For inquiries about the available upgrade, CD-ROM, or online technology, or for in-depth technical support, contact

ExamWeb Technical Support
Phone: 949-566-9375
E-mail: support@examweb.com

Career Flight Path

CompTIA's Security+ certification exam is one of the newest members of the CompTIA's certification family. The Security+ exam is vendor-neutral and the recommendation is for the exam candidate to have at least two years of networking experience.

The Security+ subject matter is organized into five domain areas:

- **Part I**   General Security Concepts (30 percent)
- **Part II**   Communication Security (20 percent)
- **Part III**   Infrastructure Security (20 percent)
- **Part IV**   Basics of Cryptography (15 percent)
- **Part V**   Operational/Organizational Security (15 percent)

Recommended Prerequisites

CompTIA recommends the candidate have the knowledge and skills equivalent of those tested for in the CompTIA A+ and Network+ certification exams.

The CompTIA A+ certification exam consists of two exams:

- A+ Core Hardware (Exam: 220–221)
- A+ Operating Systems Technologies (Exam: 220–222)

The A+ Core Hardware exam focuses on the hardware of a PC, such as Ram, CPU, SCSI, hard drives, and so forth.

The A+ Operating Systems Technologies exam focuses on Windows 9x, and Windows NT/2000, operations, organization, and troubleshooting. Basic networking and Internet configurations are also present on this exam.

The CompTIA Network+ certification exam consists of one exam:

- Network+ (Exam: NK-N10-001)

The CompTIA Network+ exam is a vendor-neutral certification exam, which is targeted at networking professionals with at least nine months of experience in network support or administration.

Security+ and Beyond

The CompTIA Security+ exam consists of one exam. Once you're certified, you're certified for life. Security+ is an excellent exam to prove your knowledge about basic network security. Security+ is also a great stepping-stone for more advanced security certification, such as the Certified Information System Security Professional (CISSP) certification.

The CISSP certification consists of ten domain areas:

1. Access Control Systems and Methodology

2. Telecommunications and Networking Security

3. Security Management Practices

4. Application and Systems Development Security

5. Cryptography

6. Security Architecture and Models

7. Operations Security

8. Business Continuity and Disaster Recovery Planning

9. Law, Investigation, and Ethics

10. Physical Security

Getting the Latest Information on Security+

Security+ is a great place to start your network security professional career. To find out the latest information about the Security+ exam, please visit www.comptia.org.

Index

K

Kerberos authentication, 15, 39, 76
key escrow, 236
key history, 239
key pairs, 233–239, 243–244
key recovery operators, 237
key systems, 130
key tokens, 16
key values, 207
key-code locks, 13–14
keys
    algorithms, 205–206
    asymmetric encryption, 211–212
    cryptographic, 232–233
    encryption. *See* encryption keys
    physical, 254, 311
    private. *See* private keys
    public. *See* public keys
    servers, 256
    symmetric encryption, 207–211
keyspace, 205–206
keystrokes, monitoring, 52

L

L2TP (Layer 2 Tunneling Protocol), 72–73
L2TP Access Concentrator (LAC), 72
L2TP Network Server (LNS), 72
LAC (L2TP Access Concentrator), 72
LANs (local area networks)
    dial-up connections, 63
    firewalls, 125–126
    segmentation, 161, 163
    VLANs, 161–163
    WLANs, 76, 107–116, 129–130
laptop computers
    locking, 140, 256
    modems and, 130–131
    passwords, 140
    physical security, 139–140, 256, 330
    security training on, 330
    theft of, 139–140, 256
Layer 2 Tunneling Protocol (L2TP), 72–73
LDAP (Lightweight Directory Access Protocol), 96–97
LDAP databases, 192
LDAP servers, 96–97
legal issues, 301, 308
lighting system, 253
Lightweight Directory Access Protocol. *See* LDAP
line conditioners, 262
LNS (L2TP Network Server), 72
local area networks. *See* LANs
lock and key systems, 254

locking items
    computers, 140, 256
    devices, 256
    electronic locks, 254
    key-code locks, 13–14
    laptops, 140, 256
    mobile devices, 139
    physical locks, 254
    servers, 256
    workstations, 139
log files
    application logs, 335
    audit logs, 335
    equipment inventory logs, 335
    event logging, 164, 166
    maintenance logs, 335
    network monitor, 164
    passive detection and, 164, 166
    used as evidence, 322
logic bombs, 48
login IDs, 8, 13–17
logins
    attempts, 18, 42, 184
    database servers, 193
    directory services, 192–193
    limiting, 42
    monitoring, 52
    network, 313
logouts, 52

M

M of N control, 237
MAC (Media Access Control), 19, 312
MAC (mandatory access control), 11
MAC address-based VLANs, 162
MAC addresses
    described, 19
    DHCP servers and, 192
    filtering, 115, 129
    machine restrictions and, 19
macro viruses, 45
macros, 45
magnetic access cards, 255, 258
magnetic card readers, 255
magnetic tape, 276–280
mail servers
    antivirus software and, 49
    authentication, 92–93
    demilitarized zones, 156
    encryption, 89
    viruses and, 49, 91
    vulnerabilities, 188
maintenance logs, 335
malicious code, 42–50
man-in-the-middle attacks, 37–38

security issues, 131–132
vs. network-based intrusion systems, 165
wireless access, 116–117
vulnerabilities
  assets, 325–326
  directory services, 192–193
  FTP servers, 188–189
  mail servers, 188
  networking devices, 41
  nonphysical, 326
  operating systems, 41, 325
  physical, 326
  remote access, 138–139
  risk assessment, 325–326
  servers, 186–193
  user accounts, 41–43
  to viruses, 325
  web servers, 187

W

WANs (wide area networks), 69, 161
WAP (Wireless Access Protocol), 110–111
war driving, 106
wardialing, 63
warm sites, 282
warm swap capability, 291
water sprinkler systems, 267
Web
  dial-up connections to, 63–64, 75
  objectionable material on, 138
  overview, 82
  privacy and, 303–304
  security, 82–88
  workstation access, 138
web applications, 84–88
web browsers
  ActiveX and, 86
  cookies and, 88
  HTTP and, 83–84
  JavaScript and, 84–85
  security and, 84–88
web of trust model, 221–222
web pages, 82–88
web servers
  demilitarized zones, 156
  firewalls and, 158
  intranets, 158
  vulnerabilities, 187
  worms, 187
web services, 154–155
web sites
  cookies, 87–88
  objectionable, 138
  security and, 82–88
  Security+ site, 344
WEP security protocol, 115

wet pipe systems, 267
wide area networks (WANs), 69, 161
Windows Internet Naming Service (WINS), 191
wireless access points, 129
Wireless Access Protocol (WAP), 110–111
wireless adapters, 108
wireless cells, 265–266
wireless devices, 110–111, 139–140
wireless LANs (WLANs), 76, 107–117, 129–130
Wireless Markup Language (WML), 110–111
wireless networks, 105–117
  access to, 108
  authentication, 76
  configurations, 106–110, 129–130
  disruption of, 265–266
  encryption, 130
  firewalls, 116
  overview, 106
  protocols, 110–116
  resource access, 109–110
  security issues, 129–130
  site surveys, 108
  SSID, 114–115
  topologies, 109–110
  VPN access, 116–117
  war driving, 106
  WLANs, 76, 107–116, 129–130
wireless phones, 111–113
Wireless Transaction Layer Security (WTLS), 111
WLANs (wireless LANs), 76, 107–117, 129–130
WML (Wireless Markup Language), 110–111
workstations, 137–139
World Wide Web
  dial-up connections to, 63–64, 75
  objectionable material on, 138
  overview, 82
  privacy and, 303–304
  security, 82–88
  workstation access, 138
worms
  e-mail, 48, 90–91
  overview, 48
  web servers, 187
Write access rights, 9
WTLS (Wireless Transaction Layer Security), 111

X

X.509 standard, 223–225
X.509-based PKIs, 225
.xls extension, 47
XTACACS (Extended TACACS)
  authentication, 75

Z

.zip extension, 47
zip files, 47

INTERNATIONAL CONTACT INFORMATION

AUSTRALIA
McGraw-Hill Book Company Australia Pty. Ltd.
TEL +61-2-9900-1800
FAX +61-2-9878-8881
http://www.mcgraw-hill.com.au
books-it_sydney@mcgraw-hill.com

CANADA
McGraw-Hill Ryerson Ltd.
TEL +905-430-5000
FAX +905-430-5020
http://www.mcgraw-hill.ca

**GREECE, MIDDLE EAST, & AFRICA
(Excluding South Africa)**
McGraw-Hill Hellas
TEL +30-210-6560-990
TEL +30-210-6560-993
TEL +30-210-6560-994
FAX +30-210-6545-525

MEXICO (Also serving Latin America)
McGraw-Hill Interamericana Editores S.A. de C.V.
TEL +525-117-1583
FAX +525-117-1589
http://www.mcgraw-hill.com.mx
fernando_castellanos@mcgraw-hill.com

SINGAPORE (Serving Asia)
McGraw-Hill Book Company
TEL +65-863-1580
FAX +65-862-3354
http://www.mcgraw-hill.com.sg
mghasia@mcgraw-hill.com

SOUTH AFRICA
McGraw-Hill South Africa
TEL +27-11-622-7512
FAX +27-11-622-9045
robyn_swanepoel@mcgraw-hill.com

SPAIN
McGraw-Hill/Interamericana de España, S.A.U.
TEL +34-91-180-3000
FAX +34-91-372-8513
http://www.mcgraw-hill.es
professional@mcgraw-hill.es

**UNITED KINGDOM, NORTHERN,
EASTERN, & CENTRAL EUROPE**
McGraw-Hill Education Europe
TEL +44-1-628-502500
FAX +44-1-628-770224
http://www.mcgraw-hill.co.uk
computing_neurope@mcgraw-hill.com

ALL OTHER INQUIRIES Contact:
Osborne/McGraw-Hill
TEL +1-510-549-6600
FAX +1-510-883-7600
http://www.osborne.com
omg_international@mcgraw-hill.com

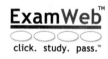